# Enjoy! again and again

## A cookbook by Fred Wix, the Gabby Gourmet

Jackie
Try some of
these and
"Enjoy"

Fred
2009

## A Few Personal Thanks

**T hanks to my** family and friends, who have served as the taste testers and critics for so many of these recipes; to *Carolyn Rose* and *Dave Midget* for their unbiased opinions and suggestions; to *Erik Ostling*, who was so quick to help with his marvelous photographic talents; to *Jonathon Hinckley* for his guidance and patience. And, to *Becky Jones*, whose design and editing talents have elevated my simple recipes to new dimensions.

Special thanks to my wife, *Jean Corley*, for her ongoing interest, many hours of research and editing, and unquestionable support. Life has certainly become far more "Enjoy!-able" with you!

First published in 1997 by Publishers Press.
Designed and illustrated by Rebecca Jones.
Photography by Erik Ostling of Erik Ostling Studios.

# Forward

**I have been involved** in the food and media world of Utah now for 19 years. My, how time flies when you're having fun! And, fun—or "ENJOY!-ment"—is what I hope all of you will have as you try out the many recipes included in this new cookbook.

It has been 14 years since the publication of my last cookbook, and our culture and tastes have changed tremendously. The old books are now out of print and many of you have requested that I once again compile recipes from recent segments of KUTV's *News at Noon*. It was hard to decide which recipes to include and which ones to leave out, but, after much sampling, re-testing, and a few late night munching sessions, I hope you will agree that we've picked some of the best. I've also noted a few of my "specialties" in each section. I hope they will soon become your favorites, too.

All recipes have previously been available either through recipe cards from *Dan's Foods*, the fax line in my office, or our Web site (www.citysearchslc.com.). As always, these recipes are intended to be easy for anyone to use, with ingredients that are readily available in our Mountain West region. If there is one word I keep in mind when messing around in the kitchen, it's *simplicity*.

With that in mind, may I just say that I hope you, too, will—

**Enjoy! again and again**

# Table of Contents

# Chapter 1

# Breakfasts and Brunches

## Gabby Specialities—Breakfasts and Brunches

# Basic Belgian Waffles

2 C all purpose flour
1 tsp. salt
8 eggs, separated

1/2 C butter, melted
1 1/2 tsp. vanilla
2 C milk

Mix flour and salt in a small bowl and set aside. In a large bowl, beat egg whites with electric mixer on high speed until stiff peaks form.

In another large bowl, beat egg yolks with electric mixer on high speed until thickened and lemon-colored, about 5 minutes. Stir in the melted butter and vanilla. Alternately add flour mixture and milk to yolk mixture, beating well after each addition. Fold egg whites into yolk mixture. Bake in preheated waffle iron.

Makes 6 waffles.

# Banana Split Belgian Waffles

1 pkg. butterscotch chips
1/3 C evaporated milk
12 large marshmallows
Belgian waffles *(see preceding recipe)*
2 cartons (8 oz.) strawberry yogurt

2 C sliced bananas
2 cartons (8 oz.) banana yogurt
2 C sliced strawberries
Chopped nuts

In a small saucepan, mix butterscotch chips, evaporated milk and marshmallows. Stir constantly over low heat until mixture is melted and smooth; set aside.

Prepare Belgian waffles. Place 1 waffle square on a plate and spoon 1/4 cup strawberry yogurt and about 2 tablespoons sliced bananas on top of waffle.

Cover with another waffle square and then add 1/4 cup banana yogurt and about 2 tablespoons sliced strawberries. Place a third waffle on top of the strawberries and top with 2 tablespoons sliced bananas and 2 tablespoons sliced strawberries.

Drizzle the entire stack with butterscotch sauce and sprinkle with chopped nuts. Repeat stacking process with remaining ingredients.

Makes 6 servings.

# Raspberry Buttermilk Pancakes

2 C fresh buttermilk
2 extra large eggs, beaten well
1/4 C light vegetable oil (canola)
2 C flour

1 1/4 tsp. baking soda
1 tsp. salt
3/4 tsp. baking powder
1 C fresh raspberries

In a medium-size mixing bowl, combine and mix well the buttermilk, eggs and oil. In a separate bowl, combine the dry ingredients and whisk well to mix. Stir the dry mixture into the buttermilk mixture. Carefully stir the raspberries into the batter. Ladle onto a lightly greased, buttered or sprayed hot (400°–425°) griddle surface.

These are a must when the Bear Lake raspberries hit the streets every summer. Serve with fresh dairy butter (the real stuff) and, of course, raspberry jam or preserves.

Serves 4.

Oh, one more idea—combine a pound of room temperature butter with 1/2 cup fresh raspberries and whip well. Spread this over the pancakes for a little raspberry overkill.

Wow, anybody ready for breakfast?

# German Oven Pancakes

1/2 C milk
1/2 C all purpose flour
3 large eggs
Dash salt
2 T butter
1 pkg. (8 oz.) frozen raspberries,
    thawed

1 can (20 oz.) pineapple chunks,
    drained
4 bananas, sliced
1/2 C (packed) brown sugar
1 carton (8 oz.) dairy sour cream

Combine the milk, flour, eggs and salt in a mixing bowl and mix with a fork or whisk. Melt 1 tablespoon of butter in each of the two 9-inch pie plates by placing them in an oven preheated to 400°. Butter should be sizzling. Swish the butter around the plates to coat the bottoms.

Increase the oven temperature to 425°. Pour batter into each pie plate to 1/4 inch deep. Bake 10–15 minutes or until golden brown and the edges are puffed. Pancake will form a well in the center. Remove the pancakes and place on serving plates.

Spoon the raspberries, pineapple chunks and bananas into the center of each pancake. Sprinkle with brown sugar and top with sour cream.

Serves 4.

# Gabby's Whole Wheat Waffles

3 3/4 C whole wheat flour
1 T (packed) brown sugar
1 3/4 tsp. baking powder
1/2 tsp. salt

5 extra large eggs, well beaten
3 C milk
1/2 C butter, melted

In a large mixing bowl, combine the flour, sugar, baking powder and salt. (*Note:* This recipe has been adapted for *high* altitude cooking, so if you are cooking at a lower altitude you might have to add more baking powder.) Whisk the mixture to blend well.

In a smaller bowl, combine the eggs, milk and cooled butter. Gradually add the liquid mixture to the dry ingredients and beat the batter until smooth.

Makes enough batter for 4–5 large round waffles.

I prefer waffles with just butter and a choice of syrups, but these can be served with whipped cream, yogurt, sour cream, fresh (or even canned) fruits, powdered sugar, and so on. If you have batter left over, make up the waffles, let cool, then freeze individually; reheat by toasting (lightly) in your toaster.

# Gabby's Weekend Creole Eggs

1 dozen hard cooked eggs, shelled,
    chilled and sliced
3 T olive oil
1 large white onion, chopped
2–3 green onions, chopped
2 green bell peppers, chopped
1/2 C celery, chopped
1 14-oz. can Cajun-style tomatoes
1/2 T chili powder

Salt and black pepper, to taste
2 T butter
2 T flour
1 C warmed milk
1/4 tsp. fresh nutmeg, grated
2 pkgs. Jimmy Dean hot sausage,
    crumbled, browned well and
    drained
1 C buttered bread crumbs

Prepare the eggs as indicated. In a large skillet or fry pan, heat the oil over medium-high heat. Add the onions, bell peppers and celery. Saute this mixture for a couple of minutes, then stir in the tomatoes and seasonings. Continue to saute until the mixture thickens.

In a separate pan, melt the butter over medium heat, then stir in the flour, forming a basic roux. Whisk in the warmed milk and nutmeg and continue to cook until the mixture thickens. Stir the tomato mixture into the white sauce, then remove from the heat.

Lightly spray a 9 x 13-inch shallow baking dish, then place a layer of half the tomato-cream sauce, then the sliced eggs, then the drained browned sausage, and finally the remaining half of the tomato cream-sauce. Top all with the crumbs. Bake, uncovered, in a preheated 350° oven for 30–35 minutes. Serve with wedges of fresh chilled melon or fruit and slices of toasted multi-grain breads.

Serves 10–12.

Great breakfast or brunch idea.

# Italian Eggs Bendito

2 T olive oil and butter combination
1/2 medium sweet onion, finely
    chopped
4–6 green onions, chopped
1 can (14 1/2 oz.) Italian-style ready
    cut tomatoes
1 tsp. Italian seasoning
Salt and fresh ground pepper, to taste
8 poached eggs, drained

4 English muffins, toasted and lightly
    buttered
16 medium-thin slices of prosciutto
    (Italian ham)
2 medium fresh tomatoes, sliced thin
1 C sini rustico cheese (Italian),
    shredded
Fresh Italian parsley, finely chopped
Wedges of fresh melon

In a medium-size skillet or fry pan, heat the oil/butter combination, then add the onion and green onions. Saute this mixture just a couple of minutes, then add the tomatoes, Italian seasoning, salt and pepper. Reduce the heat to low and simmer 8–10 minutes.

Poach the eggs as usual. Place the toasted English muffin halves on individual plates, 2 each. Layer 2 slices of prosciutto over each muffin half. Top each with 1–2 slices of tomato. Place a drained hot poached egg over the tomato. Ladle the warm tomato sauce over each. Sprinkle the rustico cheese over each and garnish with parsley. Serve immediately with wedges of fresh chilled melon.

Serves 4 (2 eggs each).

My idea of a great new Italian-style eggs benedict.

# Eggs Mornay

4 T butter
4 T flour
1 1/2 C milk
1/2 C heavy cream
1 tsp. marjoram
Salt and fresh ground pepper, to taste

1/4 tsp. fresh grated nutmeg
3/4 C Gruyere cheese, shredded
8 extra large eggs, hard cooked and
  halved
1/3 C fresh parmesan cheese, grated or
  shredded

In a medium-size saucepan, heat the butter over medium heat; when melted, stir in the flour, forming a roux. Whisk in the milk and cream and then add the seasonings.

Stir in the Gruyere cheese and continue to stir until all is melted. Spoon a small amount of the sauce over the bottom of a sprayed shallow baking dish. Arrange the halved eggs over the bottom of the dish. Spoon the remaining sauce over all and top with the parmesan cheese. Bake in a preheated 350° oven for 20–30 minutes or until lightly browned over all.

Serves 6.

# Special Holiday Eggs

2 T butter
2 T flour
1 C milk
Salt and ground white pepper, to taste
1/8 tsp. fresh nutmeg, grated
1/2 lb. fresh lobster meat, cut into
   small chunks

1 T sherry wine
1 1/2 C Swiss cheese, shredded
4 English muffins, split, toasted and
   lightly buttered
8 large thin slices of fresh tomato
8 extra large eggs, poached
Sweet Hungarian paprika for garnish

In a medium-size saucepan, heat the butter over medium heat. When melted, stir in the flour, forming a roux. Whisk in the milk, salt, pepper and nutmeg. Cook the mixture until it thickens.

Stir in the lobster, sherry and cheese, stirring until all the cheese is melted. Prepare the muffins and place on individual serving plates. Top each with a thin slice of tomato, a poached egg and a serving spoonful of the creamed lobster. Spritz each with a dash of paprika.

Serves 4 (2 muffin halves per serving).

Obviously, with the cost of lobster, this is just for special occasions.

# Scrambled Easter Sunday Eggs

12 extra large eggs, beaten
1/4 C milk
1 tsp. salt or to taste
1 tsp. fresh ground pepper
4 T butter
8 oz. fresh mushrooms, sliced and
    sauteed
1 C tender asparagus tips, cooked
1/4 C green onions, finely chopped

1/2 C pancetta (Italian bacon, cured
    with salt and spices, but not
    smoked), finely diced and fried
    crisp
1–2 C orange hollandaise sauce (*see
    instructions below*)
Fresh parsley, finely chopped for
    garnish

In a medium-size mixing bowl, combine the eggs, milk, salt and pepper. Whisk this mixture well. In a large, non-stick skillet, melt the butter over medium heat. Add the eggs and cook just until they are soft-set scrambled.

Arrange the eggs in a sprayed, shallow, 9 x 12-inch baking dish. Layer the sauteed mushrooms, asparagus tips, green onions and drained pancetta over the eggs. Prepare the orange hollandaise and pour over all. Bake in a preheated 325° oven for 10–15 minutes. Garnish with fresh chopped parsley and serve immediately.

Serves 6.

### For orange hollandaise:
Place 2 cups of orange juice in a saucepan and bring to a boil. Reduce the heat and simmer until reduced to about a 1/4 cup. Heat 1 cup butter until bubbly. Place 6 egg yolks and a teaspoon of salt in a blender and blend for a few seconds. While blending, add the orange syrup, then slowly add the melted hot butter. Blend until mixture is thick.

# Gabby's Scrambled Chippers

3–4 T butter
1/4 C shallots or green onions, chopped
10 extra large eggs, beaten
1 C small curd cottage cheese, well drained

1 1/4 C dried chipped beef, cut into strips
Fresh ground pepper, to taste
6 English muffins, toasted and buttered
Fresh parmesan cheese, grated

In a large (12-inch) fry pan, heat the butter over medium-high heat. When toasty brown, add the shallots or green onions and lightly saute a minute or so.

Combine the beaten eggs and cottage cheese, then add to the hot pan, along with the chipped beef strips; cook, scrambling over medium-low heat. Season with ground pepper to taste.

Toast the muffin halves and place 2 on each individual plate. Divide the egg mixture over each muffin half and sprinkle with parmesan cheese.

Serves 6 (two muffin halves per serving).

With wedges of fresh melon, this makes a delicious breakfast.

# Gabby's Swiss Egg Scramble

2 1/2 C (rounded) soft (fresh) 1/2-inch
    bread cubes, crusts removed
1 C milk (not skim)
8 extra large eggs, lightly beaten
2–3 T chives, chopped
1 T fresh or dried parsley flakes
2 tsp. dried sweet basil leaves
1/2 tsp. salt (optional)

1/4 tsp. fresh ground or seasoned
    pepper
3–5 drops hot pepper sauce
1/4 C butter or butter/oil combination
1/2 lb. Swiss cheese, shredded
8 slices of thick-sliced bacon, diced,
    fried crisp and well drained

In a medium-size bowl, combine 2 cups of the bread cubes and the milk. Let set about 5 minutes, then drain, reserving the excess milk.

In another bowl, combine the eggs, chives, parsley flakes, basil, salt, pepper, hot sauce and the reserved milk.

In a large skillet or fry pan, heat 2 tablespoons of the butter over medium heat. Add the egg mixture and scramble just until soft-set. Fold in the soaked bread cubes, then spoon the mixture into a sprayed or buttered 9-inch baking dish. Sprinkle the cheese over all.

Melt the remaining butter and toss with the other 1/2 cup bread cubes. Arrange the buttered cubes over the cheese, then scatter the drained bacon over all. Bake, uncovered, in a preheated 400° oven about 7–8 minutes or until the cheese has melted and is bubbly.

Serves 4–6 deliciously.

# Anytime Seafood Omelet

2 T butter, olive oil or a combination
   of both
1 can (4 oz.) sliced water chestnuts,
   drained
1/4 C green onions, chopped
1/2 tsp. fennel seeds
1/2 tsp. tarragon
1 lb. Dungeness crab or imitation crab

2 T butter, olive oil or a combination
   of both
12 extra large eggs, well beaten
1/4 C water
8 drops Tabasco or other hot pepper
   sauce
3/4 C Monterey Jack or cheddar
   cheese or a combination of both

In a small fry pan or skillet, heat the first 2 tablespoons of butter/oil over medium-high heat. Add the chestnuts, green onion, fennel and tarragon, and saute until the chestnuts are golden brown; add the crab meat and warm through. Set this mixture aside.

In a large skillet or fry pan, heat the second measure of butter/oil over medium heat. Whisk together the eggs, water and pepper sauce. Add the egg mixture to the pan and cook as you would any omelet. Sprinkle the cheese over the top of the set omelet, then ladle the crab mixture over half of the omelet. Fold omelet over and serve immediately.

Serves 6.

# Fresh Dungeness Crab, Avocado & Mushroom Omelet

9 T butter (divided)
1/4 C Walla Walla sweet onion
4 T flour
Salt and fresh ground pepper, to taste
2 C milk, heated
1/2 C Swiss or Monterey Jack cheese,
   shredded

1 1/2 T Madeira wine
Dash fresh nutmeg, grated
1/2 lb. fresh mushrooms, sliced
1 avocado, skinned and sliced
6 extra large eggs, beaten
1/3 lb. fresh Dungeness crab, picked of
   shell matter

In a medium-size saucepan, melt 4 tablespoons of butter over medium heat; add
the onion and saute just a minute. Stir in the flour and cook another minute. Add
the salt and pepper and slowly stir in the warm milk. Continue to cook the
mixture, stirring until it thickens. Stir in the cheese until all is melted, then add
the wine and nutmeg. Reduce heat to low and stir occasionally until ready to use.

In a medium-size skillet, melt 3 tablespoons of butter over medium-high heat; add
the mushrooms, saute about three minutes and remove from heat. Slice the
avocado and set aside. In a 10-inch omelet pan, melt the last 2 tablespoons of
butter over medium heat and add the beaten eggs. When the eggs start to set on
the bottom, lift them with a spatula and tilt the pan to allow the uncooked
portion to run underneath. When all is set, flip the omelet and fill half the top,
starting with crab meat, then the avocado slices, sauteed mushrooms and sauce.
Flip the unfilled half over the filling. Let set about a minute, then turn onto a
medium serving dish. Garnish with chopped green onions, more crab meat,
mushrooms and sauce.

Serve immediately to 4 hungry people.

Fresh fruit on the side really makes a wonderful breakfast or brunch.

# Breakfast Seafood Burritos

3 tsp. light (canola) vegetable oil
1 C cooked shredded potato
8 oz. imitation flaked crab (surimi)
1/2 C sweet onion, finely chopped
1 C fresh tomato, seeded and chopped
2 tsp. butter or light oil
1/4 C fresh cilantro, coarsely chopped

6 extra large eggs, beaten
1 C fresh salsa or picante sauce
3/4 C medium cheddar cheese, shredded
4 large flour tortillas, warmed
Sour cream (optional)

In a large skillet or fry pan, heat the oil over medium-high heat. Add the shredded potato, flaked crab, onion and tomato. Cook this mixture about 3 minutes, stirring often.

In a separate medium-size skillet or fry pan, heat the butter/oil over medium heat. Combine the cilantro and eggs and add to the hot pan, stirring and cooking until soft-set. Stir in the shredded cheese.

Lay out the warmed tortillas and place a row of the crab mixture down the side of each tortilla. Place a line of the soft-set cheese-eggs. Top all with an equal amount of salsa and sour cream, then fold or roll and place on a serving platter. Spoon the remaining salsa over all and serve immediately.

Serves 4 (1 burrito apiece).

Maybe not authentic Mexican, but very good and a real hit on a weekend morning.

# Gabby's Mexican Breakfast Enchiladas

8 large flour tortillas, heated
10 extra large eggs
1/4 C water
3–4 T green chilies, diced
3–4 green onions, chopped
1/4 C fresh cilantro, finely chopped

2 1/2 T picante sauce
Salt and fresh ground pepper, to taste
1 C salsa
3/4 C medium cheddar cheese, shredded

Wrap the tortillas in foil and place in a 200° oven to heat through. In a medium-size mixing bowl, combine the eggs, water, chilies, green onions, cilantro, picante sauce, salt and pepper. Whisk this mixture, then pour into a hot 10-inch skillet or fry pan, scrambling over a medium heat until soft set.

Divide the eggs onto each tortilla. Top each with a tablespoon of salsa and a tablespoon of the shredded cheddar, then roll up, enchilada-style. Place 2 on each individual plate and garnish with remaining salsa and cheese (a sprig of cilantro can be added, if desired).

Serves 4 (2 each).

Just a touch of Mexican and a nice addition to start any day.

# Mexican Weekend Brunch Bake

12–14 slices of thick-sliced bacon, diced
10 extra large eggs, beaten
1/2 C milk
5 C frozen hash brown potatoes, thawed
2 1/2 C cheddar-Monterey Jack cheese combination, shredded
1 C small curd cottage cheese, well drained

1 can (4 oz.) diced green chilies
6 green onions, chopped
1/4 C fresh cilantro, chopped
Salt and fresh ground pepper to taste
1 C (rounded) corn flakes, mixed with 2 T of the bacon drippings
Fresh salsa for each serving

Prepare the bacon as indicated, then fry until crisp. Drain off the drippings, reserving 2 tablespoons, and set aside.

In a large mixing bowl, combine and whisk the eggs and milk. Stir in all remaining ingredients except the bacon, corn flakes and salsa. Pour the mixture into a sprayed 9 x 13-inch shallow baking dish.

Mix the 2 tablespoons of reserved bacon drippings with the corn flakes, then sprinkle over the egg mixture along with the drained bacon. Cover and refrigerate overnight. Bring to room temperature an hour before baking. Bake, uncovered, in a preheated 325° oven for 65–70 minutes or until nicely browned and set in the middle. Serve with fresh salsa on the side.

Serves 10–12.

# Gabby's Sausage and Eggs Breakfast Casserole

1 C soda crackers, crushed
4 T butter, melted
1 dozen. hard cooked eggs, sliced
2 pkgs. (12 oz.) Jimmy Dean Light
    sausage, browned, crumbled, well
    drained
1 carton (1 lb.) sour cream
2 T heavy cream
1 T onion, finely minced

1 tsp. Mrs. Dash Lemon and Herb
    seasoning
Salt and fresh ground pepper, to taste
1 C medium sharp cheddar cheese,
    shredded
1/2 C seasoned bread crumbs
Sweet Hungarian paprika for color
    garnish

Crush the crackers with a rolling pin and place in a medium bowl, adding the melted butter and stirring to blend well. Spoon this mixture over the bottom of a 9 x 13-inch shallow baking dish.

Arrange the sliced eggs over the crackers followed by the cooked sausage. Combine the sour cream, cream, onion and seasonings. Spoon this mixture over all, then sprinkle the cheddar cheese over all. Top with the seasoned crumbs and spritz with paprika. Bake in a preheated 350° oven for 20–25 minutes.

Serves 6.

This may also be prepared and assembled the day before baking.

# Portuguese Sausage Breakfast Casserole

1 1/2 lbs. Portuguese sausages
(linguisa), cut into bite-size pieces
8 slices of thick sliced white bread,
crusts removed and cut into cubes
3/4 lb. medium cheddar cheese,
shredded
4–6 extra large eggs, beaten
2 1/2 C milk
1 can cream of mushroom soup
1/4 C dry vermouth (can also use
straight sherry wine)

1 tsp. Gabby's Own Mustard (*see
chapter 7, Sauces and Dressings, for
this recipe*)
or your favorite brand
3/4 C fresh mushrooms, sliced and
sauteed in butter (can also use
canned mushrooms
1/4 C fresh parsley, finely chopped

Prepare the sausages as indicated, then place in a medium-size skillet or fry pan.
Brown the sausage, then discard the extruded grease and drain on paper towels.

Lightly spray a large 9 x 13-inch shallow baking dish and arrange the cubed bread
over all. Arrange the drained sausage over the bread, then add the cheese.

In a large bowl, whisk the eggs and add all remaining ingredients, prepared as
indicated. Pour this mixture over the ingredients in the baking dish. Cover with
plastic wrap and place in the refrigerator overnight.

Bake in a preheated 300° oven for 1 1/2 hours. Remove from the oven and let
stand, uncovered, for 10 minutes before serving.

Serves 8–10.

# Summer Brunch Casserole

1 large loaf Italian or French bread,
   torn into bite-size pieces
1/2 lb. butter, melted
1/2 lb. leftover baked ham, diced
3/4 lb. Swiss cheese, shredded
1/2 lb. pepper-Jack cheese, shredded
   (can also use plain Monterey Jack)
16 extra large eggs, lightly beaten
3 C milk
1/2 C dry white wine (your choice)

1 bunch green onions, chopped
1/2 tsp. fresh ground pepper
1–2 T Gabby's Own Mustard (*see
   chapter 7, Sauces and Dressings, for
   this recipe*)
1–2 C sour cream (can use lite-style)
3/4 C fresh parmesan cheese, grated
Roasted red and yellow bell pepper,
   cut into strips, for garnish

Lightly spray two 9 x 13-inch shallow baking dishes. Divide and spread the bread pieces over both dishes, then drizzle each with the melted butter. Sprinkle the ham and cheeses over both.

In a medium-size mixing bowl, combine and beat the eggs, milk, wine, onions, pepper and mustard. Divide the mixture between the two dishes, cover each and refrigerate for up to 8 hours.

Remove from the refrigerator an hour before baking. Cover each with aluminum foil and bake in a preheated 325° oven for 1 hour. Remove from the oven and spread the top of each with sour cream and parmesan cheese. Garnish with the roasted bell pepper strips and return to the oven for 10 minutes.

Serves 18–20.

# Gabby's Fresh Mushroom Brunch Casserole

3 C (rounded) baked croutons
1/4 lb. sharp cheddar cheese, shredded
1/4 lb. Monterey Jack cheese, shredded
1/2 lb. thick sliced bacon, diced, fried
    crisp and well drained
6–8 green onions, chopped

6–8 extra large eggs, lightly beaten
2 1/2–3 C regular milk (preferably *not*
    skim)
Salt and fresh ground pepper, to taste
1/2 lb. fresh mushrooms, sliced

Lightly butter or spray a shallow 7 x 11-inch baking dish. Arrange the croutons over the bottom, then layer on the cheeses, bacon and onions.

In a 1-quart measuring cup, combine the eggs, milk, salt and pepper. Mix well and pour over the layered mixture. Cover with plastic wrap and refrigerate overnight.

Remove from the refrigerator 1 hour before baking. Arrange the sliced mushrooms over all and cover with aluminum foil. Bake in a preheated 350° oven for 45 minutes; remove cover and continue baking an additional 15 minutes.

Serves 6.

Happy brunching!

# Gabby's Fresh Apple-Raisin Coffee Cake

1 1/2 C all purpose unbleached flour
3/4 C granulated sugar
3 1/2 tsp. baking powder
1 tsp. ground cardamom
1/2 tsp. salt
3/4 C butter, chilled and finely diced
2 C cooking apples, peeled, cored and
    chopped

1 C dark raisins
1/2 C nut meats (your choice),
    chopped
2 large eggs, beaten
1 T milk
1/2 C brown sugar

In a large mixing bowl, combine the flour, sugar, baking powder, cardamom and salt, then whisk well. Add the butter chips and cut into the dry mixture using a pastry cutter until mixture is crumbly.

Stir in the prepared apples, raisins, nut meats and combined eggs and milk. This will form a stiff batter; beat well, then spread in a well-sprayed 9 x 9-inch baking dish or pan. Sprinkle the brown sugar over the top of the cake. Bake in a preheated 350° oven 55–60 minutes. Remove and allow to cool to just warm before serving.

Great for a weekend breakfast or brunch.

# Overnight French Toast

1 loaf unsliced coarse white bread,
    crusts removed
1 C (packed) light brown sugar
1/4 C butter (the real stuff)
2 T light Karo syrup
1/8 tsp. ground cinnamon

1/4 C pecan gems
5 extra large eggs, beaten
1 1/2 C milk
1 tsp. vanilla
1/4 tsp. fresh grated nutmeg
1/4 tsp. salt

Thickly slice the bread, removing and discarding the crusts.

In a small saucepan, combine the brown sugar, butter, Karo and cinnamon and heat the mixture to a simmer. When all is melted, pour the mixture into a sprayed 9 x 13-inch shallow baking dish. Sprinkle the pecan gems over the syrup. Arrange the squares of bread over the mixture.

In a medium-size mixing bowl, beat the eggs, then whisk in the remaining ingredients. Carefully pour the mixture over the bread. Cover with plastic wrap and refrigerate overnight. Remove from the refrigerator about an hour before baking. Bake, uncovered, in a preheated 350° oven for 45 minutes.

Serves 4 (2 slices each).

# Peach French Toast

3 extra large eggs
3 T peach preserves or jam
3/4 C half & half cream (can also use
    Mocha Mix)
1 tsp. cinnamon

6 thick slices of French bread
1/3 C peach preserves or jam
1/2 C butter, melted
3–4 fresh peaches, sliced
Confectioner's (powdered) sugar

In a small bowl, beat the eggs and the 3 tablespoons of preserves with a whisk. Whisk in the half & half and cinnamon.

Place the slices of bread in a large shallow baking dish. Pour the egg mixture over the bread, turning and soaking all pieces. Cover and refrigerate at least a couple of hours or overnight.

In a small bowl, beat the 1/3 cup of preserves and the melted butter with an electric mixer until fluffy. Melt 2 tablespoons of butter or spray a large non-stick fry pan, heating over medium heat. Add the bread slices to the pan and fry, turning often, until they are a golden brown (because of the thickness, this will take longer than normal or you will have soggy centers).

Serve the toast with a scoop of the butter mixture, topped with slices of fresh peaches and topped with confectioner's sugar.

Serves 3 (2 slices each).

# Weekend French Toast with Apple Sauce

1 1/2 C milk (can use skim)
2 cinnamon sticks
Zest from one fresh lemon (divided in half)
1/2 tsp. vanilla
4 extra large eggs, beaten
8 thick slices of French bread
1–2 T butter

4 medium tart cooking-type apples, peeled, cored and sliced
1 1/2 T honey
1 T lemon juice
1/4 tsp. ground cinnamon
1/8 tsp. ground allspice
4 oz. medium-sharp cheddar cheese, cut into small diced pieces

In a small saucepan, combine the milk, cinnamon sticks, half of the lemon zest and vanilla; heat and simmer for 10 minutes. Remove and discard the cinnamon sticks and let the liquid cool to room temperature.

Whisk the eggs into the cooled milk mixture. Lay out the slices of bread in a large shallow baking dish and pour the milk-egg mixture over all, turning to soak all. Cover with plastic wrap and chill overnight.

At serving time, prepare the apples as indicated. In a large skillet, heat the butter over medium-high heat, add the apples, and saute about 5 minutes. Add the honey, other half of the lemon zest, juice, cinnamon, and allspice. Continue to cook apple mixture until tender, then remove from the heat. Stir in the cheese, cover, and let set.

Preheat a large non-stick griddle over medium-high heat and spray lightly with Pam. Arrange bread slices on the hot surface and cook until golden brown, turning once. Place on individual plates and spoon the apple sauce mixture over each.

Serves 4.

# Gabby's Weekend Breakfast Cakes

1 C yellow corn meal
1/2 C all-purpose flour
1 tsp. (scant) baking soda
1 tsp. sugar
1 tsp. salt

2 C buttermilk
2 T light vegetable (canola) oil
1 extra large egg, separated (yolk,
    beaten, and white, beaten stiff)

In a large mixing bowl, combine the dry ingredients and whisk well to blend. In a smaller separate bowl, beat together the buttermilk, oil, and egg yolk. Stir the buttermilk mixture into the dry mixture.

Fold the beaten egg white into the batter, then cover and refrigerate for 10–30 minutes before preparing the cakes. Spray, butter, or grease a hot griddle, then ladle on the batter and bake, turning once until browned on both sides.

Makes a dozen cakes.

Hearty fare, and a taste of the past.

# Weekend Corn Fritters

1 1/2 C all-purpose flour
4 tsp. sugar
1 1/4 tsp. baking powder
1/4 tsp baking soda
Pinch salt

2 extra large eggs, beaten
6–8 T milk
1/2 C whole kernel corn, well drained
1/2 C creamed corn

Combine and mix the dry ingredients. In a large mixing bowl, beat the eggs and milk until frothy. Dump in the dry ingredients, stir well, then stir in the corn.

Drop by heaping tablespoons into hot (350°) oil, 3–4 inches deep, frying a few at a time until golden brown, crispy, and cooked through. Drain on paper towels and keep warm until all are cooked.

Serve with either syrups or confectioner's sugar.

# Gabby's Canola Sweet Breads

1 pkg. yellow cake mix (without
    pudding)
1 pkg. (3 oz.) French vanilla instant
    pudding mix
4 large eggs
3/4 C canola oil
3/4 C water
2 T canola seeds

2 tsp. vanilla (separated)
2 tsp. butter extract (separated)
1 tsp. cardamom
1/4 C light brown sugar
1 tsp. ground cinnamon
1/2 C confectioner's sugar
1 T milk

In a large mixing bowl, combine the cake mix, pudding, eggs, canola oil, water, seeds, vanilla, butter extract and cardamom; *reserve one teaspoon each of the vanilla and butter extract*. Using an electric mixer, beat at medium speed for 8 minutes.

Pour the batter into two sprayed regular-sized loaf pans. Combine the brown sugar and cinnamon and swirl half of the mixture into each pan. Bake in a preheated 350° degree oven for 50–55 minutes, then test for doneness.

Remove from the oven and cool 5–10 minutes before inverting on cooling racks. In a small bowl, combine the powdered sugar, milk, and reserved teaspoons of vanilla and butter extract. Mix well, then spread over the top of the still warm loaves.

These freeze well and make for a great breakfast or brunch bread.

**Chapter 2**

# Appetizers and Snacks

## Gabby Specialities—Appetizers and Snacks

# Super Bowl Party Popcorn

16 C popped pop corn (no butter added)
Butter-flavored cooking spray
3 tsp. fresh parmesan cheese, grated
1 tsp. Cajun seasoning (Joe's Stuff, Cajun Dust, etc.)

3/4 tsp. Morton Nature's Seasons seasoning blend
1/2 tsp. garlic powder
1/2 tsp. onion powder
1/2 tsp. chili powder
1/2 tsp. ground thyme leaves

Pop the pop corn following package directions and place in a large serving bowl. While the corn is still hot, coat with the butter-flavored spray.

Combine all remaining seasonings and sprinkle half of the mixture over all of the corn while tossing lightly. Repeat the procedure a second time. Serve the corn warm.

Makes 16 cups.

Easy, inexpensive, and a definite crowd pleaser!

# NFL Super Bowl Party Mix

1/4 C butter (the real stuff)
2 cloves garlic, pressed or finely
    minced
2 1/2 T Worcestershire sauce
1 1/2 tsp. Morton Nature's Seasons
    Seasoning blend or Season All
    Seasoned salt

2 C Corn Chex cereal
2 C Wheat Chex cereal
2 C Rice Chex cereal
2 C Pepperidge Farm Goldfish
2 C Cheerios cereal
2 C thin pretzel sticks
1 C salted cashew nuts

In a large roasting pan, melt the butter over medium heat, then stir in the garlic, Worcestershire and seasoned salt. When all is dissolved, add the remaining ingredients, stirring to coat well.

Bake in a preheated 250° oven for 50–60 minutes, stirring several times. Remove from the oven and spread the mixture over paper toweling to cool to room temperature. After cooling, store in air tight containers before serving.

Have a great bash!

# Smoked Trout Party Ball

1 can (7.75 oz.) Smoked Rocky
    Mountain Rainbow Trout*
1 pkg. (8 oz.) cream cheese, softened
    to room temperature
1 small Bermuda onion, very finely
    chopped
1 T dried dill weed

3 T capers, drained well
2 medium cloves garlic, pressed or very
    finely minced
Red leaf lettuce cups
Assorted party toasts, mini bagels, or
    crackers

In a medium-size mixing bowl, break up the trout, then stir in the cream cheese, onion, dill, capers and garlic. Stir well to mix.

Shape the mixture into a ball, then wrap with plastic wrap and refrigerate for several hours before serving. To serve, place the ball on a serving plate over lettuce cups and surround with the party breads or crackers.

*Trout of Paradise, Paradise, Utah (801-245-4611) is the company that makes this wonderful product. If you hadn't thought of it yet, this makes a wonderful holiday gift.

# Three Different Cheese Logs

*Each of these is quick, easy, and delicious. Choose the one that goes best with your menu.*

### Salmon Cheese Log

1 can red (not pink) salmon, picked of
  skin and bone matter
1 pkg (8 oz.) softened cream cheese
2 T lemon juice

1 tsp. horseradish
1/2 tsp. liquid smoke (Wright's)
1/4 tsp. instant minced onion
1/4 tsp. garlic powder

Combine and mix all ingredients in a medium mixing bowl. Shape into a log or ball. If desired, roll in finely chopped fresh parsley or finely chopped pecans. Wrap in plastic wrap and chill well.

### Cheddar Cheese Log

1 pkg (8 oz) softened cream cheese
1/2 lb. sharp cheddar cheese, shredded
1 small onion, very finely chopped

1–2 T fresh parsley or dried parsley
  flakes
1/8 tsp. garlic powder

In a medium bowl, combine and mix all ingredients. Form into four logs or balls, and roll each in one of the following: finely chopped pecans; chili powder; sweet Hungarian paprika; parsley flakes or finely chopped fresh basil leaves. Wrap in plastic wrap and chill well.

### Roquefort Cheese Log

1 pkg (8 oz.) softened cream cheese
1 pkg (4 oz.) crumbled blue cheese
1 C sharp Cheddar cheese, shredded

1/4 C onion, minced
1 T Worcestershire sauce

In a medium bowl, combine and mix all ingredients. Form into 4 logs or balls, then roll in finely chopped fresh parsley or pecans. Wrap in plastic wrap and chill well.

# Garden Vegetable Spread

1 pkg. (8 oz.) light cream cheese, softened
1/4 C ketchup
1 tsp. lemon juice
1/4 tsp. salt
1/4 tsp. white pepper

1/2 C carrot, finely shredded
1/2 C celery, finely chopped
1/4 C green bell pepper, finely chopped
1/4 C onion, finely chopped
Assorted vegetables or crackers

In a small bowl, blend the cream cheese, ketchup, lemon juice and seasonings until thoroughly mixed. Stir in the vegetables, cover and chill. Serve with vegetables or crackers.

# Garlic and Buttery Boursin Spread

2 cloves garlic, minced
2 pkgs. (8 oz.) cream cheese, softened
1 C butter or margarine, softened
1 tsp dried oregano
1/4 tsp dried basil

1/4 tsp dried marjoram
1/4 tsp dried dill weed
1/4 tsp dried thyme
1/4 tsp white pepper

This one is real simple. Get out the food processor and position the knife blade in the bowl. Add all ingredients, process until smooth, stopping once or twice to scrape down the sides.

Place in small crock, or two 1-cup dessert dishes, and refrigerate for several hours. Serve as cheese spread with a variety of crackers. Delicious!

# Gabby's Mustard Chicken Cubes

8 chicken breasts, skinned, boned and
    cut into 2-inch cubes
1/2 C Gabby's Own Mustard (*see
    chapter 7, Sauces and Dressings, for
    this recipe*) or your favorite brand

1/2 C honey
2–4 T soy sauce
1 1/2 T curry powder
1/4 C fresh cilantro leaves, finely
    chopped

Prepare the chicken as indicated, then place in a sprayed shallow baking dish in a single layer, skin-side down.

In a small mixing bowl, combine the mustard, honey, soy sauce and curry powder. Mix well, then pour evenly over all of the chicken. Cover with plastic wrap and refrigerate overnight.

Remove from the refrigerator about a half hour before baking. Place each piece in a baking pan, cover with foil, and bake in a preheated 350° oven for 30 minutes. Uncover, baste with the sauce and bake for 15 more minutes or until chicken is done. Place the pieces on a serving dish and sprinkle the chopped cilantro over all. Serve immediately with toothpicks.

Quick and very easy. Makes a great party pleaser.

# Fresh Herbed Mozzarella Cheese

12 1-oz. fresh mozzarella balls, well drained
1 C extra virgin olive oil (I suggest Sagra brand; you can also use a lemon olive oil)
2 T fresh sweet basil leaves, finely chopped
2 T fresh oregano leaves, finely chopped
2 T fresh chives or green onion tops, finely chopped
2–3 fresh cloves garlic, pressed or minced
1 tsp. dried red pepper flakes
1/2 tsp. fresh ground pepper
1/2 tsp. sea salt
Radicchio and endive leaves
Toasted baguette slices

Place the mozzarella balls in a shallow dish. Combine all of the remaining ingredients, except the lettuce leaves and bread slices. Whisk the mixture, then pour over the mozzarella.

Cover with plastic wrap and refrigerate about 24 hours before serving. Arrange the radicchio and endive leaves on a medium-size serving platter, then arrange the mozzarella with the marinade over all. Serve with the toasted baguette slices.

Serves 12.

Summer gathering coming up? Try this excellent hors d'oeuvre.

# Fresh Tomato-Basil Bruschetta

6–8 medium roma tomatoes, seeded
    and chopped
1/2 C red Bermuda onion, finely
    chopped
1/4 C fresh sweet basil, finely chopped
1/2 C sweet vermouth
1 1/2 T extra virgin olive oil
1 medium clove garlic, pressed or
    minced

1/2 tsp. salt, or to taste
1/4 tsp. fresh ground pepper, or to taste
1 baguette loaf bread, sliced into
    3/4-inch rounds
1–2 large cloves garlic, pressed
1/4 C extra virgin olive oil
Fresh parmesan cheese, grated

In a medium-size mixing bowl, combine all of the ingredients, except the bread, garlic, olive oil and parmesan. Mix well, cover and refrigerate for at least two hours, so the flavors can "marry."

Toast all of the slices of bread, then combine the garlic and olive oil. Mix well, then "paint" over one side of each round of toast. Drain the tomato mixture and press lightly to remove all liquid. Spoon 2 tablespoons of the tomato mixture over each toast round (oiled side only). If desired, each bruschetta can be garnished with a small basil leaf. Sprinkle each with just a small amount of parmesan cheese.

Makes 16 bruschettas.

Serve as a light hors d'oeuvre (2 per person) to a great Italian dinner.

# Crunchy Seafood Toast

1 lb. loaf of sourdough bread
    (baguette-style)
1 lb. imitation crab flakes (surimi)
1 C red bell pepper, finely chopped
5 scallions (green onion), finely
    chopped
5 T Miracle Whip Free dressing

2 T lime juice
2 T Dijon-style mustard
3 T fresh parsley, finely chopped
1 tsp. chili powder
1/4 C fresh parmesan cheese, shredded

Spray a large baking sheet. Slice the bread into 36 thin rounds. In a mixing bowl, combine the remaining ingredients and mix well to blend. Spread the seafood mixture over each of the bread rounds and place on the prepared baking sheet. Preheat your broiler and place the sheet on the first rack under the broiler. Broil for five minutes or until lightly browned. Serve immediately.

Makes 36 rounds, which serves 4–6 people.

# Basil-Cheese Bread Sticks

1 lb. round loaf of sourdough bread,
   unsliced
1/2 C butter

2 tsp. basil
3/4 tsp. garlic powder
2/3 C parmesan cheese, grated

Slice the bread into 1 1/2-inch slices, cutting to—but not through—the bottom of the loaf. Slice the bread again into 1 1/2-inch slices in the opposite direction, again cutting to—but not through—the bottom of the loaf, forming breadsticks.

Place the loaf on a sheet of heavy-duty foil. In a small saucepan, melt the butter over low heat, then stir in the basil and garlic powder. Drizzle the butter mixture between the breadsticks and over the top of the loaf. Sprinkle the cheese over all and wrap with the foil.

When ready to barbecue, place the bread on the grill 4–6 inches from the coals. Heat 15–25 minutes or until cheese is melted and bread is hot.

Serves 6.

This can also be heated in your oven at 375° for 10–12 minutes.

# Gabby's Wrapped Chestnuts

2 C light soy sauce (Kikkoman is fine)
4 green onions, sliced
1 tsp. fresh grated ginger

2 cans whole water chestnuts, drained
2 C (scant) brown sugar
1 lb. bacon slices, cut in half crosswise

Place the soy, onions and ginger in a medium-size bowl. Pour the drained chestnuts into the soy mixture and marinate for at least 30 minutes. Roll each chestnut in the brown sugar, wrap with a half slice of bacon and secure with a toothpick.

Arrange the wrapped chestnuts on a rack and place on a baking sheet or pan to catch the drippings. Bake in a preheated 400° degree oven about 20 minutes or until the bacon is browned and lightly crisp. If you are doubling this recipe for a large crowd or you want to bake ahead, just reheat in a 350° degree oven for 5–10 minutes before serving.

Serves 8–12.

These are really good, but remember they are filling—maybe too filling for a dinner party, but fine for a cocktail party.

# Artichoke Tidbits

2 jars (6 oz) marinated artichoke
    hearts
1 small onion, finely chopped
1 clove garlic, pressed
4 eggs, beaten
1/4 C fine dry bread crumbs (can be
    seasoned)

1/4 tsp. salt
1/8 tsp. fresh ground pepper
1/8 tsp. oregano
1/8 tsp. Tabasco sauce
1/2 lb. sharp cheddar cheese, shredded
2 T fresh parsley, finely chopped

Drain the marinade from one jar of artichoke hearts into a medium-size fry pan.
Drain the other jar and discard the marinade (or save for use in salad dressing).
Chop all of the artichoke hearts and set aside.

Heat the marinade in the pan, add the onion and garlic, and saute until the
onion is limp, about 5 minutes. In a medium size mixing bowl, beat the eggs,
adding the crumbs, salt, pepper, oregano, and Tabasco. Stir in the cheese, parsley,
chopped artichokes and sauteed ingredients.

Turn this mixture into a greased 7 x 11-inch baking pan or dish. Bake in a
preheated 325° degree oven about 30 minutes or until set like a custard. Let cool
in the pan and cut into 1 1/2-inch squares. Serve hot, warm or cold; these can
also be reheated as a leftover.

Serves 8–12.

# Gabby's Shiitake-Pita Crisps

3–4 T olive oil
1 tsp. oregano
2 cloves garlic, pressed or finely
    minced
4 pita breads, split apart and each side
    cut into 4 triangles
3 T butter or butter-olive oil
    combination

1/4 C red Bermuda onion
1/2 lb. fresh shiitake mushrooms,
    sliced
1/4 C fresh herbs of choice, chopped
1/2 tsp. garlic pepper
Salt, to taste (optional)
2 T straight sherry wine or brandy
3 T heavy cream

In a small bowl, combine the olive oil, oregano and garlic and mix. Prepare the pita as indicated, then brush the rough side with the olive oil mixture and place on a baking sheet. Bake in a preheated 350° oven until golden brown and crispy.

While the pita breads bake, prepare the mushroom mixture. In a medium-size skillet, heat the butter over medium heat. Add the onion and saute about three minutes, then add the mushrooms, herbs, pepper, and salt. Continue to saute a couple of minutes, then add the sherry and cream and cook for three more minutes. Spoon the mushroom mixture over each pita triangle and serve immediately.

Makes 32 crisps.

# Very Low Fat Smoked Salmon Rounds

1 can (14 1/4 oz.) red (sockeye)
    salmon, drained and picked of all
    skin and bone matter
1/2 C fresh parsley, finely chopped
1/2 C light-style mayonnaise
1/4 C currants
1/4 C toasted pecan gems
4 T chutney (your favorite)

1 T garlic red wine vinegar
1 tsp. liquid smoke (Wright's)
1/2 tsp. garlic pepper
4 medium cucumbers, scored and
    sliced
4 red and green bell peppers, seeded
    and cut into small wedges

Prepare the canned salmon as indicated and place in a medium mixing bowl or food processor bowl. Add all remaining ingredients, except the cucumbers and peppers. Mix or process the salmon mixture, cover and refrigerate until chilled and set up.

Prepare the cucumbers and peppers as indicated, then lay out the rounds and wedges. Place a small scoop of the mixture on each of the rounds and wedges and arrange on a serving platter.

This recipe can also be prepared for filling a softened lavosh round. Simply place the whole lavosh cracker between warm dampened terry toweling and let set 20 minutes or so. Place the salmon filling over the softened cracker and arrange small cucumber spears down one side. Roll up, cover with plastic wrap and refrigerate until serving. Just before serving, slice into 1-inch rounds.

Makes about 24 rounds.

# Smoked Salmon Mousse

3/4 lb. smoked salmon fillet
8 oz. pkg. cream cheese, room
   temperature
1/3 C green onions, finely chopped
3 T regular or sweet onion, finely
   chopped
3 T dill weed

Juice from 1/2 fresh lemon
3 drops hot pepper sauce (your choice)
1/2 tsp. fresh ground pepper
Cucumber, slices
Capers, drained well

Place the salmon, green onions, dill, lemon juice and hot pepper sauce into the bowl of your food processor. Place the cream cheese, cut into chunks, on top of the other ingredients in the bowl. Process the mixture on high until all is blended and pureed. Scrap the mixture into a serving bowl.

Fold in the onion, cover and chill for several hours (at least two). Place a small mound of the salmon mixture over the top of each cucumber slice and garnish each with a couple of capers.

Makes about 24 rounds.

Real nice for the summer months.

# Chicken Phyllo Hors d'oeuvres

2 T butter or margin
1/4 C finely chopped mushrooms
1/4 C finely chopped green onions
2 C finely chopped cooked chicken
2 T dried parsley flakes
1 tsp. tarragon
2 tsp. salt

1/4 tsp. fresh ground or seasoned
  pepper
1 egg, well beaten
3/4 C shredded Swiss or Gruyere
  cheese
1/3 C melted butter or margarine
2 lb. phyllo pastry sheets

Melt the butter in a skillet. Add the mushrooms and onions and saute over medium heat 7–8 minutes or until most of the moisture has evaporated. Drain the mixture on paper towels.

In a large mixing bowl, combine the mushroom/onion mixture with all other ingredients, except the phyllo and the melted butter, and blend well. Slice the phyllo into 3-inch strips. Place a rounded teaspoon of the filling mixture 1 inch from the bottom of each strip. Fold the right corner over the filling to form a triangle and continue to fold the entire strip like you would a flag, tucking the corners in tightly. Arrange the triangles on a lightly greased baking sheet. Brush the tops with butter and, if you like, sprinkle with sesame seeds.

Bake in a preheated 350° oven for 20 minutes, or until golden brown. Serve hot.

Makes 30–36 triangles … and are they good!!!

# Mexican Roll-Ups

2–3 strips of thick sliced bacon, diced, fried crisp, and drained well
1 C cheddar and Monterey Jack cheese, shredded
3 T mayonnaise (not salad dressing)
2 T green or black olives, chopped
1–2 T canned green chilies, diced
1 T fresh cilantro, finely chopped
3 green onions, finely chopped
2 tsp. chili powder
14 slices of white bread, crusts removed
2–3 T butter, melted

Prepare the bacon as indicated and place in a small mixing bowl. Combine all remaining ingredients, except the bread and butter, with the bacon. Mix well.

Prepare the slices of bread and roll flat with a rolling pin. Spread a layer of the cheese mixture over the bread, roll up, slice in half and secure each with a cocktail pick. Place on a baking sheet and brush with the melted butter. Bake in a preheated 375° degree oven about 10 minutes or until golden brown.

Makes 28 roll-ups.

# South of the Border Spicy Roll-Ups

4–6 large flour tortillas, warmed
1 pkg. (8 oz.) cream cheese, softened
   to room temperature
1–2 cloves garlic, pressed or minced
1 can (4 oz.) chopped black olives
1 C medium cheddar cheese, shredded

1 can (7 oz.) whole green chilies, cut
   into strips, lengthwise
4–6 whole green onions
8–12 fresh cilantro sprigs
Fresh salsa (your choice) for dipping

Place the tortillas in slightly moist terry toweling and "zap" in the microwave about 50 seconds just before filling.

In a small bowl, combine the softened cream cheese, garlic, olives and shredded cheese. Mix well, then spread over each tortilla. Place a couple of chili strips and a whole green onion at one end of the tortilla. Roll each tortilla tightly, cover with plastic wrap, and refrigerate to chill. Slice into 1 1/2-inch pinwheels after cutting off the ends to square. Serve the salsa for dipping with the roll-ups.

Serves 4–6.

Great for a summer party!

# Fresh Shrimp Quesadillas

1 lb. fresh medium-size shrimp,
    cooked, peeled, and coarsely
    chopped
1/2 C salsa (your choice of salsa—I
    prefer the commercial peach salsa)
1/4 C green onions, chopped
4–6 drops hot pepper sauce

4–6 sprigs of fresh cilantro, chopped
10 large flour tortillas
2 C Monterey Jack cheese, shredded
    (can also use the mixed Mexican
    cheeses by Kraft or Sargento)
Fresh cilantro sprigs for garnish

Prepare the shrimp as indicated and place in a medium mixing bowl. Add the salsa, green onions, pepper sauce and chopped cilantro. Mix well and set aside.

Lay out 5 of the tortillas on baking sheets. Sprinkle half of the shredded cheese over each of the tortillas. Divide the shrimp mixture over each tortilla, then top with the remaining cheese. Place the remaining five tortillas over each filled tortilla and press down gently. Bake in a preheated 425° oven for 7–8 minutes. Transfer to a cutting board and cut each quesadilla into 6 wedges.

Makes 30 wedges.

Makes for a quick and easy lunch, snack, or hors d'oeuvre.

# Quarterback Quesadillas

2 C cooked pork roast, chopped or shredded
1–2 medium jalapeno peppers, seeded and finely minced
1/4 tsp. ground cumin
1/4 tsp. salt or to taste
1/2 tsp. fresh ground pepper

8–10 large flour tortillas
1/2 C white onion, finely minced
1/2 C fresh cilantro, finely minced
1 1/2–2 C Monterey Jack cheese, shredded
2 C fresh salsa (homemade or purchased)

Prepare the ingredients as indicated. In a large bowl, combine the pork, peppers, cumin, salt and pepper and mix well.

Lay out the tortillas and place 1/8 of the pork mixture over half of each one. Sprinkle the onion, cilantro and cheese over each as desired. Fold each tortilla over to make a "half-moon."

Place the quesadillas on a lightly sprayed shallow baking dish or sheet, not touching. Bake in a preheated 500° oven about 5 minutes or until crisp and golden. Place each on a cutting board, slice into wedges and serve with the salsa of your choice.

Makes 8–10 servings.

Make plenty, because they'll go quickly.

# Gabby's Chile Con Queso Nachos

2 T olive oil
1 large white onion, finely chopped
3–4 large cloves garlic, pressed or
    finely minced
1–2 cans (14 1/2 oz.) Mexican stewed
    tomatoes (S&W brand)
1 can (4 oz.) green chilies, diced
1–2 jalapeno pepper, cut nacho-style
    (rings) (can also use canned
    pickled jalapenos)

2 C Monterey Jack cheese, shredded
2 C sharp cheddar cheese, shredded
1 C sour cream
1/2 C fresh cilantro, finely chopped
1 large can refried beans (with
    jalapeno), heated
1 small bunch of green onions,
    chopped
1 bag of tortilla rounds or chips,
    warmed

In a medium-size skillet, heat the oil over medium-high heat. Add the onion and garlic and saute until the onion is tender. Add the chilies, tomatoes and jalapeno peppers. Saute this mixture lightly about five minutes, then slowly stir in the cheeses.

When the cheeses are totally melted, remove from the heat and stir in the sour cream. Spread a layer of the heated refried beans over the bottom of a medium-large serving dish. Pour the chili-cheese mixture over the beans. Serve with the warmed tortilla rounds or chips to use as scoopers.

Makes about 50 rounds.

Wonderful with a cold … whatever. By the way, this can be served with a salad side dish and you've got an easy summer dinner.

# Mexican Holiday Dip

2 lbs. lean or extra lean ground beef

2–3 Mexican or Basque-style chorizo, cut into 1/2-inch rounds

2 medium white onions, coarsely chopped

2 cloves garlic, pressed or minced

2 cans (15 1/2 oz.) chili beans, smokey ranch beans or barbeque beans

2 cans (15 1/2 oz.) Mexican stewed tomatoes

1 can (4 oz.) green chilies, chopped

1/2 C jalapeno stuffed green olives, sliced

1/2 C dry red wine

1 1/2 tsp. chili powder

1 tsp. ground cumin

1/2 tsp. sugar

1/2 tsp. fresh ground pepper

1 C cheddar–Monterey Jack cheese combination, shredded

In a large fry pan, combine the ground beef, chorizo, onion, and garlic over medium-high heat. Brown the mixture well, then drain off all extruded grease.

Add the remaining ingredients, except the cheese, stirring well. Reduce the heat and simmer for 20 minutes. Pour the hot mixture into a serving bowl and swirl in the cheese, allowing it to melt. Serve with tortilla chips as dippers.

Makes enough for a midsize party.

This can be frozen or chilled for later use.

# King Crab Dip

2 lbs. king crab meat, shelled and cut into 1-inch chunks (imitation crab can be substituted)
1 1/2 T lemon juice
11 oz. (one 8-oz. and one 3-oz. pkg.) cream cheese, room temperature
3 T mayonnaise
1/2 C fresh parsley, finely chopped
1/2 small Bermuda onion, very finely chopped
1 medium red bell pepper, very finely chopped
2 ribs celery, finely chopped
3 T chives, finely chopped
2 T capers, drained
1 tsp. ground mace
1 tsp. thyme
1 tsp. fresh ground pepper
1 tsp. garlic powder
3/4 tsp. salt
Assorted crackers for dipping

Prepare the crab as indicated and place in a bowl; sprinkle the lemon juice over all and set aside.

In a large serving bowl, combine the softened cream cheese and mayonnaise and blend well. Stir in all remaining ingredients, except the crackers, mixing well. Fold the crab meat into the cream cheese mixture. Serve with the crackers.

# Holiday Crab Spread

1 pkg. (8 oz.) cream cheese, room temperature
1 T half & half cream (light cream)
1 large clove of garlic, pressed or finely minced
2 T green onions, finely chopped
1/4 C celery, finely chopped
6 oz. fresh crab meat, finely chopped

3–4 slices of thick sliced bacon, diced and fried crisp
1 T horseradish (not horseradish sauce)
Fresh ground pepper, to taste
Fresh parsley, finely chopped
Sweet Hungarian paprika, for color garnish

In a small mixing bowl, combine the cream cheese, half & half, and garlic, mixing until smooth and well blended. Mix in the remaining ingredients, except the parsley and paprika.

Pour the mixture into a medium- to small-sized decorative serving bowl. This recipe can be baked or warmed through before serving or it can be served as is, room temperature. Sprinkle the parsley and paprika over all and serve with an assortment of party crackers or breads.

Really great for a small holiday gathering.

# Holiday Bourbon Balls

1 pkg. (12 oz.) vanilla (Nilla) wafers
1 pkg. (11 oz.) chocolate chips
3 T light corn syrup
1/2 C granulated sugar

1 C pecan gems
1/3 C bourbon (rum can also be used)
1/2 C confectioner's sugar

Place the wafers in your food processor, process into fine crumbs and set aside.

In the top of a double boiler over hot—but not boiling—water, melt the chocolate chips. Mix together the corn syrup, granulated sugar, pecans, vanilla crumbs, and bourbon. Add this mixture to the melted chocolate and stir well.

Roll the mixture into 1-inch balls, then roll each in the confectioner's sugar. Refrigerate until serving time.

Makes about 3 dozen.

Just a little quickie for the holidays.

# Gabby's Boiled Shrimp

2 lbs. raw green shrimp (U15–20 in size)
10 whole peppercorns
1 clove garlic, halved

1/2 tsp thyme
2 whole cloves
1 bay leaf
2 tsp. salt (optional)

Place all ingredients except the shrimp in a saucepan with about 4 cups of water. Bring the mixture to a boil, add the shrimp and simmer, covered, 4–5 minutes, or until the shrimp turn pink and opaque. Drain and cool.

Peel off the shell matter and remove the black vein that runs down the back. Chill until serving time. Use in any recipe that calls for boiled shrimp, or serve with toothpicks, and let your guests dip them into a cocktail sauce. (*Try the "Crab and Shrimp Cocktail Sauce" recipe in chapter 7.*)

# Gabby's Marinated Veggies

4 C fresh vegetables cut into bite-size
    pieces
1/2 C cold pressed olive oil
1/4 C salad-type oil
1/3 C balsamic vinegar
1–2 cloves garlic, pressed
1 small onion, finely chopped

1 tsp. fresh parsley, finely chopped
1 tsp. Gabby's Own Mustard (*see chapter 7, Sauces and Dressings, for this recipe*)
2 tsp. dill weed
2 tsp. chervil
Salt and fresh ground pepper, to taste

You choose the combination of vegetables to marinate. (I would go for good contrasting color combinations, such as carrots, green beans, cauliflower, bell peppers, etc.) Steam all vegetables at least 10 minutes. If you use carrots, simmer them a little longer than the other vegetables.

Rinse in cold water to stop the cooking action, and place in a large covered container that contains all remaining ingredients. Refrigerate for at least 24 hours. Drain well and serve with toothpicks.

Will do well for a large party.

Well liked any time of the year.

# Marinated Party Shrimp

2–3 lbs. fresh shrimp (U-20), boiled or steamed and peeled (tails can be left on)
2 medium Bermuda onions, sliced into rings
1 C light vegetable oil
1 C tarragon white wine vinegar

2 tsp. celery seeds (crush just a bit)
1–2 cloves garlic, pressed or minced
1 T capers, drained well
4 whole bay leaves
10–15 whole peppercorns
6 whole allspice balls

Prepare the shrimp as indicated (don't over cook). While the shrimp are still warm, place in a medium-size glass bowl, add the onions and toss. Combine the remaining ingredients and mix well; pour over the shrimp and onions. Cover and refrigerate 12–24 hours.

Remove the shrimp from the marinade, garnish with fresh parsley and serve on party picks.

Now here is an easy one and something a bit different.

# Gabby's Marinated Shrimp and 'Rooms

3 lbs. medium to large-size shrimp, cooked, peeled and deveined

2 lbs. small fresh mushrooms, brushed with a damp mushroom brush and 1/8-inch of the stem removed

4 medium white onions, halved and thinly sliced

10–12 whole bay leaves

1 C herbed white wine vinegar

1 C light vegetable (canola) oil

2–4 cloves garlic, thinly sliced

4 T whole allspice balls

2 T sugar (can also use NutraSweet Spoonful)

1 tsp. whole fennel seeds

1/2 tsp. fresh ground pepper

1/2 tsp. salt (optional)

1/4 tsp. thyme

1/4 tsp. tarragon

1/4 tsp. sweet basil

In a large covered container or bowl, make four layers with the shrimp, mushrooms, onions and bay leaves. Combine all remaining ingredients, mix well and pour over the layered mixture. Cover and refrigerate at least 6 hours or up to 24–48 hours.

Makes 20 servings.

Can be served as an hors d'oeuvre or as a salad or fish course. Great for the party season.

# Marinated Sesame Chicken Wings

20 chicken wings, separated and tips discarded
2 T Japanese-style soy sauce
2 T mirin (sweet cooking rice wine)
1/2 tsp. fresh ginger, grated
2–3 extra large egg whites, beaten (not stiff)
1/4 C blanched almonds, ground
1/4 C flour
3 T toasted sesame seeds
Oil for frying in large fry pan

**Dipping sauce:**
3 T Japanese-style soy sauce
3 T seasoned rice vinegar
1 tsp. sesame oil
1 tsp. fresh ginger, grated
2 T sugar

Prepare the wings as indicated and place in a large bowl for marinating. Combine the soy, mirin and ginger and pour over the wings; marinate for 20–25 minutes, stirring often.

Lightly beat the egg whites in a medium-size bowl. Combine the almonds, flour and sesame seeds and mix well. Remove the wings from the marinade and dip into the egg whites. Then place the wings, a couple at a time, in the dry mixture and coat well.

Combine the dipping sauce ingredients in a serving bowl.

Heat about 2 inches of the oil in a large fry pan to about 360°. Fry each chicken wing until golden brown, about 5 minutes. Drain the wings on paper towels and serve piping hot with the dipping sauce.

# Gabby's Herbed Drummers

16–20 chicken drumsticks, washed in
    cold water and dried with paper
    towels
2 C cold milk
1/2 C dried bread crumbs
2 T dried parsley

2 tsp. onion granules
2 tsp. curry powder
1 tsp. garlic granules
1/2 tsp. dry mustard
1/4 tsp. sweet Hungarian paprika
Salt and fresh ground pepper, to taste

Prepare the drumsticks as indicated, place in a shallow baking dish and pour the milk over all (it is best if you can let the chicken soak in the milk for several hours).

Combine all remaining ingredients and pour into a pie tin or dish. Roll each wet drumstick in the herbed mixture. Place in a sprayed shallow baking dish or pan. Bake in a preheated 375° oven for 50–55 minutes or until browned and crispy.

These can be served hot, warm or chilled as leftovers.

# Meatballs and Chutney Sauce

2 lbs. extra lean ground beef
1 1/4 lbs. lean ground pork
3 extra large eggs, beaten
3/4 C fresh seasoned bread crumbs
3/4 C green onions, finely chopped
2 T Gabby's Own Mustard (*see chapter 7, Sauces and Dressings, for this recipe*)
2 tsp. Parsley Patch Garlic Saltless seasoning

1 tsp. coriander
3/4 tsp. ground allspice
1 1/2 tsp. salt or to taste
1/2 tsp. fresh ground pepper or to taste
1 C chutney (your favorite type)
1 C apple jelly
1/2 C whole cashews
1 T lemon juice

In a large mixing bowl, combine all the ingredients except the chutney, jelly, cashews and lemon juice; mix very well.

Form this mixture into small meat balls and place on large jelly roll pans. Cover and place in the freezer for 20 minutes. Remove from the freezer, uncover and bake in a preheated 350° oven for 20–25 minutes or until nicely browned. Drain well, place in a chafing bowl and set aside.

Combine the chutney, jelly, cashews and lemon juice in a medium saucepan and heat until jelly has dissolved. Pour this mixture over the still warm meatballs, stirring to coat all.

Makes about 6 dozen meatballs.

# Fried Lumpia (from the Philippines)

2 lbs. lean ground pork
1–2 cloves garlic, pressed or finely
    minced
1/4 C finely chopped celery
1/3 C finely chopped green onions
1 tsp. salt
1/2 tsp. fresh ground pepper

3 T soy sauce
1 small can water chestnuts, finely
    chopped
1 pkg. lumpia wrappers (you can also
    use egg roll wrappers, available in
    most stores)
Oil for frying

In a large mixing bowl, combine all ingredients except the lumpia wrappers and oil. Make sure that the chopped ingredients are indeed finely chopped. Now get in there with both hands and mix to blend well.

Remove the wrappers, one at a time, from the stack. Place about 2–3 teaspoons of the meat mixture at one end of the wrapper (the meat mixture should be rolled out in the shape of a pencil). Roll up the mixture in the wrapper and place a small amount of cold water over the end to secure the roll.

Heat about 1/4 inch of oil in a large fry pan. Add the rolled lumpia and fry until golden brown and crispy.

Makes about 50 wrappers.

# Louisiana Dipp'n Sauce

2 lbs. extra lean ground beef, browned and well drained of any extruded grease

2 cans (15 1/2 oz.) chili beans

1 can (15 oz.) chunky-style tomato sauce

3 medium fresh tomatoes, chopped (can also use more canned tomatoes)

1 large white onion, finely chopped

6 strips of thick-sliced bacon, diced fried crisp and well drained

12 large jalapeno stuffed green olives, drained and sliced

2–3 T fresh celery leaves, finely chopped

2 cloves garlic, pressed or finely minced

1/2 C burgundy wine

1 1/2 tsp. Cajun Dust or chili powder

1 tsp. salt (optional)

1 tsp. coarse ground black pepper

1/2 tsp. ground cumin

1/2 tsp. Louisiana Gold hot pepper sauce (or your choice)

1 C cheddar or cheddar-Monterey Jack cheese combination, shredded

Prepare the ground beef as indicated and place in a large deep pan. Add all remaining ingredients, except the cheese. Bring the mixture to a simmer and cook for 30 minutes.

Stir in the cheese and continue to simmer until all is melted. Serve warm with assorted corn chips, warmed tortillas or crackers.

This is large party stuff!

# Oriental Cocktail Ribs

2–2 1/2 lbs. lean pork spareribs (can use baby back), cut into 2-inch wide strips (connected)
1/2 C chicken broth
1/2 C light soy sauce
1/2 C brown sugar
3 T rice vinegar

2–3 cloves garlic, pressed or minced
1–2 T oyster sauce
1/2 tsp. fresh ginger, grated
1 tsp. fresh or coarse ground black pepper
1 T cornstarch
2 T cold water

Have your butcher cut the ribs into the desired width. Place the strips of ribs in a baking pan. Add the chicken broth, cover, and roast in a preheated 350° oven about 75 minutes.

Remove from oven and discard the extruded grease and liquid. In a saucepan, combine all remaining ingredients, except the cornstarch and water; bring the mixture to a simmer, stirring. Combine the cornstarch and water, then stir into the sauce, stirring until sauce thickens.

Cut the cooled ribs into single pieces, then pour the sauce over all and coat well. Return the sauced ribs to the baking pan, and roast uncovered for 20–25 minutes. Serve with toothpicks and lots of napkins.

Makes a big batch.

Use this one as an appetizer or a side dish to an oriental meal. Either way— delicious!

# Oriental Holiday Meat Balls

2 C fresh soft coarse bread crumbs
1/2 C milk
1/2 lb. extra lean ground beef
1/2 lb. Jimmy Dean hot country–style
    sausage
1/4 C water chestnuts, finely chopped
1 T soy sauce
1 tsp. sambal oleck (available in
    Oriental food stores)

1 tsp. garlic pepper
1/2 tsp. onion powder
Hot catsup for dipping
Gabby's Own Mustard for dipping (*see
    chapter 7, Sauces and Dressings, for
    this recipe*)

In a medium-size mixing bowl combine the crumbs and milk, mixing well. Add all of the remaining ingredients, except the catsup and mustard. Now, get in there with both hands (wash your hands first, like you mother told you), and mix well.

Roll the mixture into small, 1 1/2 inch balls, then place on a large baking pan. Place in the freezer for 30 minutes before baking. Bake in a preheated 325° oven about 20–25 minutes. Drain well and serve with toothpicks, using the hot catsup and mustard as dipping sauces.

Makes 30–35 meatballs.

Easy and great. *Note:* this recipe doubles well!

# Sweet and Sour Italian Sausage

2 lbs. Italian sausage (sweet and hot), cut into 1-inch pieces
2 cans (20 oz.) pineapple chunks, drained, but reserve 1 cup of the juice
1 C lemon juice
1/2 C (packed) brown sugar
2 T soy sauce (light or dark)
1 tsp. fresh ginger, grated
3 T cornstarch
2 medium red and green bell peppers, cut into chunks
1 bunch green onions, chopped

In a large skillet or fry pan, brown the sausage and drain well on paper towels. Discard the extruded grease, return the sausage pieces to the pan, and add the pineapple juice (reserve 2 tablespoons of the juice to mix with the cornstarch), lemon juice, brown sugar, soy sauce and ginger.

Cover and simmer for 20 minutes. Add the remaining ingredients and heat until the mixture thickens and clears (more or less). Keep warm and serve with cocktail picks and napkins.

Serves 4–6 people as a main dish or serve as an appetizer at a midsize party.

Have a great party and, yes, this can be served over steamed rice as an actual main entree—it's up to you.

# Chapter 3

# Salads, Soups and Chili

## Gabby Specialities—Salads, Soups and Chili

# Green Salad with Vanilla Vinaigrette

3/4 C olive oil
2 T white wine vinegar
1 tsp. salt
1 tsp. McCormick tarragon leaves

1 tsp. McCormick pure vanilla extract
1/2 tsp. sugar
1/4 tsp. McCormick ground black
    pepper

Whisk all of the ingredients until well blended. Chill well, then toss with mixed salad greens of choice.

Makes 1 cup of vinaigrette.

# 24-Hour Marinated Slaw

1 large head of green cabbage, cored and shredded
1 large red Bermuda onion, finely chopped
1 large green bell pepper, finely chopped
1 medium carrot, shredded
1/2 C light (canola) vegetable oil

1 C sugar
1 C cider or rice (seasoned) vinegar
2 tsp. Gabby's Own Mustard (*see chapter 7, Sauces and Dressings, for this recipe*)
1 tsp. salt
3/4 tsp. turmeric
1/2 tsp. celery seed

Prepare the cabbage, onion, pepper and carrot as indicated, place in a large serving bowl and mix well. In a medium saucepan, combine all remaining ingredients and bring to a boil, stirring until sugar is dissolved. Pour over the vegetable mixture. Cover and refrigerate to marinate for 24 hours.

Serves 8.

Take this along on your next picnic.

# Gabby's Caesar Salad

**Dressing:**
2 cloves garlic, pressed or finely
    minced
1/3 C regular salad or olive oil
3 T red wine vinegar (can also be
    garlic herb vinegar)
1 tsp. Worcestershire sauce
1/2 tsp. salt
1/4 tsp. fresh ground pepper

**Salad:**
3 qts. salad greens (mostly romaine,
    but some red leaf also)
1 coddled egg or 2 coddled egg whites

1/4 C regular salad or olive oil
1/3 C fresh parmesan or asiago cheese,
    grated or shredded
1/3 C Gorgonzola cheese, crumbled
6 strips of thick sliced bacon, diced,
    fried crisp and well drained
1 tin anchovy fillets, drained of all oil,
    chopped

**Salad toppings:**
Juice from half a fresh lemon
2 C Gabby's croutons (*recipe follows*)

*At least an hour before serving:* Prepare the dressing by mixing all of the dressing
ingredients in a shaker jar; shake well and let stand at room temperature. Also,
pull the lettuce leaves apart, place in the sink, and wash in ice cold water.

*Just before serving:* Tear the lettuce into just larger than bite-size pieces and place
on a terry towel to dry. In a large wooden salad bowl, toss the salad ingredients in
the order listed, tossing after each addition. Serve immediately.

Serves 4–6 people—and I'll guarantee, they'll come back for more!

# Gabby's Croutons

8 slices of white bread (fresh or stale)      1/2 clove garlic, minced
1 1/2 T grated parmesan cheese                1/8 tsp. oregano
1/3 C butter                                   18 tsp. parsley

Remove the crust from each slice of bread and cut the bread into 1/2-inch cubes. In a small frying pan, melt the butter. Thoroughly rub the garlic over the bottom of a cookie sheet and discard the pulp. Drizzle the melted butter over the bottom of the cookie sheet. Spread the cubes of bread over the butter and stir the cubes around. Sprinkle the cheese, oregano, and parsley over all, and again stir the cubes around.

Place the cookie sheet in a preheated 250° oven and bake 30–40 minutes or until the croutons are dry, crisp, and a dark golden color. Let the croutons cool before using, or store in an airtight container for later use. These can be used for both salads or soups.

# Shrimp-Crab-Pasta Salad

3 C sea shell pasta (small), cooked, drained and well chilled

1 medium Bermuda or sweet onion, finely chopped

1/2 C green bell pepper, finely chopped

2 hard cooked eggs, chopped

1 can (7 1/2 oz.) lump crab meat, drained (you can also use fresh crab or thawed frozen crab)

1 can (7 1/2 oz.) medium shrimp, drained (can also use fresh or frozen bay shrimp, thawed)

1/2 C celery, finely sliced

2 T fresh parsley, finely chopped

1/8 tsp. ground white pepper or to taste

1 1/2 tsp. Schilling Salad Supreme (optional)

1/2 C plain low-fat yogurt

1/4 C low-fat or light mayonnaise

Cherry tomatoes, halved, to taste

Cucumber slices, to taste

In a medium serving bowl, combine all ingredients, except the tomatoes and cucumbers, stirring to blend well. Cover and refrigerate at least two hours, or overnight. Garnish top with cherry tomatoes and cucumber slices before serving.

Makes 6 1-cup servings.

Each serving contains 240 calories, only 11 grams of fat and 176 milligrams of cholesterol. Not bad for healthy eating, eh?

# Outer Banks Shrimp Salad

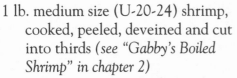

1 lb. medium size (U-20-24) shrimp, cooked, peeled, deveined and cut into thirds (*see "Gabby's Boiled Shrimp" in chapter 2*)

1 lb. elbow macaroni, boiled and drained well

4 large eggs, hard cooked, peeled and chopped

1 1/2 C Claussen kosher-style pickles, chopped

1 C sliced ripe olives (can also use green), drained

2–3 medium ribs of celery, chopped

1/2 medium sweet or red Bermuda onion, coarsely chopped

1/4 medium red sweet bell pepper, finely chopped

1 C mayonnaise (real stuff)

2 T olive oil

2 T Worcestershire sauce

2 T lemon juice

1-2 T Gabby's Own Mustard (*see chapter 7, Sauces and Dressings, for this recipe*)

1 T hot pepper sauce

1 T Old Bay Seafood Seasoning

1 tsp. Morton Nature's Seasons Seasoning blend

1 tsp. fresh ground pepper, or to taste

1/2 tsp. garlic powder

Red leaf or curly leaf lettuce

Prepare the shrimp and macaroni as indicated, then place in a large mixing bowl along with the eggs, pickles, olives, celery, onion and pepper. Toss to blend well, then cover and refrigerate.

In a smaller bowl, combine all remaining ingredients for the dressing, whisking after each addition. Cover and chill well before serving. Just before serving, combine both mixtures and mix thoroughly. Serve over lettuce cups.

# Chilled Oriental Shrimp Salad

1 pkg. (20 oz.) frozen tiny peas,
    thawed and well drained
1/2 lb. tiny bay shrimp
1 C celery with leaves, finely chopped
1/2 C carrot, finely shredded
3/4 C mayonnaise (real stuff)
1 T lemon juice

1/2 tsp. curry powder
1/4 tsp. Schilling Garlic & Herb
    Seasoning blend (salt-free)
1/2 C cashews
Chow mein oriental noodles
Chilled lettuce (your choice),
    shredded

In a large mixing bowl, combine the peas, shrimp, celery, carrot, mayonnaise, lemon juice and curry powder and toss well to blend. Cover with plastic wrap and refrigerate for 30 minutes.

Add the cashews and toss well. Arrange the Oriental noodles over the shredded lettuce, then arrange the salad mixture over the noodles. If desired, garnish with slices of roma or cherry tomatoes. Serve immediately.

Serves 6.

# Oriental Seafood Salad in a Puff Bowl

**Salad:**
1/2 lb. cooked medium (U-22) shrimp, peeled and deveined
1/2 lb. cooked bay scallops
1/2 lb. fresh crab meat (can use imitation crab—surimi), chopped
1 can (8 oz.) whole water chestnuts, drained well
1 C celery, sliced diagonally
1 C fresh mushrooms, sliced
1 C fresh bean sprouts
1/4 lb. fresh pea pods, end and strings removed
1/4 C green onions, sliced

**Dressing:**
3/4 C mayonnaise (can use light) or salad dressing
1/4 C lemon juice
1 T prepared horseradish
1 tsp. Gabby's Own Mustard (*see chapter 7, Sauces and Dressings, for this recipe*) or your favorite prepared mustard
1/2 tsp. garlic salt
Fresh ground or seasoned pepper, to taste

1 puff bowl (*recipe follows*)

Prepare the seafood as indicated and chill well. In a large mixing bowl, combine the chilled seafood and all other salad ingredients, tossing lightly to mix well.

In a small mixing bowl, combine the dressing ingredients. Whisk well, then pour over the salad mixture and toss again. Cover with plastic wrap and refrigerate.

An hour or so before serving, prepare the puff bowl, then cool to room temperature. Just before serving, spoon the salad into the puff bowl (if desired, use a regular salad bowl lined with lettuce leaves).

Serves 6.

# Puff Bowl for Salads

2 extra large eggs
1/2 C all-purpose flour
1/2 C milk

1/4 tsp. salt
2 T melted butter or margarine

In a small mixing bowl, beat the eggs until frothy. Gradually beat in the flour and continue to beat until mixture is smooth.

Add the milk, salt, and melted butter, mixing well. Pour the batter into a well-sprayed 9-inch pie plate. Bake in a preheated 425° oven for 15 minutes, then reduce the temperature to 350° and continue to bake 10–15 more minutes or until browned.

Remove and let cool to room temperature before filling.

# Let's Do Spinach and 'Rooms

3 bunches of fresh spinach, washed,
    stemmed and chopped
3 T butter and olive oil combination
1 1/2 lbs. fresh button mushrooms,
    sliced (you can also use shiitake,
    morels, etc.)

4–6 shallots, minced
1 large clove garlic, pressed or minced
1/4 tsp. fresh nutmeg, grated
Salt and fresh ground pepper, to taste

Prepare the spinach (rinse in lots of cold water and drain well) as indicated. Place the chopped spinach in a large skillet or saucepan and cook over high heat (do not add more water) until wilted, stirring often. Place the cooked spinach in a towel to squeeze out the moisture.

In a large skillet, heat the butter-oil combination over medium-high heat. Add the sliced mushrooms, shallots and garlic. Saute this mixture for 4–5 minutes, stirring often. Add the spinach, stirring to incorporate all, then add the nutmeg, salt and pepper. When all is blended and heated through, remove to a serving platter or bowl.

Serves 6.

# Special Hearts of Palm Salad

1 can (14 oz.) hearts of palm, well
    drained
1 medium avocado, seeded and diced
4–5 green onions, coarsely chopped
2 large firm ripe tomatoes, seeded and
    coarsely chopped
1/4 C pine nuts, toasted
1 1/2 T fresh parsley, very finely
    chopped

2 cloves garlic, very finely chopped
1/4 C extra virgin olive oil
3 T fresh lime juice
1 tsp Schilling Salad Supreme mix
Salt and fresh ground pepper, to taste
Mixed salad greens of choice

Drain the hearts of palm well, then slice into 3/4-inch rounds. Place the palms in a large salad bowl and add all remaining ingredients, stirring to blend well.

Taste for proper seasoning before spooning over lettuce cups. If desired, top each with fresh shredded parmesan cheese.

Serves 4–6.

A very special salad.

# Oriental-Style Spinach Salad

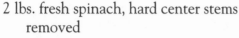

2 lbs. fresh spinach, hard center stems removed

1 C fresh mushrooms, sliced

1 1/2 C chicken breasts, skinned, boned, cooked and finely diced (can also use roasted turkey)

1/2 lb. bacon, diced, fried crisp and drained (reserve the drippings)

2 T canola oil

3/4 C herbed white wine vinegar

3 T rice wine vinegar

2 1/2 T Japanese-style soy sauce

1 egg yolk (optional)

2 T onion, grated or very finely minced

1 small wedge of fresh apple, grated

1 T lemon juice

1/2 tsp. Gabby's Own Mustard (*see chapter 7, Sauces and Dressings, for this recipe*) or your favorite

1/2 tsp. sweet Hungarian paprika

Salt and fresh ground pepper, to taste

Toasted sesame seeds, to taste

Wash the spinach in ice cold water, then dry well, tear into bite-size pieces and place in a large salad bowl. Add the mushrooms, chicken and bacon. Toss lightly. Sprinkle the oil over the salad ingredients and toss lightly again.

Combine the remaining ingredients in a shaker jar and shake well. Pour the dressing in the pan with the bacon drippings and heat to the bubbly stage. Pour over the salad ingredients, toss and serve immediately.

Serves 4–6.

# Grapefruit and Spinach Salad

2 bunches of fresh spinach, thick stems removed, rinsed in ice cold water
2–3 pink grapefruit, cut into sections
1–2 large avocados, seeded and diced
1/2 lb. thick-sliced bacon, diced and fried crisp
1 bunch of radishes, sliced
1/2 lb. Swiss cheese, shredded
1/2 C sugar or sugar substitute

5 1/2 T seasoned rice vinegar
1 T Gabby's Own Mustard (*see chapter 7, Sauces and Dressings, for this recipe*)
2 1/2 tsp. poppy seeds
2 tsp sweet onion, grated
1 tsp. salt
1/2 tsp. fresh ground pepper
1 C light (canola) salad oil

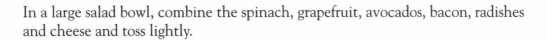

In a large salad bowl, combine the spinach, grapefruit, avocados, bacon, radishes and cheese and toss lightly.

In a small mixing bowl or shaker jar, combine the remaining ingredients and mix well. Add the dressing to taste to the basic salad mixture and again toss lightly. Serve immediately.

Serves 4–6.

# Super Supper Salad

**Meatball ingredients:**
1 lb. extra lean ground beef
1/2 lb. lean ground pork
1/2 C wheat germ
1/2 C sweet onion, finely chopped
1/4 C chili sauce or ketchup
1 extra large egg, beaten lightly
1–1 1/2 tsp. chili powder
1 tsp dried parsley flakes
1 tsp. garlic pepper
1 tsp garlic salt
1/2 tsp. ground cumin

**Salad ingredients:**
1 large head red lettuce, torn into
    pieces
4 medium tomatoes, sliced into wedges

2 medium avocados, skinned and cut
    into slices
2 medium green and red bell peppers,
    sliced
1 1/2 C red kidney beans, well drained
1 C peperoncini peppers, drained
1/2 C whole pitted black olives
1/2 C Italian-style green olives

**Dressing:**
1/2 C Gabby's Super Italian Salad
    Dressing (*see chapter 7 for this
    recipe*)

1/4 C fresh parmesan cheese, shredded
    or grated

In a medium-size mixing bowl, combine the meatball ingredients and mix well to blend. Form into 1 1/2-inch meatballs, place in a shallow baking pan, cover and chill about an hour. Bake in a preheated 400° oven for 15 minutes. When done, discard the extruded grease and let meatballs cool to room temperature.

Place the lettuce leaves over the bottom of a large serving platter and arrange the rest of the salad ingredients around the sides. Place the meatballs in the center, pour the dressing over all, sprinkle the parmesan cheese over the top and serve.

Serves 8–10 as a great side dish or luncheon salad.

# Chicken and "Broc" Pasta Salad

2 chicken breasts, skinned, boned, seasoned (garlic powder, herbed lemon pepper, seasoned salt and sweet Hungarian paprika), sauteed and cut into strips

1/2 lb. penne or rotelle pasta, cooked and well drained

2–3 C small fresh broccoli flowerets, steamed or boiled and drained

4 roma tomatoes, cut into wedges

3/4 C celery (with leaves), finely chopped

1/2 C walnut pieces, lightly toasted

1 C mayonnaise (the real stuff)

1/2 C fresh basil leaves, lightly chopped

1/2 C fresh parmesan or asiago cheese, grated

1 T lemon juice

2–3 tsp. garlic, very finely minced

1/2 tsp. fresh ground pepper (or to taste)

Red or curly leaf lettuce

Prepare the chicken breasts as indicated, set aside to cool, then cut into strips. In a large mixing bowl, toss the chicken strips with the cooked pasta, broccoli, tomato wedges and celery.

In your food processor container, combine the toasted walnuts, mayonnaise, basil, cheese, lemon juice, garlic and fresh ground pepper and process until fairly smooth. Add about 3/4 cup of the dressing to the salad ingredients and toss lightly to blend. Make a lettuce border on a serving plate, spoon the salad in the center and dust with a spritz of paprika. Retain the remaining dressing to serve on the side.

Makes up to 6 luncheon-sized salads.

I have also prepared this recipe with the addition of halved green Thompson grapes.

# Days of '47 Pasta Salad

**Dressing:**
1/4 C herbed white wine vinegar
   (tarragon or sweet basil)
3–4 cloves garlic, minced or pressed
1 T Gabby's Own Mustard (*see chapter
   7, Sauces and Dressings, for this
   recipe*)
1 tsp tarragon or sweet basil leaves (to
   go with the vinegar)
1 tsp. sweet Hungarian paprika
Salt and fresh ground pepper, to taste
1 C extra virgin olive oil

**Salad ingredients:**
3 C cooked chicken, boned, skinned
   and diced
2 jars (6 oz.) marinated artichoke
   hearts
12 oz. pasta (your choice), cooked and
   well drained
1 can sliced black olives, drained (can
   also use Kalamata olives)
1/2 C green onions, chopped
1/2 large red Bermuda onion, thinly
   sliced
Large lettuce leaves (your choice)
Large avocado, sliced
Cherry tomatoes, halved
1–2 jars marinated mushrooms
   (optional)

Prepare the dressing at least the day before by combining the ingredients in a
shaker jar, shaking well, and refrigerating. In a large mixing bowl, combine the
chicken, artichoke hearts and pasta. Pour about 3/4 cup of the dressing over all
and toss well. Just before serving, add the olives and onions and toss again. Line a
large pasta serving bowl with the lettuce leaves, add the chicken/pasta mixture,
garnish with the avocado slices, cherry tomatoes and marinated mushrooms.

Makes 6–8 large salads.

# Summer Time Cheese Tortellini Salad

**Salad ingredients:**
1/2 lb. cheese tortellini (can use the tricolor variety)
2 T olive oil
3/4 C celery, finely sliced with the leaves
3/4 C green onions, sliced
1 medium red, yellow, or purple bell pepper, finely diced
1 jar marinated artichoke hearts, drained and chopped
4–6 roma tomatoes, chopped

**Dressing:**
1/2 C mayonnaise (the real stuff)
1/2 C plain yogurt
2 T lemon juice
1 T dried basil flakes
Salt and fresh ground pepper, to taste

Bring 4 quarts of salted water to a rolling boil, add the tortellini and cook until done and all are floating. Drain well, place in a large bowl, sprinkle the olive oil over all and toss. Add the vegetables, prepared as indicated, and toss again well.

Combine the dressing ingredients in a small mixing bowl, whisk well and pour over the salad. Toss one more time, cover with plastic wrap and refrigerate for several hours before serving. Serve the well-chilled salad on a bed of red leaf lettuce.

Serves 4.

# Freddie's Fettuccine Salad

1 lb. fettuccine pasta, cooked al dente, then drained well and kept warm
1/2 C olive oil
1/2 C (rounded) pine nuts (shelled)
2–4 large cloves garlic, pressed or finely minced
1 large fresh firm tomato, seeded and chopped
1 large piece of pimiento, chopped
1 can (small) black ripe olives, chopped

1–2 T fresh Italian parsley, finely chopped
3/4 C fresh basil, finely chopped
2 T balsamic vinegar
1–2 T olive oil
Salt and fresh ground pepper, to taste
Fresh asiago or parmesan cheese, shredded or grated, to taste

Prepare the pasta as indicated, then cover to keep warm. In a large skillet or fry pan, heat the oil over medium-high heat, then add the pine nuts and garlic to the hot oil. Saute this mixture until the nuts are just lightly browned, then add the warm pasta and toss well to coat the pasta.

Pour the mixture into a large salad bowl. Add all remaining ingredients, tossing after each addition. When everything has been added, sprinkle the cheese over all.

Serves 4.

This is best if served at room temperature with warmed Italian bread or rolls. Serves great all year round.

# Gazpacho Salad

1 C long grain rice, uncooked
2 1/2 C water
1/2 tsp. salt
1/2 C chunky-style salsa sauce
1/2 C V8 juice
1 T olive oil
1 T garlic red wine vinegar
1/2 tsp. chili powder

1/2 lb. imitation crab (surimi)
1 C cucumber, seeded, chopped
1/2 C tomato, seeded, chopped
1/2 C green pepper, chopped
1/2 C celery, chopped
1/4 C green onion, chopped
Red leaf lettuce leaves
Fresh lemon or lime, sliced thinly

In a medium saucepan, combine the rice, water, and salt; cover and cook according to package directions, then set aside. In shaker jar, combine the salsa, V8, olive oil, red wine vinegar, and chili powder and shake well; refrigerate to chill until you are ready to prepare the salad.

In a medium mixing bowl, combine the cooked rice, imitation crab, and all remaining ingredients, except the lettuce and lemon/lime slices. Toss lightly, add the chilled dressing and toss well. Cover and refrigerate for a couple of hours before serving. Place a lettuce leaf on individual serving plates, spoon a serving of the salad on each plate, and garnish with a thin slice of fresh lemon or lime.

Serves 6.

# Gabby's "No Egg" Potato Salad

4 C cooked new red potatoes, unpeeled and diced into 1/2- to 3/4-inch pieces
1 C celery, chopped (with leaves)
1/2 C sweet onion, coarsely chopped
1/4 C radishes, sliced
1/4 C fresh parsley, finely chopped
1/4 C green bell pepper, finely chopped

1 C mayonnaise (the real stuff)
1 T mustard, either your favorite brand or "Gabby's Own Mustard" (*see chapter 7, Sauces and Dressings, for this recipe*)
1 T cider vinegar
1/2 tsp. celery seeds
Salt and fresh ground pepper, to taste
Sweet Hungarian paprika, to taste

In a large mixing bowl, combine the potatoes, celery, onion, radishes, parsley and bell pepper and mix well. In a small bowl, combine all remaining ingredients except the paprika. Whisk well and pour over the salad mixture. Mix well again, cover with plastic wrap and chill several hours before serving. Place the salad in a large serving bowl and dust with paprika just before serving.

Serves 6–8.

Just make sure the potatoes are cooked through, not hard.

# Hot Dilled Potato Salad

1 T butter or olive oil
1 T flour
1 tsp salt
1 tsp dill weed
1 tsp Salad Supreme seasoning mix
Fresh ground pepper, to taste

1 C milk
1/2 C mayonnaise
1/4 C onion, finely chopped
5 medium potatoes, cooked, peeled
    and diced

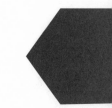

In a small saucepan, melt the butter over medium heat. Stir in the flour, salt, dill weed, Salad Supreme and pepper and cook about a minute, stirring constantly. Add the milk all at once and continue to cook, stirring until the mixture thickens and is bubbly.

Whisk in the mayonnaise and onion, followed by the diced potatoes. Heat through and spoon into a serving dish. If desired, you can garnish the dish with finely chopped parsley and paprika. Serve immediately.

Makes 4–6 servings.

# Oriental Chicken-Asparagus Salad

6 chicken breasts, boned, skinned,
    seasoned, sauteed and cooled
2 lbs. fresh asparagus
1 can chicken or beef consomme
2 T soy sauce
1/2 C rice wine vinegar

1/2 C light (canola) vegetable oil
1/2 tsp. fresh ginger, grated
Fresh red leaf lettuce leaves
3 hard cooked eggs, sliced, for garnish
1 can (2 oz.) pimento, sliced
Sweet Hungarian paprika

Prepare the chicken breasts as indicated; after cooling to room temperature, carve into 1/2-inch thick slices and set aside. Break asparagus at the tender spot on each spear. Place the spears in a shallow baking dish and add the consomme. Cover with plastic wrap, place in your microwave and "nuke" on high about 8–9 minutes or until tender crisp. Drain and cool.

Combine the soy, vinegar, oil and ginger and pour over the asparagus. Chill for a couple of hours; when ready to serve, drain asparagus again. Place several leaves of lettuce on individual salad plates. Place several chicken strips and several asparagus spears on each plate. Top with three slices of hard cooked egg and several strips of pimento. Spritz each with paprika. Serve with marinade on the side, if desired.

Serves 6.

# Chicken Salad in Avocados

6 medium chicken breasts, seasoned,
    sauteed, cooled, skinned, and
    chopped
1 C celery, with leaves, finely chopped
1/2 C sweet or regular onion, finely
    chopped
1/4 C fresh parsley, finely chopped
2 T capers
1 T lemon juice
1 tsp. dry mustard

1/2 tsp. fresh grated nutmeg
1 1/2 C mayonnaise (the real stuff)
Salt and fresh ground pepper, to taste
6 large, ripe avocados, halved and
    pitted
6 hard cooked eggs, shelled and
    quartered
Shredded lettuce for each serving
Sweet Hungarian paprika for garnish

Prepare all of the ingredients as indicated and place all but the avocados, eggs, lettuce, and paprika in a large mixing bowl. Toss until well mixed.

Place a bed of shredded lettuce on each plate. Place two avocado halves over each bed. Fill each half with the chicken salad. Arrange a quartered egg around the avocado. Spritz paprika over each for color garnish.

Serves 8–10.

# Hot Chicken Salad

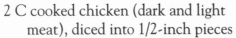

2 C cooked chicken (dark and light meat), diced into 1/2-inch pieces
2 C celery, diced and cooked until barely tender
2 C long grain rice, cooked in chicken broth
1 C frozen petite peas, thawed
2 cans cream of chicken soup
1 1/4 C mayonnaise (can be light, but don't use salad dressing)

1 medium sweet Bermuda or regular onion, chopped
6 hard cooked eggs, chopped
6 T lemon juice
1/2 tsp. fresh ground or garlic pepper
1/4 C butter
3/4 C toasted slivered almonds
1 C cornflakes, lightly crushed

Prepare the chicken, celery, rice and peas as indicated, then set aside. In a medium mixing bowl, combine the soup, mayonnaise, onion, eggs, lemon juice, and pepper, stir to blend, then add to the prepared ingredients, mixing well.

Spoon the mixture into a 4-quart casserole or baking dish. Taste for proper seasoning (add salt, if desired). In a small skillet, heat the butter, adding the almonds. Pour this mixture over the casserole, then top all with the cornflakes. Bake in a preheated 350° oven for 45 minutes.

Serves 12.

Great for a typical pot luck …. Bet they like your dish best.

# Garden Seafood Pasta Salad

1/2 lb. fresh green beans, snapped into
   bite-size pieces
1 pkg. dry Italian salad dressing mix,
   prepared as directed
3 T fresh basil, finely chopped
3 T fresh oregano, finely chopped
12 oz. corkscrew (fusille) pasta,
   cooked, drained, and chilled well
   (this can also be tricolor fusille)

1/2 lb. surimi seafood, chunk-style
1/2 C fresh parmesan cheese, shredded
   or grated
1/3 C sliced ripe olives, drained well
2 T green onions, chopped

Prepare the green beans as indicated, then place in a large fry pan and add
enough water to cover the bottom of the pan. Bring the mixture to a boil, cover,
and let simmer two minutes. Drain in a colander, rinse with cold water, and set
aside. Prepare the salad dressing mix, following the package directions. Stir the
herbs into the dressing mixture.

In a large salad bowl, combine the cooled beans, pasta, and all remaining
ingredients. Toss the mixture, adding the dressing. Cover with plastic wrap and
refrigerate for several hours before serving. Toss well just before serving.

Makes 8 servings.

# Gabby's Real Navy Bean Soup

1 lb. dry navy or great northern white
    beans
Water to cover beans
1 ham bone or 2 ham hocks (can be
    smoked) with plenty of ham and
    well trimmed of fat
1 C white onion, finely chopped
2/3 C celery with leaves, chopped
1 medium potato, peeled and cut into
    a 1/2-inch dice

1 C carrot, finely chopped
2 T fresh parsley, finely chopped
2 whole bay leaves
8 C chicken stock or broth
8 slices of thick sliced bacon, diced,
    fried crisp and well drained
1 tsp. garlic salt
1/2 tsp. seasoned pepper
1/2 tsp. Tabasco sauce (optional)

Pick through the dry beans and discard the culls. Place in a large soup pot, cover with water and soak overnight.

Bring the beans to a simmer and add the ham bone/hocks, onion, celery, potato, carrot, parsley, bay leaves and stock/broth. Return to a simmer, cover, reduce the heat and simmer until the beans are tender. Remove the ham bone/hocks from the soup, then remove and chop the meat. Remove and discard the bay leaves, then place about half of the soup in your food processor and process until smooth, then return to the pot. Add all remaining ingredients, including the chopped ham, simmer until heated through, and serve. Or, you can refrigerate for a couple of days before serving.

Serves 8.

Great for winter dining.

# French Canadian Leek and Potato Soup

3 large russet potatoes, peeled and
    diced
2 large leeks (white and light green
    portion only), chopped
1 small yellow onion, chopped
3 C vegetable stock or broth
1/2 C fresh parsley, finely chopped

1/4 C. (packed) fresh basil leaves,
    chopped
1 C half & half cream or milk
4 T unsalted butter (can use less)
Dash of hot pepper sauce
Salt and fresh ground pepper, to taste
2 T straight sherry wine (optional)

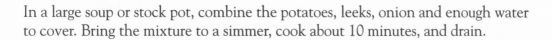

In a large soup or stock pot, combine the potatoes, leeks, onion and enough water to cover. Bring the mixture to a simmer, cook about 10 minutes, and drain.

Replace the liquid with the vegetable stock/broth and heat to the simmering point, cooking for 10 more minutes. Add the parsley, basil, cream/milk, butter, pepper sauce, salt and pepper. Stir well, then place the mixture in your blender or food processor and puree until all is liquefied. Return to the pan over medium heat and check for proper seasoning to your taste.

Makes 6 servings and can be served hot or cold, as desired.

# Tortellini in Broth with Chives and Wild Mushrooms

1 1/2 lbs. fresh tortellini (cheese, meat, or spinach)
1 1/2 qts. chicken broth
2–3 T olive oil
1/2 lb. fresh Portobelo, shiitake, or chanterelle mushrooms (or a mixture of all three), sliced

2 medium roma tomatoes, diced
1 bunch fresh chives, chopped
Salt and fresh ground pepper, to taste

In a soup pot, bring a pot of water to a rapid boil, adding a little salt. Add the tortellini and boil until done, then drain well, place in a bowl, and toss with a little of the olive oil. Set aside.

In the same soup pot, heat the broth to a simmer. In a skillet, heat the rest of the olive oil and saute the mushrooms. In six large soup bowls, place a portion of the cooked tortellini, ladle the hot chicken broth over all, and spoon in the mushrooms, tomatoes, and chives. Add the salt and fresh ground pepper to taste. Serve immediately.

Makes 6 servings.

Present with chunks of fresh hot bread, rolls or garlic bread.

# Golden Pumpkin Soup

1 medium fresh pumpkin
3 T butter
1 medium onion, finely chopped
1 lb. fresh pumpkin, steamed until soft
and pureed
2 cans cream of chicken soup
2 cans (soup cans) milk or half & half
cream

1/2 tsp. fresh nutmeg, grated
2 T straight sherry wine
1 1/2 T Worcestershire sauce
Fresh ground pepper, to taste
1 T fresh chives or green onion tops
Sour cream (a dollop per serving)

Prepare the pumpkin as you normally would for a jack-o-lantern, but instead of carving an appropriate face, use large felt-tip pens to paint the face (make sure all seeds and pulp are removed from the pumpkin). Set the pumpkin shell aside.

In a 4-quart saucepan, melt the butter over medium heat, add the onion and saute until tender, but not browned. Have the fresh pumpkin steamed before starting on the basic recipe (make sure the skin is removed before you puree). Add the pumpkin to the pan and stir in all remaining ingredients, except the chives and sour cream. Bring the mixture to a simmer, stirring.

Place the prepared pumpkin shell on a sturdy baking sheet, fill with the soup, and place the top on the pumpkin. Bake in a preheated 325° oven for about one hour. Serve in individual bowls, sprinkling with chives and topping with a small dollop of sour cream.

Serves 6–8.

Well worth the extra effort!

# Mexican Tortilla Soup

4–5 fresh corn tortillas, cut into 1-inch strips
Salt to taste
2 T light (canola) oil
3 T olive oil
1/2 medium white onion, thinly sliced
4–6 green onions, chopped
2 cloves garlic, pressed or minced
1 fresh jalapeno pepper, seeded and finely chopped
2 qts. chicken stock or broth

1 can (14 1/2 oz.) Mexican stewed tomatoes, with liquid
1 medium red bell pepper, very finely chopped
1 tsp. Worcestershire sauce
2 tsp. ground cumin
4 medium chicken breasts, boned, skinned, seasoned, cooked and cut to a medium dice
1/2 C Monterey Jack cheese, shredded

In a large skillet, heat the canola oil, add the tortilla strips and fry until crispy. Remove, drain on paper towels and salt as desired.

In a large soup pot, heat the 3 tablespoons of olive oil over medium-high heat. Saute the onions, garlic and jalapeno pepper until tender and lightly browned. Add chicken stock, tomatoes, bell pepper, Worcestershire and cumin. Bring this mixture to a boil, reduce the heat and simmer for 25–30 minutes. Add the chicken and heat thoroughly.

Place a couple of tortilla strips in the bottom of eight individual soup bowls, ladle in the soup, sprinkle on more tortilla strips and top with the Jack cheese. Serve with hot squares of corn bread.

Makes 8 servings.

# Cream of Tortilla Soup

2 cans (14 1/2 oz.) chicken broth
1/4 C butter
1 medium onion, diced
1/2 C celery, diced
2 cloves garlic, pressed or finely
    minced
1 medium tomato, chopped
2 T fresh chives, minced
1 1/2 C unsalted tortilla chips, crushed
1 T flour

1/4 C whipping cream
1 C Monterey Jack cheese (about
    4 oz.)
1 C cheddar cheese, shredded (about
    4 oz.)
2 tsp. chili powder
2 tsp. ground cumin
Additional crushed unsalted tortilla
    chips for garnish

In a small saucepan, bring the broth to a boil. Melt the butter in a heavy saucepan over medium heat and saute the onion, celery and garlic until the onion is translucent (about 4 minutes). Add the tomato and chives, reserving a tablespoon for garnish.

Add the crushed chips and saute two minutes. Reduce the heat to low. Sprinkle the flour over the mixture and stir for two minutes. Stir in the broth, cover and bring to a boil, then reduce the heat and stir in the cream. Add the cheeses and stir until all is melted. Add the chili powder and cumin. Season to taste with salt and pepper.

Ladle into bowls and sprinkle each serving with reserved tomatoes, chives, and tortilla chips. Serve immediately.

Makes 4–6 servings.

# Chowdered Carp, Yes Carp!

2 C boiling water
4 slices of bacon
1/2 C onion, chopped
1/2 C green bell pepper, chopped
2 cloves garlic, pressed or minced
2 medium potatoes, peeled and cut
  into a small dice

2 lbs. carp fillets, skinned
1 can (14 1/2 oz.) stewed tomatoes
  with juice
1 tsp. salt
1/4 tsp. black pepper
1 T fresh cilantro, finely chopped

Place the water on to boil. In a large skillet, fry the bacon slices until crisp, then remove and drain. Add the onion, green pepper and garlic to the hot drippings. Saute this mixture until tender. In order, add the potatoes, fish, tomatoes and carefully add the simmering water. Season with the salt and pepper. Simmer the mixture for 20 minutes or until the potatoes are tender. Top with the cilantro and crumbled bacon.

Serves 6.

Note: The carp fillets should be eaten from one end or the other by flaking the meat off with a fork, removing the bones as you go. Place a towelette and a small plate for the bones at each setting to facilitate the process.

Thanks to Dan Potts for sharing this recipe. You have to try it to believe it.

# Gabby's Soup-er Bowl Sea Bass Gumbo

3 T olive oil
2 T flour
1 medium green bell pepper, finely
    chopped
1 rib celery (with leaves), finely
    chopped
1 medium white onion, finely chopped
1/2 C green onions, chopped
2 cans (14 1/2 oz.) Cajun-style stewed
    tomatoes
32 oz. defatted chicken broth

1 pkg. frozen sliced okra
1 pkg. frozen whole kernel corn
1/4 C Italian-style flat leaf parsley,
    finely chopped
1 T Worcestershire sauce
1 tsp. salt
1 tsp. thyme
1/4 tsp. cayenne pepper
1 bay leaf
1 lb. white sea bass, cut into chunks
8 C hot steamed long grain rice

In a large stock pot, heat the olive oil over medium heat and stir in the flour to form a roux. Cook for 10–15 minutes or until the roux reaches a dark brown color, stirring constantly.

Stir in the bell pepper, celery and onions cook over low heat, stirring occasionally, for 10 minutes or until tender. Add the remaining ingredients, except the fish and rice, and bring to a boil. Reduce heat and simmer about 10 minutes. Add fish and cook through.

Place a half cup of rice in each serving bowl and ladle soup on top. Serve immediately.

Makes 8–10 servings.

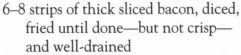

# Down-Maine Clam Chowder

6–8 strips of thick sliced bacon, diced, fried until done—but not crisp—and well-drained
1/4 lb. butter or margarine
1 C onion, finely chopped
1 C celery (with the leaves), finely chopped
1 C all-purpose flour
5 C bottled clam juice

1/2 C milk, heated
1/2 C half & half cream, heated
1/2 lb. boiled potatoes, skinned & cut into cubes
3 cans (62 oz.) chopped clams with juice
1 tsp. dried thyme, crushed just a bit
1 tsp. salt
1/2 tsp. fresh ground pepper or to taste

Prepare the bacon as indicated and set aside. In a medium-size pan, heat the butter/margarine over medium-high heat. Add the onion and celery and saute about 35 minutes.

Add the drained bacon, stir in the flour and continue to cook about 5 minutes, forming a roux; remove from the heat. In a heavy-bottomed pan, heat the clam broth over medium-high heat. Whisk in the roux mixture until all is added. Whisk in the milk and cream, then add the potatoes, clams and seasonings. Heat through and serve steamy hot with oyster crackers, if desired.

Serves 4-6.

Everyone in the state of Maine has a favorite recipe for "chow-da," and this is another great one if you like it thick and creamy.

# Gabby's Real Low Fat Vegetable Soup

1 small head of green cabbage, cut into small wedges

2 C celery (with leaves), chopped

1 large yellow or white onion, chopped

3–4 small zucchini, ripple cut into 1/4-inch rounds

3 medium carrots, ripple sliced

1/2 lb. fresh asparagus, cut into 2-inch lengths

1 can (28 oz.) ready-cut tomatoes with juice

1–2 medium cloves garlic, pressed or minced

1 can (142 oz.) green beans with liquid

1 can (10 1/2 oz.) defatted beef broth

9 beef bouillon cubes (I prefer Wyler's brand)

1–2 tsp. Italian seasoning

Salt and fresh ground pepper to taste

Throw all of the ingredients (in any order) into a large (8–12 quart) stock pot or kettle. Cover the mixture with water and bring to a boil. Reduce the heat, cover and simmer about 30 minutes.

Remove from the heat and let set all day (on top of the stove, but not over the heat). Reheat when ready to serve.

Serves *lots* with lots left over.

Who says you need all that fancy stuff to make a great soup?

# Busy Times Italian Goulash

1/2 lb. lean or extra lean ground beef
1/2 lb. lean ground pork (can use bulk
    Italian sausage)
1 large onion, chopped
2 cloves garlic, pressed or minced
1 medium green or red bell pepper,
    finely chopped
1 small carrot, finely shredded
2 cans (14 1/2 oz.) Italian-style ready
    cut tomatoes
1 can (6 oz.) Italian-style tomato paste

1 can (8 oz.) sliced mushrooms
    with liquid
1 bay leaf
1 T parsley flakes
2 tsp. Italian seasoning
1/2 tsp. oregano
Salt and fresh ground pepper, to taste
1–2 C elbow macaroni, cooked al
    dente, well drained
1/2 C fresh parmesan cheese, grated

Spray a large skillet with olive oil-flavored Pam and heat over medium-high heat. Add the crumbled meats, onion, garlic and bell pepper. Saute this mixture until the meats are browned.

Drain excess grease and add the remaining ingredients, except the macaroni and parmesan, stirring well. Bring to a boil, reduce the heat, cover and simmer 20–25 minutes.

During this cooking period, boil the macaroni and drain well. Stir the drained macaroni into the meat sauce, cover and continue to cook 5 more minutes. Serve with parmesan cheese sprinkled over each serving.

Serves 4–6.

# Black Bean Chili

5 cans (1 lb.) black beans (turtle), undrained
2 T whole cumin seeds
2 T dried oregano leaves
2 T olive oil
1 large white onion, finely chopped
2 large green bell peppers, finely chopped
2 cloves garlic, pressed or minced
1 tsp. cayenne pepper
1 1/2 T sweet or hot Hungarian paprika
3 C crushed whole tomatoes with juice
1–3 small jalapeno peppers, finely chopped
2/3 C low fat yogurt
6 sprigs of fresh cilantro

Pour the beans and liquid into a large kettle and heat until simmering. Place the cumin seeds and oregano in a small pan and bake in a preheated 325° oven for 10–12 minutes or until toasted.

In a medium-size pan, heat the oil over medium-high heat. Add the onions, green peppers and garlic and saute a minute, then add the cayenne and paprika. Continue to saute until vegetables are tender. Add the tomatoes and peppers. Add this mixture to the simmering beans and stir well. Continue to cook until heated through. Serve with a dollop of yogurt and a sprig of fresh cilantro.

Makes 6 large servings.

# Spicy Chili Con Carne

6 thick slices of bacon, diced
2 large white or sweet onions, chopped
4–6 cloves garlic, pressed or minced
3 lbs. lean pork shoulder, cut into
    1/2-inch cubes
1 tsp. chili powder (plus or minus),
    your choice of brand
1/2 tsp. ground cumin
2 cans ready cut tomatoes (S&W
    brand)
1 can (4 oz.) diced green chilies

1 C beer (your choice)
2 fresh jalapeno peppers, seeded and
    very finely chopped
1 tsp. oregano
1 bay leaf
2 cans (15 1/2 oz.) chili beans
1 can (4 oz.) sliced black olives,
    drained (optional)
Chopped onion, shredded cheese,
    chopped avocado, sour cream and
    green onion, garnishment for each
    serving, as desired

In a large Dutch oven, brown the bacon, remove and drain on paper towels. In 2 tablespoons of the drippings, saute the onions and garlic until soft; remove and drain on paper towels.

Add remaining bacon drippings to the pan and over medium-high heat, brown the pork lightly. Remove and drain on paper towels. Wipe all the fat from the pan, then return the bacon, onions and pork. Stir in the chili powder and cumin and cook over medium heat for two minutes, stirring occasionally. Add tomatoes, chilies, beer, jalapenos, oregano and bay leaf. Simmer uncovered for 1 hour, stirring occasionally. Add beans and olives and simmer until pork is tender and sauce has thickened. Discard the bay leaf and garnish.

Serves 6+.

# Cincinnati Chili

2 lbs. lean or extra lean ground beef
2 medium white onions, coarsely
    chopped
2 C beef broth
2 C water
2 cans chunky-style tomato sauce
2–3 cloves garlic, pressed or finely
    minced
4 T chili powder (your favorite brand)
2 T red wine garlic vinegar
1/2 oz. unsweetened chocolate (don't
    substitute)
1 bay leaf

2 tsp. Worcestershire sauce
2 tsp. ground cinnamon
1 tsp. ground cumin
1 tsp. salt
1/2 tsp. fresh ground pepper
1/2 tsp. ground allspice
1/2 tsp. red pepper flakes
1/4 tsp. ground cloves
4 drops of hot pepper sauce
1 lb. spaghetti or thin pasta of choice
2 cans chili beans (optional)
1–2 white onions, finely chopped
2 C cheddar cheese, shredded

In a large deep skillet, break up the ground beef and add the onions, broth and water. Simmer this mixture for about 30 minutes.

Stir in the tomato sauce and the remaining ingredients, except the pasta, beans, white onions and cheese. Simmer, uncovered, stirring often for 2–3 hours; it should be quite thick. Refrigerate overnight before serving.

Boil the pasta and drain well. Place on individual plates and cover with the reheated chili and a layer of the canned chili beans (optional). Sprinkle with the finely chopped onion and cover all with a layer of the shredded cheese.

Serves 6–8.

# Southwest White Chili

1 T olive oil
1 lb. chicken breasts, boned, skinned
    and cut into cubes
1/4 C onion, chopped
1 C chicken broth
1 can (4 oz.) green chilies, diced
1 tsp. California-style garlic powder
1 tsp. ground cumin

1/2 tsp. oregano leaves
1/2 tsp. cilantro leaves
1/4 tsp. ground red pepper (can use
    less)
1 can (19 oz.) white kidney beans
    (cannellini), undrained
Monterey Jack cheese, shredded
Green onions, sliced

In a 2- or 3-quart saucepan, heat the oil over medium-high heat. Add the chicken and saute 4–5 minutes, stirring often. Remove from the pan, drain on paper toweling and cover to keep warm.

Add the onion to the pan and saute 2 minutes. Stir in the broth, chilies, and seasonings. Let the mixture simmer 30 minutes. Return the chicken to the pan and add the beans. Continue to simmer 10 minutes. Serve in individual bowls, garnished with cheese and onions.

Makes 4 servings.

# Gabby's Timberline Chili

3 lbs. beef round steak, trimmed well, tenderized and cut into bite-size cubes (can use pork cubes, too)
5 T olive oil (divided)
2 large white onions, chopped
4 cloves garlic, pressed or minced
3–5 T chili powder (your choice of brands)
1 1/2 tsp. dried oregano
1 1/2 tsp. ground cumin
1 tsp. dried red pepper flakes, or to taste
1 can (7 oz.) green chilies, diced
4–5 fresh tomatillos, chopped

1 can (28 oz.) ready-cut tomatoes with juice
1 can (6 oz.) Italian tomato paste
2 C small dried red beans (soaked in cold water overnight and drained well)
4 C beef stock or broth
1 tsp. sugar
1 T salt or to taste

**Garnish:**
Sour cream, shredded cheddar cheese, chopped green and white onions

Prepare the beef as indicated. In a large kettle or soup pot, heat 2 tablespoons of the oil. When hot, add beef and brown well. Remove the meat and drain on paper towels. Discard pan drippings, add remaining oil and saute onions and garlic until tender.

Add the remaining ingredients, stirring well. Return the meat to the sauce, cover and simmer about an hour or until beans are tender. If a thicker chili is desired, simmer the mixture over low heat, uncovered. Taste for proper seasoning and adjust to your taste. Cool the chili, cover and refrigerate for at least 24 hours before serving. Reheat over low, then ladle into individual bowls and serve with garnishes as desired.

Serves 6–8.

# Gabby's Chili for Twenty

3 T olive oil

3 lbs. extra lean chili-grind, ground beef

2 lbs. lean round steak, trimmed of all fat and cut into small cubes

1 lb. hot-style bulk Italian sausage meat

3 large white onions, chopped

2–3 medium green bell peppers, finely chopped

4–6 cloves garlic, pressed or finely minced

4 dried Anaheim chilies, cut into small strips (or equal amount of dried flakes)

4 T Worcestershire sauce

2–3 T cumin seeds

6+ T chili powder (your favorite)

1–2 tsp. sugar

3 cans (15 oz.) chunky-style tomato sauce

1 qt. water

6 cans (16 oz.) red kidney beans, drained

2 cans (30 oz.) chili beans, half drained

2 cans (28 oz.) ready-cut tomatoes, drained (S&W brand)

1 can (7 oz.) green chilies, diced

In a heavy 12-quart stock pot, heat the oil over medium-high. Add meats and brown well. Drain off most of the grease. Add onions, bell peppers and garlic and cook until onion is limp. Add the chilies, Worcestershire sauce, cumin, chili powder, sugar, tomato sauce and water, blending well and heating to a simmer. Cover, reduce heat to low and simmer for 3 hours, stirring occasionally.

Add all remaining ingredients and adjust seasoning to your taste. Simmer for 2 more hours, stirring occasionally. Serve with bowls of shredded sharp cheddar and parmesan cheeses, green and white chopped onions and sour cream as individual garnishes.

You've got it—this serves 20!

# Chapter 4

# Pastas and Pizzas

## Gabby Specialities—Pastas and Pizzas

# Sausage Pesto Pasta

1/2 lb. bulk Italian sausage (regular or turkey Italian sausage)
12 oz. fresh angel hair pasta (Contadina brand)
2 T olive oil
1/2 C fresh pesto sauce (*recipe follows*)

3 extra large eggs, well beaten
1/2 C fresh parsley, finely chopped
1/3 C fresh parmesan cheese, grated
1/2 tsp. red pepper flakes
Fresh ground pepper, to taste
Fresh parmesan cheese, shredded

Crumble the sausage into a medium-size skillet, then brown over medium-high heat. During this cooking period, boil the pasta following the package directions and drain well (remember, fresh pasta cooks in just a few minutes).

In a large skillet , heat the oil over medium-high heat. Add the drained pasta and pesto sauce, tossing well to coat. Reduce the heat to low and add the well-drained sausage. Mix together the beaten eggs, parsley, grated parmesan cheese, pepper flakes and pepper. Again, toss to coat well. When all is absorbed, serve with shredded cheese over all.

Serves 4.

# Pesto Sauce for Pasta

2 C freshly picked basil leaves, washed
   in cold water
2 cloves fresh firm garlic, pressed
2 T pine nuts, shelled
4 T fresh parmesan cheese, grated

4 T fresh Romano cheese, grated
Salt and finely ground fresh ground
   pepper to taste
1/2 C fine olive oil

Pick the basil leaves from the plants and strip the large leaves from the stems (discard the stems). Wash as indicated.

Combine all ingredients in a blender container and blend at a low, chopping speed. Stop the machine often and scrape the sides down, so that all blends well. A smooth mixture is the desired consistency (about the same as a tomato sauce).

Prepare and cook your pasta as you normally would. Drain well and place in a large pasta bowl. Pour the sauce over the hot pasta and toss lightly to blend well. Serve immediately.

This recipe prepares enough sauce for 1 pound of pasta.

This pesto "holds" well in the refrigerator. Place in a small jar and cover the sauce with a bit more olive oil.

# Sun-Dried Tomato Pesto

3 C (packed) sun-dried tomatoes
   (reconstituted in water)
1 1/2 C extra virgin olive oil
1 C fresh parmesan cheese, grated

1/2 C toasted pine nuts
1 C (packed) fresh parsley
3 cloves garlic

Prepare all of the ingredients as indicated, then place in a food processor and process until pureed. Place 2–3 tablespoons of the mixture over hot drained pasta. Toss well and serve immediately.

Makes enough to cover one pound of cooked pasta.

If you have a hunk of fresh Italian bread on hand, just dip it in this sauce and feed your face.

*This wonderful pesto is an original from Tony Caputo.*

# Sauced 'Chokes and Fettuccine

2 T olive oil (can use butter, if desired)
1 medium onion, finely chopped
2 cloves garlic, pressed or minced
12 small canned or frozen artichoke
    hearts, drained and quartered
1/2 C dry white wine
2 T lemon juice
11/2 C heavy whipping cream or
    Mocha Mix non-dairy creamer

1/8 tsp. fresh nutmeg, grated
Fresh ground pepper, to taste
12 oz. fettuccine pasta, boiled and well
    drained
1/2 C pine nuts, toasted
1/2 C fresh parmesan cheese, shredded
    or grated
2 T fresh parsley, very finely chopped

In a large skillet or fry pan, heat the oil over medium-high heat, then add the onion and garlic. Saute just until the onion is golden, then add the drained chokes, wine and lemon juice.

Continue to saute about 2 minutes, then add the cream, nutmeg and pepper. Simmer, uncovered about 2 minutes, then add the pasta and pine nuts. Toss lightly and add the cheese, place on a warmed serving platter and sprinkle the parsley over all. Serve immediately.

Serves 4.

# A Real Man's Lasagna

1 lb. ground beef
1 medium yellow onion, ground
2 ribs celery, ground
2 medium carrots, ground
2 cloves garlic, ground
1 T fresh parsley, chopped
1 T fresh thyme, chopped
1 tsp. salt

1/2 tsp. pepper
1 can (14 oz.) tomato sauce
2 cans (14 oz.) whole peeled tomatoes
1 pkg. lasagna noodles, boiled to al
   dente stage
1 medium container of ricotta cheese
1 lb. mozzarella cheese, sliced
1 C fresh parmesan cheese, grated

Brown the ground beef, then add the onion, celery, carrots, garlic, parsley, thyme, salt and pepper and continue to simmer approximately 30 minutes.

Add the tomato sauce and whole tomatoes. Simmer slowly for 2 hours, stirring occasionally, adding additional salt and pepper, if desired. In a medium-size glass baking dish, spread a thin layer of the sauce, then noodles, ricotta, mozzarella and parmesan. Repeat until dish is full. Spread generous layers of parmesan and mozzarella on top. Bake in a preheated 350° oven for 25 minutes.

Serves 6.

# Gabby's Super Bowl Lasagna

1 lb. fresh or dried large lasagna
  noodles, boiled, rinsed in cold
  water and drained well
5 C Gabby's Red Sauce for Anything
  Italian (see this recipe in chapter 7,
  Sauces and Dressings)
1 lb. ricotta cheese (can use light, low
  or no-fat versions)
2 extra large eggs, beaten

2 T fresh Italian-style flat leaf parsley,
  chopped
1 lb. sweet Italian sausage, cut into
  rounds, fried and well drained (can
  also use bulk, crumbled)
1 lb. mozzarella cheese (can use light),
  cut into 1/4-inch slices
1 C fresh parmesan cheese, grated

Prepare the noodles as indicated, then drain into a large colander and rinse with cold water until chilled. Drain well and pat dry with paper towels. In a large mixing bowl, combine the ricotta, beaten eggs and parsley. Stir to mix well. Pour a cup of the red sauce over the bottom of a 9 x 13-inch baking dish, then top with a layer of the drained noodles, just barely over lapping them. Using a large spatula, spread a layer of the ricotta mixture over the noodle layer. Arrange the mozzarella slices next and sprinkle parmesan cheese over all. Pour another layer of the red sauce. Arrange some of the browned sausage meat over the sauce, then repeat the remaining layers, creating 4 layers in all, ending with a generous layer of red sauce, several slices of mozzarella cheese and a good sprinkling of parmesan cheese.

Bake in a preheated 350° oven for 1 1/4 to 1 1/2 hours (should be bubbly and lightly browned over the top). Remove and set on a cooling rack 10–20 minutes before cutting into serving-size squares.

Serves 6–8.

A great tossed Italian salad and toasty warm garlic bread will round out the meal, and what a meal it will be!

# Vegetarian Lasagna Supreme

1 T olive oil
1 large onion, chopped
2 cloves garlic, pressed or minced
1/2 lb. fresh mushrooms, sliced
1 can (6 oz.) tomato paste (Contadina, Italian)
1 can (14 1/2 oz.) thick and chunky tomato sauce (Hunt's Special is a good one)
1 small carrot, very finely shredded
1/2 C chicken broth
1 1/2 tsp. salt, or to taste
3 T fresh basil, lightly chopped

1 tsp. Italian seasoning
1 tsp. oregano
1 tsp. sugar
1/2 tsp. fresh ground pepper, or to taste
12 oz. lasagna noodles
1 lb. mozzarella cheese, sliced or shredded
1 lb. fresh spinach, cooked, well drained and chopped
16 oz. low-fat ricotta cheese
2/3 C fresh parmesan cheese, grated or shredded

In a medium-size fry pan, heat the oil over medium heat. Add the onion and garlic and saute until transparent. Add the mushrooms and continue to saute another 5 minutes, then add the tomato paste, sauce, carrot, broth and seasonings, stirring well to blend. Simmer the mixture about 1 hour (red wine can be added to the mix, if desired), stirring occasionally.

Meanwhile, prepare the noodles according to package directions and drain. Spray a large 9 x 15-inch shallow baking dish. Layer the ingredients as follows: 1/3 sauce, 1/3 noodles, all the mozzarella cheese, 1/2 spinach, 1/3 noodles, 1/3 sauce, ricotta cheese, remaining spinach, remaining noodles, and remaining sauce. Top all with the parmesan cheese. Bake uncovered in a preheated 350° oven for 1 hour. Let rest 10 minutes before cutting into serving-size squares.

Makes 8–10 wonderful servings.

# Easy Ziti Primavera

8 oz. ziti pasta, uncooked
3 qts. water
2 C fresh broccoli flowerets
2 C fresh cauliflower
1 C carrot, cut into julienne strips
1 small red bell pepper, cut into
    julienne strips
1/4 C green onion, sliced

1/2 pt. heavy whipping cream (room
    temperature)
3/4 C fresh parmesan cheese, grated
1 tsp. basil leaves
1/2 tsp. garlic powder
1/2 tsp. seasoned salt
1/8 tsp. ground white pepper

Bring the 3 quarts of water to a boil, then add the pasta and cook according to
the package directions. Add the veggies during the last 4 minutes of cooking.
Drain all.

Place the mixture in a Dutch oven over very low heat. Add half of the cream and
parmesan cheese, stirring well. Toss well to coat all. Add the remaining cream,
cheese and seasonings. Toss well and heat through. Serve immediately.

Serves 6–8.

# Three Pepper Pasta

3 large bell peppers (1 green, 1 red and 1 yellow), cored and sliced into julienne slices
1 1/2 T olive oil
1 medium sweet onion, sliced
1–2 cloves garlic, pressed or minced
2–3 T balsamic vinegar
2–3 T fresh sweet, opal or lemon basil, finely chopped

2 medium roma tomatoes, chopped
1 1/2 tsp. sugar (optional)
Salt and fresh ground pepper, to taste
12–16 oz. pasta (your choice), boiled and well drained
Fresh parmesan or asiago cheese, shredded or grated

Prepare the peppers as indicated, then set aside. In a large fry pan, heat the olive oil over medium-high heat. Add the peppers, onion and garlic. Saute this mixture just until the peppers are tender crisp.

Add all remaining ingredients, except the pasta and cheese. During this cooking period, prepare the pasta according to package directions. Place the hot drained pasta on a serving platter and top with the pepper mixture. Sprinkle the cheese over all as desired.

Serves 4.

Inexpensive, easy and delicious!

# Gabby's Fettuccine Vegetarian

1 lb. fettuccine pasta
3 T butter (can use olive oil and
    butter)
2-3 cloves garlic, pressed or finely
    minced
1/2 lb. fresh mushrooms, sliced
2–3 small fresh firm zucchini,
    julienne-sliced
1 can (2 oz.) pimento, drained
    and sliced

1/4 C Italian green olives, pitted and
    chopped
3-4 T butter, cut into small cubes
1 C heavy cream
3/4 C fresh parmesan cheese
1/2 C fresh parsley, finely chopped
Fresh nutmeg, grated, to taste
Fresh ground black pepper, to taste

In a large 8-quart pot, boil the pasta following the package directions, then drain well and hold. In a large skillet or fry pan, melt the 3 tablespoons of butter, adding the garlic. Add the mushrooms and saute over medium-high heat for 2 minutes. Add the zucchini, pimento and olives. Saute this mixture about a minute, then add the butter cubes and cream.

Cook the mixture at a full simmer for 3 minutes. Add the well-drained pasta and toss lightly. Add about 1/2 cup of the parmesan, most of the parsley, nutmeg and pepper. Again, toss the mixture, then place on a warmed serving platter or pasta bowl. Garnish with remaining parmesan and parsley and serve immediately.

Serves 6.

Serve with a warm Italian-style salad and warm bread … if you can stand any more calories.

# Gabby's Baked Penne Pasta and Tomato Sauce

1 lb. penne pasta, boiled until just about done, but not quite and well drained
1–2 T butter, melted
Salt and fresh ground pepper, to taste
2 C meatless tomato sauce (your favorite)

1/2 C fresh parmesan cheese, shredded (divided)
1/2 lb. mozzarella cheese, shredded
1/2 C dry sour dough bread crumbs, toasted

Prepare the penne as indicated, drain well and place in a medium-size bowl. Drizzle the butter over the pasta and season to taste with salt and fresh ground pepper.

Mix 1 cup of the tomato sauce and half the parmesan cheese with the pasta. Arrange half of the pasta in a shallow baking dish or large au gratin dish. Sprinkle the mozzarella cheese and remaining sauce over the pasta. Cover all with the remaining pasta. Combine the remaining parmesan cheese and toasted bread crumbs. Sprinkle this mixture over all, then place on a baking sheet. Bake in a preheated 425° oven for 20–25 minutes or until lightly browned and slightly crusty on top.

Serves 4–6.

One of my favorite pasta dishes when I want something quick, easy and delicious. Obviously, cooked meats can also be added, but try it like this the first time.

# Gabby's Pasta and Pecans

1 lb. linguine pasta, cooked and well
    drained
2–3 T olive oil
1/2 C butter
1 1/2 C pecan gems
1/2 C fresh spinach, finely chopped
2 T Parsley Patch Seasoning
    (garlic-saltless)

1 tsp. fresh ground pepper
1–2 T fresh basil, finely chopped
Salt to taste (optional)
4 T fresh parmesan cheese, shredded
    or grated

Prepare the pasta, following the package directions, then drain well and keep hot. In a large fry pan, heat the oil and butter over medium-high heat. Add the drained pasta and toss with the butter-oil.

Add all of the remaining ingredients, except the parmesan, and toss well to blend. Place the mixture in a large pasta bowl and sprinkle the parmesan over all. Serves immediately.

Serves 4.

So easy and wait till you taste it ….

# Sauteed Shrimp and Capillini Pasta

1/2 lb. capillini pasta, cooked and well
    drained
2 T butter and olive oil combination
12 oz. medium-size (U20-22) shrimp,
    peeled, deveined and cut in thirds
2 large cloves garlic, pressed or minced
3/4 C heavy whipping cream
1/2 C dry white wine (a Riesling
    would work well)

1 C frozen tiny peas, thawed
1/2 C pine nuts, toasted
1/4 C fresh parsley, finely chopped
1/2 C fresh parmesan cheese, shredded
    or grated
1 tsp. dried basil flakes
1/2 tsp. fresh ground pepper or to taste
1/4 tsp. dried crushed red pepper flakes
Salt to taste (optional)

Prepare the pasta following the package directions, then drain well and keep warm. While boiling the pasta, heat the butter-oil mixture in a large fry pan. Add the shrimp pieces and garlic. Saute, stirring often, until shrimp are pink and firm. Remove the shrimp from the pan and keep warm.

Add the cream, wine, peas, pine nuts and parsley to the pan over medium-high heat and cook about 1 minute; reduce the heat and add the remaining ingredients (reserve 1/4 cup of the parmesan cheese). Let the mixture just bubble in the pan for 2 minutes, then return the shrimp and add the drained pasta, tossing well to mix. Pour the mixture on a serving platter and top with the remaining parmesan. Serve immediately.

Serves 4, unless they're real eaters.

# Linguine with Dungeness Crab and Garlic

1/2 C olive oil (a good extra virgin oil)
2–3 cloves garlic, pressed or finely
   minced
1 medium dried hot chili pepper (seeds
   discarded), crushed
1 C (rounded) fresh Dungeness crab
   meat, picked of all shell matter

Salt and fresh ground pepper to taste
1/2 C dry white wine (your favorite)
1/4 C fresh basil, chopped
1/2 C fresh parsley, finely chopped
   (divided)
1 lb. linguine, cooked and well drained
Fresh parmesan cheese, to taste

Set a large pot of slightly salted water on to boil. In a large saute pan, heat the olive oil over medium heat; when hot, add the garlic and red pepper. When the garlic just starts to turn golden in color, add the crab meat, salt, pepper and wine. Simmer this mixture lightly until slightly reduced. Add the basil and half the parsley. Remove from the heat and set aside.

Boil the pasta in boiling water until it reaches the al dente stage, then drain well, add to the sauce and toss. Serve immediately with fresh parmesan cheese to taste.

Serves 2–4.

This is so good!

# Gabby's Leftover Salmon Capillini

12 oz. capillini pasta, cooked and
    well-drained
2 T olive oil and butter combination
1/4 C onion, finely chopped
1 medium clove garlic, pressed or
    minced
1 pkg. frozen petite peas, thawed (use
    fresh peas if they're in season)

2 C leftover salmon, small pieces
1 1/2 C heavy cream
1/2 T dried dill weed
1/2 tsp. ground white pepper
1/2 tsp. fresh nutmeg, grated
1/4 C fresh parsley, finely chopped
3–4 T fresh asiago, parmesan or
    Romano cheese, grated

Start the pasta boiling before beginning on the sauce. In a medium-large skillet, heat the butter-oil combination over medium heat until sizzling. Add the onion and garlic and saute just a minute, then add the peas and continue to cook another minute. Stir in the salmon, cream, dill, pepper, nutmeg and parsley. Simmer this mixture about 3 minutes, then stir in the cheese and continue to cook over low heat until cheese is totally incorporated into the sauce.

Drain the pasta well and pour into a large pasta bowl. Pour the sauce over the pasta. Don't toss. Sprinkle more parsley and cheese over all, if desired, and serve immediately.

Serves 4.

Serve with a green salad of choice, a piece of garlic toast, and maybe a glass of chilled whatever … and who said leftovers aren't delicious?

# Penne Pasta and Sausages

1 lb. sweet or hot Italian sausages, cut into 1/2-inch rounds
2 T olive oil
1 bulb of fennel, trimmed and cut into thin strips about 1/4-inch wide
1/4 C pine nuts
1 1/2 qts. Gabby's Marinara Sauce (*see chapter 7, Sauces and Dressings, for this recipe*)
1 tsp. red pepper flakes

Salt and fresh ground pepper, to taste
1 lb. penne pasta, boiled and well drained
1/2 C green Kalamata olives, pitted and chopped
1/2 C (packed) fresh sweet basil leaves, chopped
Fresh asiago cheese, grated, for each serving

Place the sausage rounds in a large skillet over medium-high heat. Brown the sausage, drain on paper towels and discard the extruded grease in the pan. In the same pan, heat the olive oil over medium heat. Add the fennel and pine nuts and saute until lightly browned. Add the marinara sauce, drained sausages, red pepper flakes, salt and pepper. Stir well and simmer, uncovered, about 10 minutes.

Boil the pasta, drain well, place in a warmed pasta bowl or platter and cover to keep warm. Add the olives (these are available in Italian food stores) and basil to the sauce, heat through, then pour over the pasta. Sprinkle some asiago, over all and serve immediately.

Serves 6.

Ah, pasta and red sauce. It's still hard to beat!

# Sweet Italian Sausage with Roasted Pepper and Garlic Rotelle

3 T olive oil
1 medium onion, finely chopped
3 cloves garlic, pressed or minced
1/2 lb. cooked sweet Italian sausage,
 bulk, crumbled
2 C mixed mushrooms, sliced and
 sauteed in butter or olive oil
2 cans Italian-style ready cut tomatoes
1 C chunky-style tomato sauce
1/4 C ricotta cheese

1 C cooked petite peas
1 C half & half cream
1 T dried parsley flakes
2 tsp. Italian seasoning
Salt and fresh ground pepper, to taste
2 pkgs. (12 oz. each) Pasta LaBelle
 Roasted Bell Pepper *or* Roasted
 Garlic Rotelle (or your choice)
2/3 C fresh Parmigiano-Reggiano
 cheese, grated

Prepare the sausage and mushrooms as indicated, then set aside. In a large skillet or saucepan, heat the olive oil over medium-high heat. Add the onion and garlic and cook until onion is limp. Add the cooked sausage and mushrooms, then add the tomatoes and tomato sauce. Simmer this mixture about 10 minutes over medium-low heat.

Add the ricotta cheese, peas and light cream. Continue to simmer 5 more minutes, then stir in the seasonings. During this cooking period, prepare the pasta, following the package directions, then drain well and place in a large pasta bowl. Carefully spoon the sauce mixture over the pasta. Sprinkle the cheese over all and serve immediately.

Serves 6–8.

# Penne Pasta with Gabby's Fresh Mushroom-Meat Sauce

1 lb. extra lean ground beef
1/2 lb. lean ground pork
1 T olive oil
1/2 lb. fresh mushrooms, sliced
1 small zucchini, thinly sliced
1 small red bell pepper, finely chopped
4–5 pieces of sun-dried tomatoes,
   thinly sliced
2–3 cloves garlic, pressed or minced
1 qt. thick spaghetti sauce (homemade
   is best)

1/4 C bold dry red wine (Burgundy)
3 T fresh sweet basil, finely chopped
   (can use 1 tablespoon of dried)
Salt and fresh ground pepper, to taste
12 oz. penne pasta, cooked until just
   barely tender and well-drained
2 C mozzarella cheese, shredded
1 C fresh parmesan cheese, shredded

In a large skillet, brown the beef and pork in the olive oil. Remove the meat from the pan and add the mushrooms, zucchini, bell pepper, dried tomatoes and garlic to the drippings. Saute this mixture 4–5 minutes over high heat, stirring often. Return the meat mixture to the pan and stir in the sauce, wine, basil, salt and pepper. Let this mixture come to a simmer, then remove from the heat.

Lightly spray a large shallow baking dish. Layer half of the penne pasta into the dish, then half of the sauce mixture, followed by half of the cheeses. Repeat the layers, then bake in a preheated 325° oven for 60 minutes.

Serves 6–8.

A crispy cold tossed salad and a loaf of crusty-warm Italian bread and you've got a wonderful meal .... Oh, yes, a red beverage of your choice will really make it complete.

# Layered Italian Casserole

1/2 lb. spaghetti, capillini or your
   favorite pasta, cooked and
   well-drained
1 T olive oil
1 lb. extra lean ground beef
1 medium onion, finely chopped
1–2 cloves garlic, pressed or minced
1–2 carrots, shredded
1/4 C fresh parsley, finely chopped

1 tsp. oregano
1/2 tsp. Italian seasoning
1 can (14 1/2 oz.) Italian-style
   ready-cut tomatoes
3 T Italian-style tomato paste
Salt and fresh ground pepper, to taste
3/4 C half & half cream
1/4 C fresh parmesan cheese, grated

Prepare the pasta following the package directions, then drain well and keep warm. In a large skillet, heat the oil over medium-high heat. Add the beef, onion and garlic. When the beef is browned, add the carrot, parsley, oregano, Italian seasoning, tomatoes, tomato paste, salt and fresh ground pepper. Simmer this mixture for 5 minutes, then check for proper seasoning.

Spray a 2-quart casserole dish. Starting and ending with the pasta, alternate layers of pasta and meat mixture. Pour the cream over all and top with the parmesan cheese. Bake, uncovered, in a preheated 400° oven for 30–35 minutes or until bubbly and lightly browned on top.

Serves 6.

Hey, the kids are going to love this one! By the way, if you want to add small crumbles of feta cheese over the meat layers, it really adds a nice flavor.

# Oven-Baked Chicken with Linguine

1/2 C butter or margarine (can also use half olive and half butter)
1 medium onion, finely chopped
2 cloves garlic, pressed or finely minced
3 T fresh basil, finely chopped
3/4 tsp. dried red chili flakes
3 lbs. chicken thighs and breasts

4–5 small zucchini, cut into 1/4-inch rounds
1/4 C lemon juice
8-10 oz. linguine pasta, cooked and well-drained
1 lb. fresh spinach, cooked, drained well and chopped
3/4 C fresh parmesan cheese, shredded

In a large (12 x 15-inch) shallow baking dish, place the butter or butter-oil combination and heat in a preheated 400° oven until the butter is melted and sizzling. Remove from the oven and mix in the onion, garlic, basil and chilies. Turn the pieces of chicken in the butter mixture until well-coated.

Add the zucchini to the pan, stirring well, then arrange the chicken pieces in the pan, skin-side up and sprinkle the lemon juice over all. Return to the 400° oven and bake, uncovered, about 45 minutes (chicken should be well-browned).

Remove the chicken from the pan and add the pasta and spinach to the pan, stirring to mix well with the pan drippings. Pour the pasta onto a warmed serving platter, arrange the chicken pieces over all, sprinkle with parmesan cheese and serve immediately.

Serves 6.

# Key West Pasta and Grilled Chicken

4 chicken breasts, skinned, boned and
    scored on both sides
1/4 C olive oil
1 T lime juice
1/2 tsp. hot pepper sauce
1 T olive oil
1–2 cloves garlic, pressed or finely
    minced

2 C fresh salsa (your favorite)
12 oz. linguine or your favorite pasta,
    cooked and well-drained
2 T butter
1 can (11 oz.) mandarin orange
    sections, drained
2–3 T fresh cilantro, finely chopped
1 T fresh lime zest

Prepare the chicken as indicated and place in a shallow glass dish. Combine the olive oil, lime juice and pepper sauce and pour over the chicken. Refrigerate and let marinate for 20–30 minutes. Remove and grill the chicken until done, then slice into 1/2-inch slices.

Heat the olive oil in a medium skillet, add the garlic and salsa and heat through. In a large bowl, toss together the pasta, butter, orange slices, cilantro and zest. Arrange the mixture on 4 individual plates, top each with a sliced chicken breast, then spoon the warmed salsa over the chicken.

Serves 4.

# Spicy Baked Chicken and Pasta

1/2 C butter
1 medium onion, halved and thinly
    sliced
2 cloves garlic, pressed or minced
1 T dried basil leaves
1 tsp. dried crushed red chilies
3 lbs. chicken breasts and thighs

4–6 sprigs of fresh rosemary
1/2 lb. spaghetti or linguine pasta,
    boiled and drained
2 pkgs. frozen chopped spinach,
    thawed and squeezed dry
3/4 C fresh parmesan cheese, grated
1 small orange, cut in half

In a large shallow baking pan, melt the butter over medium-high heat. Add the onion, garlic, basil and chilies to the melted butter and mix. Remove from the heat and roll each piece of chicken in the butter mixture, coating well.

Arrange the chicken in the pan, skin-side up and place the rosemary sprigs over the chicken. Bake, uncovered, in a preheated 400° oven for 40–45 minutes or until chicken is nicely browned.

Boil the pasta while the chicken bakes. When the chicken is done, remove from the pan and keep warm, then add the prepared spinach to the same pan and stir to scrape up the browned crispies from the bottom of the pan. Add the drained pasta and all but 1/4 cup of the parmesan cheese, mixing well with the spinach. Arrange the chicken pieces over all and sprinkle with the remaining parmesan cheese. Return to the oven for 5 minutes, then serve immediately with the fresh orange squeezed over all.

Serves 6.

# Gabby's Chicken and Basil Sauce with Penne Pasta

3 T olive oil
4 chicken breasts, skinned, boned, diced and seasoned as desired
2 T olive oil
1 medium onion, halved and finely chopped
2–3 cloves garlic, pressed or finely minced
2 cans (15 oz.) chunky-style tomato sauce
1/2 can (6 oz.) Italian-style tomato paste

1/2 C sun-dried tomatoes in olive oil, sliced
1/2 C dry white wine
1/4 C fresh basil, chopped
1 T fresh chopped or dried parsley flakes
1 tsp. Italian seasoning
1 C (as needed) chicken broth
Salt and fresh ground pepper, to taste
1 lb. penne pasta, boiled and well-drained

In a large fry pan, heat the olive oil over medium-high heat, then add the chicken, prepared as indicated, seasoned lightly as desired (try garlic pepper, oregano or other herbs and a small amount of lemon juice). Saute the chicken until nicely browned, then remove from the pan and drain on paper towels.

In the same pan, heat the remaining measure of oil, then add the onion and garlic. Saute until onion is limp, then add the drained chicken and all remaining ingredients, except the pasta. Reduce the heat to low and simmer about 30 minutes. Prepare the pasta as indicated, then place on a large serving platter. Spoon the chicken mixture over the pasta, sprinkle the parmesan cheese over all and serve hot immediately.

Serves 6.

# Fettuccine Ratatouille

1 lb. fresh broccoli, cut into flowerets and steamed until tender crisp
2–3 small zucchini, sliced and steamed until tender crisp
1 lb. fettuccine pasta, boiled and well-drained
1/4 C olive oil
1/2 lb. fresh mushrooms, sliced
3 cloves garlic, pressed or finely minced
2–3 fresh tomatoes, seeded and chopped

3/4 C fresh parsley, finely chopped
3 T fresh basil, chopped
1 T fresh oregano, chopped
1 T lemon juice
Salt and fresh ground pepper, to taste
2–4 T butter, melted
1/2–1 C fresh parmesan cheese, grated or shredded
1/2 C heavy whipping cream, warmed (optional)

Prepare the broccoli, zucchini and fettuccine as indicated, then set aside. In a large fry pan, heat the olive oil over medium-high heat and add the mushrooms and garlic. Stir fry this mixture about a minute, then add the tomatoes, parsley, basil, oregano, lemon juice, salt and pepper. Continue to stir fry another 2–3 minutes.

Place the drained pasta (pasta must still be hot) into a large pasta bowl and toss with the melted butter, parmesan and cream. Pour the vegetable mixture, with juices, over the pasta and toss. Serve immediately with warm crusty rolls or garlic bread.

Serves 8.

An eggplant-less ratatouille for eggplant-haters! This is really tasty and there is no need for any meat addition.

# Fettuccine Alfredo with Chicken and Pecans

1 lb. fettuccine pasta, cooked according to package directions and drained well
2 T butter or a butter-olive oil combination
2 chicken breasts, boned, skinned and cut into 1/2-inch strips
1 medium red bell pepper, julienne sliced
1 bunch green onions, sliced

1–2 cloves garlic, pressed or minced
1/2 C butter
1 T flour
2 T dry white wine
1 1/2 C heavy whipping cream
1 C fresh parmesan cheese, shredded
1/4 tsp. fresh nutmeg grated
Fresh ground pepper, to taste
1/2 C toasted pecans, chopped

Prepare the pasta as indicated, toss lightly with a small amount of olive oil, then set aside, but keep warm. In a medium-size fry pan, heat the butter over medium-high heat, then add the chicken strips and lightly brown. Add the bell pepper, green onions and garlic to the pan and saute until chicken is done, then hold in the pan.

During this period, melt the 1/2 C butter in another large skillet and stir in the flour until smooth. Whisk in the wine, then slowly whisk in the cream until all is added and the sauce is smooth. Stir in the cheese, nutmeg and pepper. Add the pasta and toss lightly.

Turn the pasta mixture onto a serving platter, then spoon the chicken mixture over the pasta. Arrange the chopped pecans around the outer edge of the dish and serve immediately.

Makes 4 servings.

# Summer Seafood Primavera

1 T butter, olive oil or combination
6 oz. medium (U-20-26) shrimp,
    peeled
6 oz. bay scallops, rinsed and drained
1 C fresh broccoli flowerets
1 C small fresh mushrooms, sliced
1/2 medium sweet onion, sliced
1/4 medium green or red bell pepper,
    chopped
2 cloves garlic, pressed or minced

2 T butter
2 T flour
2 C milk
1/2 tsp. ground white pepper
1/4 tsp. fresh nutmeg, ground
1/2 C Swiss or Gruyere cheese,
    shredded
3–6 drops hot pepper sauce of choice
1/2 C fresh parmesan cheese, shredded
12 oz. hot cooked pasta of choice

In large skillet, heat the butter/olive oil over medium heat. Add the seafood and saute until shrimp are totally pink, then remove from the skillet and keep warm.

In the same pan, add the broccoli, mushrooms, onion, bell pepper and garlic. Saute this mixture until tender crisp, then remove from the pan and keep warm with the seafood.

Add the butter to the still-hot pan and heat until melted, then stir the flour into the butter. Cook for 1 minute, stirring, then stir in the milk, until the mixture is smooth and thickens. Stir in the seasonings, cheese and hot sauce. Stir in the seafood and vegetables and heat through. Stir in the pasta, heat and serve.

Serves 4.

# Gabby's Jumbo Stuffed Shells

2 T olive oil
1/2 lb. extra lean ground beef (can use fresh ground turkey, if desired)
1/3 lb. bulk Italian sausage (can use turkey sausage)
1 medium onion, finely chopped
2 cloves garlic, pressed or minced
3/4 pkg. (10 oz.) frozen chopped spinach, thawed and well-drained
1/3 C seasoned bread crumbs
1/3 C parmesan cheese
1/4 C toasted pine nuts
Salt and fresh ground pepper to taste
3 extra large eggs, beaten
25 jumbo pasta shells for stuffing
1 recipe batch of Gabby's Marinara Sauce for Jumbo Stuffed Shells (*see chapter 7, Sauces and Dressings, for this recipe*)
1/2 lb. mozzarella cheese, shredded or crumbled

In a large fry pan, heat the olive oil over high heat, then crumble and add the ground beef and sausage. Brown well, then drain off and discard any extruded grease. Return the pan to the heat (adding more oil if desired) and saute the onion and garlic until the onion is limp. Return the meat to the pan and mix in the spinach, bread crumbs, parmesan, pine nuts, salt and pepper. Turn off the heat.

During this cooking period, place the shells (don't use cracked or broken shells) in boiling water and parboil for 9 minutes, then drain well. Spoon the meat mixture into the drained shells and set aside. Pour a cup of the marinara sauce over the bottom of a shallow baking dish. Arrange the stuffed shells over the sauce, then pour the remaining sauce over all and top with the mozzarella cheese. Cover with aluminum foil and bake in a preheated 350° oven for 45 minutes, then remove the cover and bake an additional 5–10 minutes.

Serves 6–8.

Just a real nice recipe!

# Quicky Shrimp and Pesto Pizza

1–2 large Boboli pizza crusts
1 1/2 C fresh pesto sauce (homemade
   or purchased)
1 lb. small cooked salad shrimp
1–2 bottles (14 oz. each) marinated
   artichoke hearts, drained
1–2 medium tomatoes, seeded and
   chopped

1/2 medium onion, cut into thin rings
1 1/2 C mozzarella cheese, shredded
3–4 T fresh parmesan cheese, grated
3–4 T fresh basil, coarsely chopped
1–2 tsp. Italian seasoning
1 tsp. garlic pepper
1–2 T olive oil

Lay out the Boboli crusts on a baking sheet and spread the pesto sauce over all, leaving a 1/2-inch outer rim. Arrange the shrimp over all, then top with artichoke hearts, tomatoes and onion rings.

Sprinkle the remaining ingredients over the pizzas, ending by lightly drizzling the olive oil over all. Bake in a preheated 450° oven until cheeses are melted and bubbly and crust is crisp. Slice and serve.

Serves 4–6.

Good stuff!

# Easy Mexican Pizzas

2 chorizo sausages (I prefer the Falls Brand Basque-style), sliced or crumbled
1/2 lb. extra-lean ground beef
6–8 large flour tortillas
2–3 T butter
1 can (16 oz.) refried beans with green chilies
Taco or picante sauce (your choice, hot or mild)
1/2 lb. mild cheddar cheese, shredded
1/2 lb. mozzarella cheese, shredded
1/2 C onion, finely chopped
1/2 tsp. dried oregano leaves (for each pizza)
Hot pepper sauce, to taste (optional)
2 medium fresh tomatoes, thinly sliced
1/2 small head of iceberg lettuce, shredded

In a medium-size skillet, combine and brown the chorizo and ground beef. Drain the meats on paper towels.

Spread 3–4 tortillas with a small amount of butter and top each with another tortilla. Spread the top tortilla with a layer of the refried beans. Pour the taco or picante sauce over the beans and spread evenly. Sprinkle with the cheeses, onions and meat layers, then top each with oregano and hot sauce.

Place on baking sheets or pizza pans and bake in a preheated 425° oven for 12–15 minutes. Remove from the oven and top with tomato slices and shredded lettuce. Slice each tortilla into 4–6 slices.

Serves 6–8.

# Gabby's Mexican Pizza

2 lbs. lean or extra lean ground beef
1 medium white onion, finely chopped
1/2 medium green bell pepper, finely chopped
2 cloves garlic, pressed or finely minced
1 can (4 oz.) green chilies, diced
1 C green or red taco sauce (hot to mild—you can also use a favorite fresh salsa instead)
1/2 C black ripe olives, sliced

1 can tomato sauce (Mexican-style if available)
1 C sour cream
1 C sharp cheddar cheese (can also use Monterey Jack or mozzarella)
1 C iceberg lettuce, shredded
1 medium tomato, finely diced
1 medium avocado, peeled and finely diced
1 large Boboli pizza crust (thick or thin)

In a large fry pan, crumble the ground beef, then add the onion, pepper and garlic. Brown this mixture over medium-high heat, then drain off the extruded grease. Add the taco sauce and olives.

Lay out the Boboli crust on a baking sheet or pizza pan and spread with the tomato sauce. Spread the meat mixture over the tomato sauce, then the sour cream and finally the shredded cheese of choice. Bake in a preheated 375° oven for 20–25 minutes. Remove from the oven and sprinkle the lettuce, tomato and avocado over the hot pizza. Cut into wedges and serve immediately.

Makes 1 pizza (6 wedges).

# Pizza by the Yard

1 loaf of French, sourdough or Italian-
　style bread, cut in half lengthwise
1/2 lb. lean or extra lean ground beef
1/2 lb. bulk Italian sausage
1 medium onion, finely chopped
1–2 cloves garlic, pressed or minced
2 cans (6 oz.) Italian-style tomato
　paste

1/3 C parmesan cheese, grated
1/4 C onion, finely chopped (optional)
1/3 C chopped ripe olives, drained
2 large tomatoes, thinly sliced
6 oz. mozzarella cheese, sliced
6 oz. medium cheddar cheese, sliced

Slice the bread as indicated and set aside. In a medium-size skillet, combine the beef, sausage and onion. Saute this mixture until just about done and drain well.

Spread the tomato paste over both cut sides of the bread. Sprinkle the meat mixture over the paste. Sprinkle on the parmesan, the second measure of chopped onion and olives. Top with the thin slices of tomato followed by alternating and overlapping slices of mozzarella and cheddar cheese. Broil on the second rack down for 12 minutes or until all cheeses are melted, lightly browned and bubbly on top.

Serves 4 kids or 6 adults.

Kids just love this easy recipe.

# Macaroni Pizza

1 C elbow macaroni
2 extra large eggs, well beaten
2/3 C milk
1 tsp. salt
1/2 tsp. fresh ground or seasoned
    pepper
1 pkg. (12 oz.) Jimmy Dean Light
    sausage
1 stick pepperoni, thinly sliced

1 can (8 oz.) chunky-style tomato
    sauce
1 tsp. parsley flakes
1/4 tsp. oregano
1/4 tsp. sweet basil
1/4 tsp. thyme
1 can (4 oz.) mushroom stems and
    pieces, drained
1 C mozzarella cheese, shredded

Prepare the macaroni following package directions, then drain well. In a medium-size mixing bowl, combine the eggs, milk, salt, pepper and drained macaroni. Pour this mixture into a sprayed 9 x 9-inch baking dish. Bake in a preheated 400° oven about 10 minutes or until set.

While the macaroni is baking, fry the crumbled sausage and sliced pepperoni until well browned, then drain on paper towels. Remove the macaroni from the oven. Add the herbs to the tomato sauce and spread over the macaroni. Spread the sausage mixture over the sauce and the mushrooms over the sausage. Top all with the shredded cheese. Return to the oven and bake until the cheese has melted and is bubbly.

Serves 4–6.

Let the junior chefs give this one a try and keep this in mind when you're going out and need something for a kid-loving meal.

# Gabby's Pizza Puff

1/2 lb. lean ground beef, crumbled
1/2 lb. bulk Italian sausage, crumbled
1 medium onion, finely chopped
1–2 cloves garlic, pressed or finely minced
2 C spaghetti sauce (meatless) or pizza sauce

1/2 lb. mozzarella cheese, sliced
2 extra large eggs, beaten
1 C milk
1 T light vegetable oil (canola)
1 C flour
1/2 tsp. salt
1/2 C fresh parmesan cheese, grated

In a large fry pan, brown the combined meats, onion and garlic. Pour off any extruded grease. Add the spaghetti sauce and simmer for 8–10 minutes.

Pour the mixture into a large (9 x 13-inch) shallow baking dish and arrange the slices of mozzarella on top. Bake in a preheated 400° oven for 10 minutes.

In a medium-size mixing bowl, combine the eggs, milk, oil, flour and salt, in the order listed, and whisk well. Remove the meat mixture from the oven and pour the batter mixture over all, then sprinkle the parmesan cheese on top. Return the dish to the oven and bake an additional 25–30 minutes or until the batter has puffed and is lightly browned. Cut into squares and serve.

Serves 4.

# Upside Down Pizza

1/2 lb. lean or extra lean ground beef, crumbled
1/2 lb. bulk ground pork sausage, crumbled
2–3 cloves garlic, pressed or minced
1 can (15 oz.) Italian-style tomato sauce
2 cans (3 oz.) Italian-style tomato paste
2 T flour

1 1/2 tsp. Italian seasoning
1 lb. Mozzarella cheese, sliced about 1/4-inch thick
1 C flour
3 extra large eggs
1 C milk
1 T light vegetable (canola) oil
1/4 tsp. salt
1/2 C fresh parmesan cheese, grated

In a large skillet, brown the ground beef, pork sausage and garlic. Drain off and discard the excess grease. Stir in the garlic, tomato sauce, tomato paste, 2 tablespoons flour and Italian seasoning and heat to a simmer. Continue to cook for another couple of minutes.

Pour this mixture into a 9 x 13-inch shallow baking pan. Arrange the mozzarella slices, overlapping, over the meat sauce. In a medium-size mixing bowl, beat the 1 cup of flour, eggs, milk, oil and salt. Pour this egg mixture over the cheese and sprinkle the parmesan over the top. Bake in a preheated 425° oven for 25–30 minutes or until puffy and cheese has melted. Remove from the oven and invert onto a platter for serving.

Serves 4–6.

# Chapter 5

# Main Dishes

# Gabby Specialities—Main Dishes

# Chicken Pommodoro

1 T olive oil
4 chicken breasts, julienne sliced
1/4 C onion, finely chopped
1/4 C celery, with leaves, finely
    chopped
1/2 C dry vermouth
1 C chicken broth (defatted)

2 T capers, drained
1 tsp. dried tarragon
1/3 C oil cured Italian olives, drained,
    pitted and chopped
2 tsp. butter, cut into small pieces
8 oz. cooked pasta (your choice)
3–4 T sun dried tomato pesto

In a large skillet or fry pan, heat the oil over medium heat. Add the chicken and saute for 3 minutes, stirring often. Add the onion and saute until chicken is done. Remove the chicken-onion mixture and cover to keep warm.

Deglaze the pan with the vermouth and reduce the liquid. Add the chicken broth, capers, tarragon and olives. Bring the mixture to a simmer, then add the butter, piece by piece. Return the chicken to the pan, along with the cooked pasta and the pesto. Stir well; when all is heated through, transfer to a pasta bowl and serve.

Serves 4.

Awfully good!

# Gabby's Chicken Mozzarella

3 T butter and olive oil combination
8 oz. fresh mushrooms, sliced
2 cloves garlic, pressed or minced
Salt and fresh ground pepper, to taste
2 T Madeira, port or sherry wine
1/2 C seasoned flour (flour and
    Schilling Salt-Free seasoning mix)

4 chicken breasts, boned and skinned
3 T butter and olive oil combination
1/2 C dry white wine
1/2 lb. mozzarella cheese, sliced
2–3 T parsley flakes

Heat the butter/oil combination in a medium-size skillet. Add the mushrooms, garlic, salt and pepper. Saute this mixture over medium-high heat about 2 minutes, then add the Madeira; continue to saute, reducing the liquid by half.

Place the seasoned flour in a medium-size paper or plastic bag. Add the chicken breasts, one at a time, and shake to coat well. In a large skillet, heat the remaining butter-oil combination over medium-high heat. Add the coated chicken breasts and cook about 3 minutes; turn and continue to cook an additional 3–5 minutes.

Arrange the browned breasts in a shallow baking dish. Spoon the mushrooms over the breasts. Deglaze the chicken pan with the white wine, reducing the liquid by half, then pour over the chicken. Place the cheese slices over the chicken and garnish with the parsley flakes. Bake in a preheated 375° oven for 15 minutes or until chicken is done and cheese is bubbly and golden brown.

Makes 6 servings.

# Chicken Mediterranean

1/2 c. lemon juice
1/2 C dry white wine
2 T ground cumin
4 chicken breasts, boned and skinned
1 red bell pepper, cut into thin strips
1/4 red Bermuda onion, thinly sliced
1 T garlic puree
1 T vegetable oil
1 T ground cumin

1 tsp. lemon pepper seasoning
1 C dry white wine
1 tsp. chicken base
1 1/2 tsp. course ground black pepper
1 T brown sugar
1 C water
1 T cornstarch, dissolved in small
    amount of water

Combine the lemon juice, wine and cumin, then place the chicken breasts in the mixture and marinate for 4 hours. Drain well, then grill chicken for 6 minutes per side.

In a saucepan, saute the bell pepper, onion and garlic paste in the oil until pepper is tender. Add the second measure of cumin, lemon pepper, lemon juice, wine, chicken base and black pepper. Continue to cook until the mixture reduces by 1/4. Add just a bit of water and continue to simmer. Check for proper seasoning, and bring mixture to a boil. Add the diluted cornstarch and cook until the mixture thickens. Serve this sauce over the cooked chicken.

Serves 4.

# Apple-Glazed Chicken Thighs

8–10 chicken thighs, skinned and
   boned
3 T butter and olive oil combination
1 C seasoned flour (flour, garlic powder
   and select herbs)
1/2 C apple jelly
1/2 C dry white wine of choice
2 T lemon juice
1 T dried onion flakes

1 clove of garlic, pressed or finely
   minced
8 whole cloves
1/2 tsp. madras curry powder (can use
   more, if desired)
Salt and fresh ground pepper, to taste
Cherry tomatoes, green onion tops
   and fresh parsley sprigs for garnish

Prepare the chicken as indicated. In a large fry pan, heat the butter-oil combination over medium-high heat. In a shallow dish, place the flour and dredge each of the thighs.

Place the coated chicken in the hot pan and brown, turning often, 8–10 minutes or until well-browned over all. Pour off any excess grease in the pan. In a small saucepan, combine all remaining ingredients except the garnishes. Heat just until the jelly dissolves. Pour the sauce over the browned chicken, cover and simmer, basting occasionally, about 15 minutes. Remove the cover and continue to simmer an additional 5 minutes or until the chicken is glazed. Place the pieces of chicken on a warmed serving platter and garnish with tomatoes, green onion tops and parsley.

Makes 4 servings.

# Oven-Roasted Garlic Chicken

1/2 C chicken broth
6 T Worcestershire sauce
6 T lemon juice
3 T butter, melted
1/4 C fresh parsley, finely chopped
4 cloves garlic, pressed or finely
   minced

2 tsp. Italian seasonings
Salt and fresh ground pepper, to taste
Pinch cayenne pepper
4 chicken breasts, boned and skinned
1 loaf of Italian or French bread,
   warmed and cut into chunks

Combine all the ingredients except the chicken and bread in a 9-inch square baking dish. Lay out the chicken breasts, prepared as indicated, then score each about 1/4-inch deep in a cross patch pattern.

Place the breasts in the pan, scored-side down, spooning some of the sauce over the top portion to coat. Bake in a preheated 375° oven for 25–30 minutes. Serve, scored-side up, with a tablespoon of the sauce over each. Pass the remaining sauce and dip in the chunks of warmed bread.

Serves 4.

# Broiled Hoisin Chicken Thighs

12 chicken thighs, boned and skinned
1/2 C Hoisin sauce
1 1/2 C hot mango chutney
1 T fresh ginger, shredded
3 T cloves garlic, pressed or minced
1 1/2 T seasoned or regular rice
    vinegar

1 1/2 T sesame oil
3/4 tsp. coarse or fresh ground black
    pepper
1/4 C sesame seeds, toasted

Prepare the thighs as indicated, then place in a large zip lock plastic bag. In a mixing bowl, combine all remaining ingredients, except the sesame seeds. Mix well, then pour the sauce into the bag with the thighs. Shake well to cover all, then place in the refrigerator to marinate for several hours or overnight.

Place the marinated thighs on a sprayed broiler pan. Place 3 inches under the broiler and broil for 3 minutes; turn once and continue to broil an additional 3–6 minutes, depending on the size of the thighs and desired doneness.

Remove from the broiler and press each into the sesame seeds and serve immediately.

Serves 4, *maybe* (you might want to double this recipe, 'cause they're well liked).

# Baked Pignoli Chicken

3 T butter and olive oil combo
6 chicken breasts, boned and skinned
    preferred
1 C seasoned flour (flour, paprika,
    garlic powder, salt and pepper)
1/2 lb. fresh mushrooms, sliced
1 can cream of mushroom soup (light)
1/2 C dry white wine

1/2 C chicken broth
2 T fresh parsley, finely chopped
1/4 tsp. dried thyme
1/4 C toasted pignoli (pine) nuts
Sweet Hungarian paprika
6 C cooked long grain rice (can use
    brown rice, if desired)

In a large fry pan, heat the butter and oil combination over medium-high heat. Dredge each breast in the seasoned flour mixture and place in the hot pan. Brown the breasts on each side, then remove and place in a sprayed shallow baking dish, skinned-side up.

In the same skillet, brown the mushrooms in the pan drippings (add more butter, if too dry). Spoon the browned mushrooms over the breasts. Add the soup to the same pan, then whisk in the wine, broth, parsley and thyme and heat through. Sprinkle the pignoli nuts and paprika over the mushrooms and chicken. Spoon the sauce over all. Cover and bake in a preheated 350° oven for 20 minutes, then uncover and bake an additional 20–25 minutes. Serve over rice.

Serves 6.

# Gabby's Sherried Chicken Paprika

8 medium chicken breasts (skinned
   and boned, if desired)
1 C straight sherry wine
1/4 C melted butter
1 T lemon juice

1 tsp. sweet Hungarian paprika
1/4 C green onions, chopped
1/4 C fresh parsley, finely chopped
2 tsp. salt
1/2 tsp. fresh ground pepper

Place the chicken breasts skinned-side down in a shallow baking dish. In a 2-cup measure, mix the remaining ingredients and pour over the chicken. Cover with foil and bake in a preheated 350° oven for 1 hour. Uncover, turn the chicken, and continue to bake for 30 more minutes.

Makes 8 servings.

# Almond-Chicken with Parmesan Crumbs

1/2 C dry seasoned bread crumbs
1/2 C fresh parmesan cheese, grated
1/4 C almonds, finely chopped
2 T fresh parsley, finely chopped
1 tsp. salt
1/2 tsp. thyme, crushed just a bit
1/4 tsp. seasoned pepper

1/2 C butter, melted (you can
    substitute olive oil)
1 clove of garlic, pressed or finely
    minced
8 pieces of chicken (your choice),
    skinned and boned

Combine the crumbs, cheese, almonds and seasonings, and mix well; pour into a pie tin or shallow dish. Combine the melted butter and garlic and place in a shallow dish. Dip the pieces of chicken into the butter first, then roll in the crumb mixture.

Arrange the coated chicken on a baking sheet. Bake in a preheated 400° oven for 45 minutes or until tender. Baste with any remaining butter/olive oil during the baking period.

Serves 4.

# Gabby's Chicken a l'Orange

4–6 chicken breasts, boned, but not
   skinned
1/4 tsp. ground cinnamon
1/4 tsp. ground cloves
Salt and fresh ground pepper, to taste
3 T olive oil
1 medium sweet onion, chopped
1–2 cloves garlic, pressed or minced

2 C fresh orange juice
Pinch of saffron threads
1/2 C golden raisins
1/2 C sliced almonds, toasted
4–6 C hot steamed rice
2 large fresh oranges, peeled and sliced
   into sections

Prepare the chicken breasts as indicated, then lay out and season on both sides with the cinnamon, cloves, salt and pepper.

In a large non-stick pan, heat the oil over medium-high heat. Add the seasoned chicken and brown lightly on both sides. Add the onion and garlic and continue to saute until well browned. Add the orange juice, saffron and raisins; cover, reduce heat, and simmer about 35–40 minutes.

Place the hot rice on a warmed serving platter, then arrange the chicken mixture on top of it. Sprinkle the toasted almond slices over all and arrange the orange sections around the rim of the platter as garnish.

Serves 4–6.

# Glazed Ginger Chicken Breasts

4–6 chicken breasts, boned, skinned and slightly flattened
1/2 C seasoned flour (flour, seasoned salt, fresh ground pepper and garlic powder)
2 T butter
1 T olive oil
1 C orange juice
2 green onions, finely chopped

1 T brown sugar
1/2 tsp. fresh ginger, grated
2–3 tsp. Gabby's Own Mustard (*see chapter 7, Sauces and Dressings, for this recipe*)
1 can (15 oz.) mandarin orange sections, drained
2–3 T fresh orange zest

Prepare the chicken breasts as indicated. Combine the ingredients for the seasoned flour and coat each chicken breast with the flour mixture.

In a large non-stick skillet, heat the butter and oil over medium heat. Add the floured chicken and saute about 5 minutes on both sides, then remove and keep warm. Pour off the excess fat from the pan, place over high heat and add the orange juice, green onions, sugar, ginger and mustard. Cook the mixture, stirring until the sauce reduces and thickens. Add the orange sections to the pan.

Return the chicken to the pan, turning in the sauce several times to coat well. Arrange the breasts on a serving plate and spoon the sauce and orange sections over all. Garnish all with the orange zest.

Makes 4–6 servings.

# Chicken and Pine Nuts in Madeira Sauce

2 T olive oil
6 chicken breasts, boned and skinned
Salt and fresh ground pepper, to taste
1–2 T butter
1/4 C onion, finely chopped
1–2 cloves garlic, pressed or minced
1 lb. fresh mushrooms, thickly sliced

1/2 C toasted pine nuts
1 T lemon juice
1 1/2 T flour
3/4 C Madeira wine
3/4 C heavy whipping cream
3/4 C Swiss cheese, shredded (divided)

In a large skillet, heat the oil over medium-high heat. Add the chicken breasts to the hot pan and brown on both sides. Salt and pepper to taste. Drain well on paper towels, then place in a 9 x 13-inch shallow baking dish.

In the same skillet, melt the butter in the chicken drippings and add the onion and garlic. Saute this mixture about 3 minutes, then add the mushrooms, pine nuts and lemon juice. Cook for 5 minutes, then sprinkle the flour over all. Stir in the Madeira and then the cream. Cook about 2 minutes and when the liquid thickens, stir in 1/2 cup of cheese and let melt. Spoon the mixture over the breasts, then top with the remaining cheese. Bake, uncovered, in a preheated 400° oven for 20 minutes or until the chicken is tender.

Makes 6 servings.

A great company dish!

# Gabby's Chicken Swiss

4–6 chicken breasts, boned and
   skinned (thighs can also be used)
1/2 C flour
1 tsp. rosemary, crush lightly
1/2 tsp. sweet Hungarian paprika
1/4 tsp. garlic pepper
1/4 tsp. salt

1/4 C olive oil and butter combination
1/2 lb. fresh mushrooms, sliced
1/4 C green onions, chopped
1/3 C dry white wine
1/2 lb. Swiss cheese, sliced
1/4 C fresh parsley, finely chopped

Prepare the chicken as indicated, then wash in cold water and dry on paper towels. Place the flour and seasonings in a paper bag or a pie plate. Add the chicken, a couple of pieces at a time and shake or dredge to coat well.

In a large fry pan, heat the oil-butter combination over medium-high heat. Add the floured chicken and saute 3–5 minutes on each side or until lightly browned. Place the browned chicken in a shallow baking dish and set aside.

Add the mushrooms and green onions to the pan, adding more butter, if necessary, and saute 5–7 minutes. Pour this mixture over the chicken pieces. Deglaze the pan with the wine and let the liquid reduce to half. Pour this over all in the dish. Place a slice of cheese on each piece of chicken. Sprinkle the parsley over all. Bake uncovered in a preheated 350° oven about 30 minutes.

Serves 4–6.

# Chicken Breasts with Tarragon Cream and Rice

6–8 chicken breasts, boned and
    skinned
1/2 C flour
1 tsp. sweet Hungarian paprika
1/2 tsp. salt
1/2 tsp. fresh ground pepper
3 T butter and olive oil combination
2 C fresh mushrooms (preferably
    wild), sliced

2–3 shallots, chopped
1/4 C heavy whipping cream
2 T fresh tarragon leaves (without
    stems)
3 T dry white wine
6 C hot steamed long grain rice
Fresh tarragon sprigs for garnish

Prepare the chicken breasts as indicated (make sure all fat is removed from the meat along with the skin), then set aside. In a medium-size paper or plastic bag, combine the flour, paprika, salt and pepper. Add the chicken breasts, a couple at a time, shake well to coat.

In a large skillet, heat the butter-olive oil combination; when hot, add the coated chicken breasts and brown well over medium heat. When all are browned, add the mushrooms, stir well, cover and cook about 10 minutes. Add the cream and tarragon leaves, stir well, and simmer about 10 more minutes. Arrange the cooked rice on a serving platter, then place the chicken on top. Add the wine to the sauce, stir well, and simmer, uncovered, over low heat about 3 minutes; ladle sauce over the chicken and rice. Garnish with more fresh tarragon sprigs.

Makes 6–8 servings.

# Green Noodles and Chicken Parmesan

1/4 lb. butter
2 cloves garlic, pressed/minced
1/2 lb. fresh mushrooms, thickly sliced
2 tsp. dried tarragon leaves
1 pint heavy cream
2 T straight sherry wine
6 chicken breasts, skinned, boned,
    seasoned, cooked and cut
    into strips

2 T butter, room temperature
2 T flour
12 oz. green noodles, boiled according
    to package directions and drained
    well
Parmesan cheese, grated or shredded
Sweet Hungarian paprika

In a medium-large saute pan, melt the butter over medium-high heat, then add the garlic, mushrooms and tarragon. Saute this mixture about 5 minutes, then stir in the cream, sherry and chicken strips. Bring to a simmer.

Make a paste with the softened butter and flour, then stir into the chicken mixture, and cook until thickened. In a large, shallow, sprayed baking dish, arrange the drained noodles, followed by the chicken-mushroom mixture. Sprinkle the parmesan cheese over all and spritz with a touch of paprika for color garnish. Bake in a preheated 350° oven for 30–35 minutes.

Makes 6 servings.

# Herbed Roasted Holiday Chicken

1 6–8 pound whole roasting chicken
   or capon
1 small onion, skinned and cut into
   quarters
1 small cooking apple, cut into
   quarters
2 large cloves garlic

Zest from one lemon
1 large sprig of fresh rosemary
1/4 C olive oil
2 T mixed fresh herbs, chopped
   (parsley, thyme, rosemary, basil,
   and oregano)
Salt and fresh ground pepper, to taste

Rinse out the chicken with cold water, then pat dry with paper towels. Place the onion, apple, garlic, zest and rosemary in the cavity of the bird.

In a small bowl, combine the olive oil and the mixed fresh herbs. Paint this mixture over the outside of the chicken, then season generously with salt and fresh ground pepper. Cover with plastic wrap and refrigerate for 1 hour.

Place the chicken on a roasting rack in a roasting pan. Bake in a preheated 400° oven for 1 1/4 to 1 1/2 hours, or until the juices run clear when pierced with a fork. Let rest 10–15 minutes before slicing or cutting into parts. Discard the flavoring ingredients in the cavity.

Serves 4–6.

This is a great substitute for the traditional holiday turkey.

# Gabby's Sesame Chicken

5–6 chicken breasts, skinned, boned
    and cut into bite-size pieces
1/2 C seasoned flour mixture
1/2 C peanut oil
1/4 C sugar

1/4 C soy sauce
1 tsp. sesame oil
3–4 T toasted sesame seeds
1/4 C green onions, finely chopped

Prepare the chicken as indicated, then dredge each piece in the seasoned flour. In a large fry pan or oriental wok, heat the peanut oil until it is 365° to 375°. Add the pieces of chicken and fry until done. Drain on paper toweling, cover and keep warm.

In a small saucepan, combine the sugar, soy sauce and sesame oil. Heat the mixture, stirring until the sugar dissolves. Add the chicken pieces to the sauce, then roll in the sesame seeds and green onions. Serve immediately.

Serves 4–6.

Easy and very tasty, but don't over cook the chicken!

# Gabby's New "Oven-Qued" Game Hens

2 T olive oil
1/2 medium sweet onion, very finely
　chopped
1–2 cloves garlic, pressed or minced
1/2 C celery (with leaves), very finely
　chopped
1/2 C green bell pepper, very finely
　chopped
1 1/2 C chili sauce

1/2 C water
2 T Worcestershire sauce
2 T brown sugar
1 T lemon juice
1 tsp. Wright's liquid smoke (or your
　favorite)
1/4 tsp. fresh ground pepper or to taste
4 Rock Cornish game hens, split in
　half

In a medium-size saucepan, heat the olive oil over medium heat, then add the onion, garlic, celery and bell pepper. Saute this mixture until the onion is tender. Add all of the remaining ingredients, except the hens. Reduce the heat to low and barely simmer, uncovered, for 40–45 minutes.

Prepare the hens as indicated, then wash in cold water and pat dry with paper towels. Spray a shallow baking pan with Pam. Lightly salt all sides of the hen halves, then arrange in the baking pan. Spoon all of the sauce over the birds and bake in a preheated 350° oven for about 1 hour or until they test done.

Makes 8 servings.

# Greek-Style Game Hens

4 Rock Cornish game hens or other
    game bird (quail, thrush, etc.)
1/2 C olive oil
1/2 T oregano leaves
1/4 T salt
1/4 T fresh ground pepper
1/2 C Nea Fytini or other vegetable oil
1 small onion, diced

2 green onions, thinly chopped
1 lb. fresh mushrooms (preferably wild
    types), sliced
2 T Metaxa or other brandy
4 T fresh parsley, finely chopped
2 C watercress sprigs
1 T lemon juice

Wash and drain the birds. Split each lengthwise from tail to neck and lay them on a cutting board, breast up. Press down firmly with palm to break the breast bone. Slit the skin between the two legs with the tip of a sharp knife and thread leg tips through. Brush each bird with olive oil and rub with oregano, salt and pepper. Cover and refrigerate for 2 hours.

In a heavy frying pan, heat the remaining olive and vegetable oils over medium-high heat. Add the birds and fry until well browned on both sides (7–8 minutes per side). Remove the birds to a platter and keep hot.

Saute the onions and mushrooms over high heat until the liquid evaporates. Add the Metaxa, parsley, more salt, and pepper, stirring for 1 minute. Cover the center of the platter with the mushroom mixture, surrounded by the birds and garnished with the watercress. Sprinkle lemon juice over all just before serving.

Serves 4.

# Gabby's Gringo Enchiladas

2 T olive or canola oil
1 medium white onion, finely chopped
1 clove of garlic, pressed or minced
1 can (15 oz.) chunky-style tomato
    sauce
1 can (7 oz.) diced green chilies
1/4 C fresh cilantro, chopped
1/2 tsp. ground cumin

2 C cooked chicken, shredded
12 large flour tortillas
Canola oil for softening tortillas
2 C half & half or whipping cream,
    heated
6 tsp. chicken bouillon granules
1/4 lb. Monterey Jack cheese, shredded
1/4 lb. sharp cheddar cheese, shredded

In a medium-size skillet, heat the oil over medium-high heat. Add the onion and garlic and saute just a couple of minutes. Add the tomato sauce, chilies, cilantro and cumin. Simmer this mixture over medium-low heat about 10 minutes. Add the shredded chicken and heat through.

In a medium-size saucepan, combine the cream and bouillon granules and heat until the bouillon has dissolved. Heat the remaining oil and soften each tortilla in the oil for just a second, then remove and dip in the warmed cream. Fill each tortilla with the chicken mixture, then roll and place in a sprayed shallow baking dish, seam down. When all of the tortillas are filled, rolled and arranged in the dish, pour the remaining cream mixture over all and top with the shredded cheeses. Bake in a preheated 350° oven for 30–35 minutes or until just lightly browned over the cheese.

Serves 6 (2 enchiladas per person).

# Family Tortilla Bake

5 medium (6-inch) flour tortillas
3/4 lb. lean or extra lean ground beef
    (you can also use ground white
    turkey meat)
1 small white onion, finely chopped
1/4 C salsa (your choice)
1 can (4-oz.) diced green chilies
1/2 C medium sharp cheddar cheese,
    shredded

1 egg plus 2 egg whites
1/2 C non-fat skim milk
2 T flour
1/2 tsp. baking powder
1/2 tsp. ground cumin
1/4 tsp. chili powder
Fresh tomato slices
Fresh cilantro sprigs, for garnish
Plain yogurt or sour cream

Spray a 9-inch pie plate with cooking spray, then line with the tortillas. Brown the ground beef and onion, drain well, and then combine with the salsa, chilies and cheese. Spoon this mixture over the tortillas.

Combine the eggs and the milk, flour, baking powder, cumin and chili powder, whisking well, then pour over the beef mixture. Bake in a preheated 350° oven for 40–45 minutes or until set in the middle. Remove from the oven and top with the tomato slices and sprigs of cilantro. Serve each slice with dollops of yogurt, sour cream or a mixture of both.

Serves 4–6.

# Gabby's Best Italian-Stuffed Peppers

8 medium green bell peppers, topped, seeded and steamed

**Meat mixture:**
2 T light vegetable (canola) oil
1 medium onion, finely chopped
2 ribs celery, finely chopped
3 cloves garlic, pressed or minced
1 1/2 lbs. lean ground beef
1 8 oz. can mushrooms with liquid
1 can (14 1/2 oz.) S & W brand ready-cut Italian peeled tomatoes
2 cans (14 1/2 oz.) Hunt's brand Special Chunky tomato sauce
1/2 C tomato ketchup

1/4 C dry red wine
1 tsp. Italian seasoning
1 tsp. Worcestershire sauce
1/2 tsp. dried basil leaves
2 C cooked long grain rice
1/2 bottle Mancini brand fried peppers with onions

**Sauce:**
2 cans (14 1/2 oz.) Hunt's chunky tomato sauce with garlic and herbs
1 tsp. worcestershire sauce
1 tsp. Italian seasoning
1 tsp. sugar

In a large saute pan, heat the oil over medium-high heat. Add the onion, celery and garlic and saute until onion is soft. Crumble the ground beef, add to the pan and cook until browned. Add the rest of the meat mixture ingredients, except the rice and peppers, and simmer over medium heat. Stir in the cooked rice and bottled peppers and simmer about 10 minutes.

Steam the bell peppers in an inch of water about 6 minutes. Invert on paper towels and drain well. Stuff each pepper with the meat mixture, rounding over the top. In a medium saucepan, combine the sauce ingredients. Heat through, then spoon over the filled peppers in a shallow baking dish, just large enough to snugly hold the filled peppers. Bake, covered, in a 350° oven for 40 minutes.

Serves 8.

# Gabby's Picadillo

2 lbs. extra lean ground beef
2 medium white onions, finely
    chopped
2 large cloves garlic, pressed or finely
    minced
3 jalapeno or serrano peppers, seeded
    and minced
1/4 C fresh cilantro, finely chopped
3 large fresh ripe tomatoes, seeded and
    chopped

2 medium cooking-type apples, pared,
    cored and coarsely chopped
1/2 C stuffed green olives, halved
1/2 C raisins
1/8 tsp. ground cloves
1/8 tsp. ground cinnamon
2–3 ripe avocados, sliced
12 fajita flour tortillas, heated

In a large fry pan, combine the ground beef, onion and garlic and brown over medium-high heat. Add all of the remaining ingredients, except the avocados and tortillas, stirring well. Reduce heat to low, cover, and simmer 20–25 minutes.

Pour the mixture in a colorful shallow serving bowl and garnish with the avocado slices around the rim. Serve with the tortillas.

Serves 6.

If desired, this can be "heated up" by adding the hot sauce of your choice while it cooks.

# Cheesy Meat Loaf with Mustard Mushroom Sauce

2 1/2 lbs. lean or extra lean ground beef
2 C soda cracker crumbs
1 C medium cheddar cheese, diced into small cubes
2/3 C onion, finely chopped
1/4 C green bell pepper, finely chopped
1 rib celery, finely chopped with leaves
1 T salt
1 tsp. thyme

1 tsp. garlic pepper
2 1/2 C chunky tomato sauce
3 eggs, beaten
6 bay leaves (3 for each loaf)
2 cans cream of mushroom soup
1 can (4 oz.) sliced mushrooms, drained
2 tsp. Gabby's Own Mustard (*see chapter 7, Sauces and Dressings, for this recipe*)
1/4 tsp. thyme

In a large mixing bowl, combine the beef, cracker crumbs, cheese, onion, bell pepper, celery, salt, thyme and garlic pepper and mix well. Combine the tomato sauce and eggs. Blend this mixture into the meat mixture.

Divide the meat mixture into two sprayed loaf pans, then arrange three bay leaves over each. Bake in a preheated 350° oven for 60–70 minutes. During the baking, prepare the mushroom sauce. In a medium-size saucepan, combine the soup, mushrooms, mustard and second measure of thyme, stirring well and heating through. Serve the sauce over slices of the meat loaf (remove and discard the bay leaves before serving).

Makes 10–12 servings.

# Gabby's Glazed Meat Loaf

1 lb. lean or extra lean ground beef
1 lb. pork sausage meat
1/2 C fresh seasoned bread crumbs
1/2 C sweet onion, very finely chopped
3 green onions, chopped
1 T dried parsley flakes
1 tsp. oregano
1 1/2 tsp. salt
1 tsp. fresh ground pepper

1/4 tsp. fresh grated nutmeg
1 egg yolk, lightly beaten
3/4 C beer
1 C brown sugar
1/4 C beer
2 tsp. Gabby's Own Mustard (*see chapter 7, Sauces and Dressings, for this recipe*)

In a large mixing bowl, combine the beef and sausage and mix until well blended. Add the crumbs, onions, parsley, seasonings, egg yolk and 3/4 cup beer and mix well. Place the mixture on a baking sheet or in a shallow baking dish and shape into a loaf. Bake in a preheated 350° oven for 1 hour.

While the loaf is baking, prepare the glaze by combining the brown sugar, 1/4 cup beer and mustard in a small saucepan. Bring to a boil over medium heat and cook 5 minutes, stirring.

After the loaf has baked for 1 hour, pour the glaze mixture over the meat, return to the oven and continue baking for 15 more minutes, basting often. Remove from oven and cool for 10 minutes, then slice as desired.

Serves 6–8.

# Just a Nice Meat Loaf, Italian-Style

1 lb. lean ground beef
1/2 medium sweet onion, chopped
3/4 C fresh seasoned bread crumbs
1/2 C milk
1 extra large egg, lightly beaten
2 T catsup
1 T horseradish
1/2 T Gabby's Own Mustard or your
    favorite (for "Gabby's Own
    Mustard," see chapter 7, Sauces and
    Dressings)

1 tsp. salt
1 tsp. Italian seasoning
1/2 tsp. fresh ground pepper
1 medium green bell pepper, sliced
    into rings
1/2 C Italian-style chunky tomato
    sauce
3/4 C cheddar cheese, shredded

Place the beef in a large mixing bowl and add and mix well all of the remaining ingredients, except the bell pepper, tomato sauce and cheese. Form this mixture into a loaf shape, then place in a loaf pan, forming somewhat of a moat around the sides of the loaf about 1 inch deep.

Arrange the bell pepper rings over the top of the loaf, overlapping. Bake in a preheated 350° oven for 45–50 minutes, then remove from the oven, and pour off any grease extruded around the sides. Pour the tomato sauce over the top, then sprinkle the cheese over all. Return to the oven and bake about 15 minutes. Let set 10–15 minutes before removing from the pan, then slice and serve.

Serves 6–8.

# Fresh Mushroom Pot Roast

4–5 lb. beef pot roast
1/2 C seasoned flour
Olive oil for browning meat
3–4 large onions, halved, sliced
1 28-oz. can ready-cut tomatoes with
    liquid
1/2 C dry red wine
1/2 C chili sauce
2–3 cloves garlic, pressed or finely
    minced
1 T Bovril (beef seasoning base)
2 tsp. Gabby's Own Mustard (*see
    chapter 7, Sauces and Dressings, for
    this recipe*)

1 bay leaf
1 tsp. thyme
1/2 tsp. marjoram
1/2 tsp. rosemary
Salt and fresh ground pepper, to taste
1 lb. fresh mushrooms, thickly sliced
2 T flour (can use any remaining
    seasoned flour)
1/4 C cold water
1 lb. extra wide egg noodles, boiled,
    drained and buttered

Dredge the beef in the seasoned flour mixture. Heat the oil in a large Dutch oven over high heat. Add the meat and brown well on all sides. Add the onions and brown them, too. Combine and add the tomatoes, wine, chili sauce, garlic, and seasonings. Reduce the heat to low, cover, and simmer 2 1/2 to 3 hours (depending on size of the roast) or until the meat is tender. About 15 minutes before serving, add the mushrooms.

Just before serving, remove the meat and mushrooms and arrange over the noodles on a warmed serving platter. Combine the flour and water, then stir into the pan juices over medium heat. Let this mixture simmer, stirring until thickened. Pour the sauce over everything on the platter.

Should serve 8 with some leftovers.

# Gabby's Fresh Herbed Pot Roast

1 medium (4–5 lb.) beef pot roast
1/4 C seasoned flour (flour, seasoned salt, pepper and sweet Hungarian paprika)
2–3 T light cooking (canola) or olive oil
2 large onions, halved and sliced
1/2 C beef broth
1/2 C catsup
1/3 C straight sherry wine
1 T Worcestershire sauce
1 tsp. Gabby's Own Mustard (*see chapter 7, Sauces and Dressings, for this recipe*)
1 medium sprig fresh rosemary
1 medium sprig fresh marjoram
1 medium sprig fresh thyme
1–2 bay leaves
Salt and ground pepper, to taste
1/2 lb. fresh mushrooms, sliced
1 1/2 T cornstarch
1/2 C cold water

Dredge the roast with the seasoned flour. In a large Dutch oven, heat the oil over medium-high heat, then add the meat and brown well on both sides. Add the onions. Combine the broth, catsup, wine, Worcestershire, and mustard, and pour over the roast. Cover and simmer about 1 hour, then add the herbs, salt, pepper and mushrooms. Cover and continue to simmer another 1 to 1 1/2 hours.

When tender, remove the meat and place on a large serving platter. Combine the cornstarch and cold water, stir into the pan juices and continue to cook until thickened. Sauce can be served with the roast or on the side.

Serves 6 with some leftovers.

Needs a green vegetable or two and warm crusty bread. Small red new potatoes and carrots can be added with the herbs, if desired.

# Gabby's Crock Pot Beef

1 1/2 lbs. beef tenderloin,
    well-trimmed
1 lb. fresh mushrooms, sliced
1 C pearl onions, trimmed
2–3 cloves garlic, pressed or minced
1/2 C dry red wine
1/4 C soy sauce

3 1/2 T Worcestershire sauce
2 T light vegetable (canola) oil
1 tsp. lemon juice
2 T fresh parsley, finely chopped
2–3 sprigs of fresh oregano
Salt and fresh ground pepper, to taste
Buttered noodles

Arrange the beef over the bottom of your crock pot. In the order listed, place all of the remaining ingredients, except the noodles, over the meat. Turn the crock pot on its low setting, cover and let cook for 5 hours.

Remove the beef and carve into 8–10 slices. Arrange the beef slices over the buttered noodles. Ladle the juices over the meat. Serve immediately.

Serves 4–6.

# Gabby's Chili-Beer Pot Roast

3 1/2–4 lbs. beef pot roast
2 T olive oil
2 cans (14 1/2 oz.) Cajun or Mexican
   stewed tomatoes
1 can (4 oz.) diced green chilies
1/2 C beer
2–3 cloves garlic, pressed or finely
   minced

2–3 onions, halved and chopped
2 tsp. ground chili powder
2 tsp. Bovril beef seasoning base
6 large red new potatoes, cut into
   quarters
6 medium carrots, halved and cut into
   quarters

In a large Dutch oven, heat the oil over high heat. Add the meat and brown well on both sides. In a medium-size bowl, combine the tomatoes, chilies (with juices), beer, garlic, onions, chili powder and Bovril. Pour this mixture over the browned roast and bring to a boil. Reduce the heat, cover and let simmer 2 to 2 1/2 hours.

During the last hour, add the potatoes and carrots, cover, and continue to simmer until all is tender. Serve as is or you can remove the meat and vegetables to a warmed serving platter, add 1–2 tablespoons flour to cold water, whisk into the pan juices, making a thickened gravy.

Serves 6–8.

Nothing like doing something different with a pot roast.

# Delicious Barbequed Beef Brisket

4–5 lbs. beef brisket, well trimmed
14 oz. Heinz Hot Ketchup
1/2 C hot boiling water
2 cloves garlic, pressed or minced
4 T Worcestershire sauce
3 T brown sugar
2 T onion, finely minced
2 T instant coffee granules (mix with
the hot water above)

2 T light vegetable oil (canola)
2 T Wright's Liquid Smoke
2 T Gabby's Own Mustard (*see chapter
7, Sauces and Dressings, for this
recipe*)
2 tsp. celery seed

In a large Dutch oven, brown the brisket in a small amount of oil. While browning the beef, prepare the barbecue sauce. Combine all of the remaining ingredients in a medium-size saucepan. Bring the mixture to a boil, stirring occasionally. Reduce the heat to low and simmer about 5 minutes, then pour over the browned brisket in the pan.

Cover the pan and bake in a preheated 325° oven for 3–4 hours. When done to your liking, remove the meat to a cutting board and carve against the grain into 1/4-inch slices. Serve with the sauce (defatted).

Serves 8.

Grab some hot crusty rolls and serve this at the next tailgate party.

# Marinated Flank Steak

3–4 lb. beef flank steak, tenderized if
   desired
1/2 medium onion, finely chopped
6 T frozen orange juice concentrate
1/4 C light vegetable (canola) oil
1/4 C seasoned rice vinegar
2 T soy sauce

2 cloves garlic, pressed or finely
   minced
1/2 tsp. rosemary
1/2 tsp. thyme
1/2 tsp. celery salt
Salt and fresh ground pepper, to taste

Lay out the flank steak and tenderize, then place in a medium-sized shallow baking dish. In a small bowl, combine all of the remaining ingredients, whisk well, and pour over the steak. Cover with plastic wrap and refrigerate to marinate up to 12 hours, turning several times during the period.

Remove meat from the marinade and place on the grill about 5–6 inches above the heat source and grill to desired doneness, basting often with the marinade.

Serves 6–8.

I prefer to slice the steak against the grain in about 1/4-inch thick strips and serve over toast points. This marinade can also be used for fish, such as fresh tuna, swordfish, or salmon.

# Korean-Style Flank Steak

1 beef flank steak (about 1 1/2 lbs.),
    tenderized as desired
1/2 C dry white wine
1/2 C soy sauce
1/4 C honey

2 green onions, chopped
1–2 T sesame oil
1 T fresh ginger, grated
1 clove garlic, pressed/minced

Prepare the flank steak as indicated, place in a small shallow baking dish and set aside. Combine all of the remaining ingredients, whisk well, and pour over the steak. Cover and place in the refrigerator to marinate 1 hour, turning once. Grill over hot coals to desired doneness. Slice diagonally against the grain.

Serves 6.

# Flank Steak and Mushrooms

1 1/2–2 lbs. beef flank steak
1 lb. fresh mushrooms, sliced
1 medium onion, halved and sliced
1 large red or green bell pepper,
    chopped
4 T olive or light salad-type oil
2 cloves garlic, pressed or finely
    minced
2 T flour

3/4 C beef bouillon or broth
1 can (14 1/2 oz.) ready-cut tomatoes
2 tsp. Worcestershire sauce
1 tsp. Mrs. Dash original seasoning
    mix
1/2 tsp. fresh ground pepper or to taste
12 oz. egg noodles, boiled, drained,
    buttered and parslied

Lay the steak out flat and slice on the diagonal into thin strips. Prepare the vegetables as indicated and set aside.

In a large skillet, heat the oil over medium-high heat. Add a single layer of meat and brown over all, remove from the pan and drain on paper towels. When all the meat has been browned, add more oil to the pan and saute the onion, pepper, mushrooms, and garlic for about 5 minutes. Stir in the flour and continue to cook for one minute. Stir in the bouillon, tomatoes, Worcestershire, Mrs. Dash, and pepper. Reduce the heat to medium and let simmer about 3 minutes, then return the meat to the mixture and continue simmering another 3 minutes. Serve over boiled noodles prepared as indicated.

Serves 4–6.

Really a great quickie dinner idea!

# Gabby's Sunday Beef Short Ribs

3 T light (canola) oil
5 lbs. lean beef short ribs (bone in is a
　　must)
1 C lightly seasoned flour mixture
　　(flour, paprika, salt and pepper)
3–4 onions, peeled and cut into
　　wedges
2–3 cloves garlic, pressed or minced
3 cans (15 oz.) Italian-style ready cut
　　tomatoes, with the juice
1 1/2 C dry red wine

4–6 medium carrots, cut into 1/4-inch
　　ripple slices
4 T fresh basil leaves, coarsely
　　chopped
1 large sprig of fresh thyme
Salt and fresh ground pepper, to taste
1 lb. curly egg noodles, cooked, well
　　drained, and lightly buttered
1/4 C fresh Italian parsley, finely
　　chopped

In a large Dutch oven (preferably non-stick), heat the oil over medium-high heat. Lightly coat the ribs in the seasoned flour, then add to the hot oil and brown well. Remove the browned ribs to a holding platter. Reduce the heat to medium and add the onions, browning, stirring occasionally. Add the garlic, then return the short ribs and any juices collected in the platter.

Add the tomatoes, wine, carrots, basil, thyme, salt and pepper. Bring the mixture to a boil, cover with a tight lid, then braise in a preheated 350° oven for 2 1/2 hours (check periodically to make sure there is proper liquid, and stir a few times, too). The meat should be very tender.

Prepare the noodles as indicated, then arrange on a warmed serving platter. Ladle the ribs and pan juices over the noodles, sprinkle with the parsley, and serve.

Serves 6–8 with some leftovers, *maybe*.

# Ginger-Orange Barbequed Beef Back Ribs

6 lbs. beef back ribs, well trimmed
2 tsp. fresh lemon zest
1/3 C fresh lemon juice
3/4 C fresh orange juice
1 T fresh ginger, grated
4 cloves garlic, pressed or finely
    minced

1/2 C Hoisin sauce
1/4 C honey
1 tsp. salt
2 T dark soy sauce
Zested orange and lemon rind for
    garnish

Separate the beef into individual ribs. Combine all of the remaining ingredients, except the zest, and mix well; pour into a zip lock bag. Add the ribs, seal and refrigerate for 12 hours before roasting, turning several times.

Remove the ribs from the marinade and place on a rack over a shallow pan with hot water. Bake in a preheated 425° oven for 30 minutes, turning once. During this baking time, pour the marinade in a small saucepan. Bring the mixture to a simmer and cook until reduced to the thickness of a glaze.

After the 30 minutes of baking, reduce the temperature to 375° and brush the ribs with the reduced marinade; continue to roast an additional 10–15 minutes. Place the ribs on a serving platter and garnish with the orange and lemon zest.

Serves 4.

# Gabby's Smokey Beef Short Ribs and Beans

3–3 1/2 lbs. beef short ribs, cut into singles
1/4 C light vegetable oil
1 can (28 oz.) ready cut tomatoes
2 cans (15 oz.) red kidney beans, drained
2 medium onions, halved and sliced
1 medium green bell pepper, chopped
3 cloves garlic, pressed or finely minced
1/4 C beef broth
1/4 C lemon juice
1/4 C brown sugar
1 T Worcestershire sauce
2–2 1/2 tsp. Wright's Liquid Smoke
1 tsp. hot pepper sauce
1 tsp. chili powder
Salt and fresh ground black pepper, to taste
Steamed long grain rice

Trim and prepare the short ribs as indicated. Heat the oil in a large Dutch oven, add the ribs and brown over all, braising well. Drain off all extruded grease.

Add the tomatoes, beans, onions, bell pepper, and garlic, and heat through. Combine all remaining ingredients, except the rice, mix well, and pour over all in the pan. Cover tightly, bake in a preheated 325° oven for 2–2 1/2 hours. Place the steamed rice on a large warmed serving platter and arrange the meat mixture over it.

Serves 6.

*Note:* This recipe has almost a barbecue flavor, and the beans go so well with the addition of the rice.

# Oh, Those Wonderful Beef Short Ribs

5–6 lbs. meaty beef short ribs, cut into serving pieces
1–2 large onions, cut into small wedges
1/2 C garlic red wine vinegar
1 T celery seeds
1 T mixed peppercorns
1 T thyme
3–4 cloves garlic, slightly mashed
1 T salt
2 bay leaves
1 C red currant jelly
1 C Japanese-style soy sauce

1/2 C straight sherry wine
1/2 C garlic red wine vinegar
3 T Worcestershire sauce
2 T Gabby's Own Mustard (*see chapter 7, Sauces and Dressings, for this recipe*)
1 T Wright's Liquid Smoke
3 cloves garlic, pressed or finely minced
1–2 tsp. fresh ground black pepper or to taste
1/2 tsp. Tabasco sauce (optional)

In a large stock pot, combine the meat, onions, vinegar, seasonings and bay leaves and cover with water. Bring to a boil, reduce heat, cover, and simmer 1 1/2 hours, adding more water if needed to cover the ribs.

In a small saucepan, combine all remaining ingredients and cook over medium-low heat for 30 minutes or until thickened. Drain the ribs, place in a shallow baking pan, and cover with the hot sauce. Bake in a preheated 350° oven, uncovered, basting often for 40 minutes.

Serves 6 with leftovers.

# Gabby's Holiday Swiss Steak

3 lbs. beef round or boneless chuck
    steak (cut thin)
1/2 C flour
1 tsp. sweet or hot Hungarian paprika
1 tsp. salt
1/2 tsp. garlic powder
1/4 tsp. fresh ground pepper

3 T (scant) canola oil
1 medium onion, halved and sliced
2 cans (15 oz.) chunky-style tomato
    sauce
1 package onion soup mix
1 T Worcestershire sauce
1 C sour cream

Cut the meat into serving-size pieces. In a pie plate, combine the flour and seasonings and mix well to blend. Tenderizer each piece of meat, then dredge in the flour mixture.

In a large fry pan, heat the oil over medium-high heat. Add the pieces of meat and brown on both sides (add more oil, if necessary). Add the onion slices to the pan along with the tomato sauce, soup mix, and Worcestershire sauce. Reduce the heat to low, cover and simmer 2–2 1/2 hours or until meat is fork tender. Remove the meat and keep warm. Skim off rendered grease and discard. Stir in the sour cream and heat just till hot, not boiling. Return meat to the sauce and serve when ready.

Serves 6–8.

Can be prepared in advance and served with boiled egg noodles.

# Gabby's Madagascar Steak

4–6 thick-cut rib eye, top sirloin, tenderloin, or New York strip steaks

4–6 cloves garlic, pressed or very finely minced

1/2–1 C butter, softened to room temperature

1–2 egg yolk(s)

2–4 T (rounded) soft green peppercorns, drained

2–3 T green onions or chives, finely chopped

1 T fresh parsley, finely chopped

1/2 tsp. tarragon leaves

1 tsp. lemon juice

1 tsp. Worcestershire sauce

1 tsp. Gabby's Own Mustard (see chapter 7, Sauces and Dressings, for this recipe)

1 tsp. sweet Hungarian paprika

One hour before cooking, remove the meat from the refrigerator, prepare the garlic, and rub over each piece of meat. Cover and let stand at room temperature.

In a small mixing bowl, combine all remaining ingredients and blend well. Set the mixture aside. Preheat your broiler oven. Place the beef on a broiler pan, then slip under the broiler and broil to just under desired doneness. Remove from the oven and thickly spread about 4 tablespoons of the pepper mixture over each steak. Slip under the broiler again, broiling until the mixture glazes. Serve at once.

Serves 4–6.

A marvelous piece of meat!

# Gabby's Quickie Sirloin Tips

2 T butter and olive oil combination
1 lb. beef sirloin tips, cut into 1 1/2 to
    2-inch cubes
1/4 C seasoned flour (flour, seasoned
    salt, Parsley Patch Saltless Garlic,
    and pepper)
2 T butter and olive oil combination
1 medium onion, halved and sliced

1–2 cloves garlic, pressed or minced
1 T dried marjoram flakes
1/2 lb. fresh mushroom, sliced
1 1/2 T tomato paste
1/2 T Gabby's Own Mustard (*see
    chapter 7, Sauces and Dressings, for
    this recipe*)
1 C defatted beef broth

In a large skillet, heat the butter-oil combination over medium-high heat. Lightly dredge the beef cubes in the seasoned flour, then place in the pan, brown well, then remove from the pan.

In the same pan, add the other butter-oil combination and saute the onion, garlic, mushrooms and marjoram until the onion is tender. Remove from the pan and add to the meat. Add the remaining ingredients to the pan and heat to boiling, then let simmer until liquid has reduced by half, stirring often. Return the beef and mushroom mixture to the hot pan and bring to serving temperature. Serve with steamed rice or lightly buttered noodles.

Serves 4.

# Gabby's Marinated Tri-Tip Steaks

2–4 beef tri-tip steaks (also known as beef loin or bottom sirloin butt)
1/2 C light vegetable (canola) oil
1/2 C dry red wine
1/4 C lemon juice
1/4 C sweet onion, very finely chopped
2–3 cloves garlic, pressed or finely minced

2 bay leaves
3 T cracked black pepper
1/2 tsp. oregano leaves
1/2 tsp. rosemary needles
1/2 tsp. thyme leaves

Place the steaks on a flat surface and pierce with the tines of a fork or a commercial tenderizer like the Jaccard tenderizer. Place the steaks in a shallow baking dish.

In a small bowl, combine all remaining ingredients, mix well, and pour over the steaks. Cover with plastic wrap and place in the refrigerator to marinate for up to 48 hours, turning several times during the period.

Place the meat on a hot grill, 8 inches above the heat source. Grill to your desired doneness, then remove and slice in 1/4-inch thick slices, against the grain. Serve immediately.

Serves up to 12 people.

This is just one of the most flavorful cuts of beef. You must normally ask your meat cutter for this cut because of the limited supply available—one to each side of beef.

# Gabby's No-Peek Prime Ribber

1 prime rib beef roast, 4–7 ribs long
(large or small end—small end has
the least waste)
Worcestershire sauce, to taste
Fresh minced garlic, to taste

Sweet Hungarian paprika
Seasoned or fresh ground pepper, to
taste
Flour to coat the roast

The secret to this preparation is the method of roasting, as you will see.

The weight of this roast does not matter, as long as it is between 4 and 7 ribs long. Rub the Worcestershire, garlic, paprika and pepper over the outside of the entire roast (bone side, too). Dust with the flour, then set the meat on a roasting rack inside a roasting pan.

Bake in a preheated 500° oven for 5 minutes for each pound (you must know the exact weight of the roast) if you want rare meat, 5 1/2 minutes per pound for a more medium to well-done roast. After this roasting period, turn the oven off, *but don't you dare open the oven door!* In fact, the oven door must not be opened for exactly 2 hours. Now, open it up, place the meat on a warmed serving platter, and carve away.

Serves 6–12.

Oh, this is so good, especially if you have chosen a Certified Angus Beef roast.

# Great Baked Pork Chops

2 T oil
6 large thick, center-cut pork chops,
    well trimmed
Salt and fresh ground pepper, to taste
1 T onion soup mix (Lipton)

2–3 T rosemary, crushed just a bit
1 jar (1 lb.) chunky-style applesauce
1 C whole cranberry sauce
1/4 C dry vermouth

In a large fry pan, heat the oil over medium-high heat. Season the chops with the seasonings. Add the seasoned chops to the hot pan and brown well on both sides.

Layer the applesauce and cranberry sauce in a shallow glass baking dish or casserole. Layer the chops, over lapping just a bit, over the sauces. Sprinkle the vermouth over all. Cover with foil and bake in a preheated 325° oven for 90 minutes.

Makes 6 servings.

# Summer Grilled Pork Tenderloins

2 pork tenderloins, well trimmed
1/2 C light vegetable (canola) oil
1 C light or dark soy sauce (your
    choice)
1/4 C garlic red wine vinegar
3 T lemon juice
2 T Worcestershire sauce

2–3 cloves garlic, pressed or minced
1 T fresh parsley, finely chopped
1 T Gabby's Own Mustard (*see chapter
    7, Sauces and Dressings, for this
    recipe*)
1 1/2 tsp. coarse ground black pepper
1 tsp. fresh ginger, grated

Prepare the tenderloins as indicated and set aside in a large plastic zip lock bag. In a medium-size bowl, combine all remaining ingredients and whisk well; pour the mixture over the loins. Close the bag and refrigerate to marinate for several hours before grilling.

Remove the loins from the marinade and cook on a hot grill about 5–7 minutes per side, depending on desired doneness; brush with the marinade several times during the grilling.

Serves 6–8, depending on the size of the tenderloins.

Serves well with just about any summer side dishes.

# Sweet and Sour Pork Chops

6–8 center cut pork chops (about 1 3/4 pounds), trimmed well of fat and seasoned as desired (salt, pepper, garlic, etc.)
1–2 T olive or canola oil
1/2 C sweet onions, chopped
1/2 C lemon juice
3 T cornstarch
1/2 C (packed) brown sugar
1 T soy sauce

1 tsp. instant chicken-flavored bouillon
1 can (20 oz.) pineapple chunks, drained, but reserve the syrup
1 C carrots, thinly ripple sliced
1 large green bell pepper, thinly sliced
1/4 C slivered almonds, toasted
1/4 C green onions, sliced
6–8 C hot cooked long grain rice

Prepare the chops as indicated and set aside. In a large skillet, heat the oil over high heat, add the chops and brown on both sides. Arrange the chops in a large (9 x 13-inch) shallow baking dish.

Add the onion to the drippings in the skillet and saute until lightly browned. Combine the lemon juice and cornstarch and add to the pan, reducing the heat to medium. Mix well and add the brown sugar, soy, bouillon, plus reserved pineapple juice. Cook and stir this mixture until it thickens and the bouillon is totally dissolved. Stir in the carrots, bell pepper and almonds. Pour this mixture over the chops in the baking dish.

Cover with foil and bake in a preheated 350° oven for 60 minutes. Remove the cover, arrange the pineapple chunks over all, and bake an additional 10 minutes. During the baking period, prepare the rice. Arrange the rice on a serving platter and when done arrange the chops and vegetable mixture over the rice. Garnish with green onions and serve immediately.

Serves 6–8.

# Gabby's Holiday Roast Pork

1 (4–5 lbs.) boneless pork roast, tied
7–8 cloves garlic, slivered
Kosher salt and fresh ground pepper, to
    taste
1/4 C Hoisin sauce

1 T fresh ginger, grated
1 tsp. ground sage
1 tsp. thyme leaves, crushed
1 can chicken broth
2 whole bay leaves

Lay out the roast on a cutting board and insert the blade of a paring knife deep into the roast, then carefully slide a sliver of the garlic down the blade, covering the whole roast. Rub the roast with the salt and pepper.

Combine the Hoisin sauce, ginger and sage and baste over the pork. Place the pork, fat cap up, on a roasting rack in a shallow roasting pan. Pour the broth in the pan and add the bay leaves. Insert a meat thermometer and roast in a preheated 350° oven until the temperature of the meat reaches 175°, then remove and let rest about 15 minutes before carving.

Serves 6–8.

Garnish the plattered roast with parsley and spiced crab apples or whole cranberry sauce.

# Chinese Pork Chops and Onions

2 T light (canola) oil
8 thick, center-cut pork chops
Salt and fresh ground pepper, to taste
2 large onions, halved and sliced
    (prefer sweet onions)
1 can (8 oz.) sliced water chestnuts,
    drained
1 can (8 oz.) sliced mushrooms,
    drained
1 medium bunch fresh cilantro
1 medium red bell pepper, cut into rings

1/4 C soy sauce (your favorite)
1/4 C oriental broth (available in most
    stores, soup section)
2 T lemon juice
1 T Gabby's Own Mustard or your
    choice *(for "Gabby's Own
    Mustard," see chapter 7, Sauces and
    Dressings)*
1 T fresh ginger, grated
1-2 cloves garlic, pressed/minced

In a large skillet, heat the oil, season the chops, then brown well on both sides over high heat. Arrange the chops in a large shallow baking dish or pan. Top the chops with the onion slices, water chestnuts, mushrooms, a few cilantro sprigs (chopped) and the bell pepper slices.

In a small bowl, combine the remaining ingredients, except the remaining cilantro sprigs. Mix well, then pour over all. Cover with foil and bake in a preheated 350° oven for 40–45 minutes or until pork is done.

Serves 4–8 depending on serving size.

Serve with steamed long or short grain rice.

# Gabby's Grilled Lamb Kabobs

5–7 lb. leg of lamb, trimmed well, boned and cut into 1 1/2-inch cubes
2–3 medium onions, diced
3/4 C dry red wine
1/2 C olive oil
4–6 cloves garlic, pressed or finely minced
3 bay leaves
1 T Worcestershire sauce
1 T oregano
1 tsp. sweet basil
1 tsp. dill weed
1 tsp. marjoram
1 T seasoned or fresh ground pepper
4–6 C steamed long grain rice

*The day before serving:* Prepare the lamb as indicated, then place the cubes in a large glass bowl or deep dish. Combine all remaining ingredients, except the rice, and pour over the lamb. Stir well and cover with plastic wrap. Refrigerate to marinate at least 24 hours, stirring several times during the period.

When ready to prepare, place the lamb on either metal or bamboo skewers (can be separated with wedges of onion, if desired), then grill over hot charcoal, brushing with the remaining marinade during the grilling. Serve over regular steamed rice or Greek-style lemon rice.

Serves 6–8.

You will really ENJOY!

# Gabby's Balsamic Grilled Leg of Lamb

1 leg of lamb (6–7 lbs.), deboned and butterflied
3/4 C light soy sauce
1/4 C olive oil
1/4 C balsamic vinegar
1/4 C lemon juice
2 T Worcestershire sauce
2 T Gabby's Own Mustard or your favorite brand (*for "Gabby's Own Mustard," see chapter 7, Sauces and Dressings*)

10 bay leaves
2–3 cloves garlic, pressed or finely minced
1 T fresh ground pepper, or to taste
1 T dried parsley flakes
1 T dried rosemary, crushed slightly

Have your meat cutter prepare the leg of lamb as indicated. Place the leg in a large zip lock plastic bag and set aside. In a medium-size mixing bowl, combine the remaining ingredients, mix well and pour over the lamb. Close the bag and place in the refrigerator to marinate at least overnight.

Remove the lamb from the bag and reserve the marinade for basting the meat. Place the lamb over grey-hot coals, about 8 inches above the heat source. Grill, turning about every 10 minutes until reaching desired doneness (about 50–60 minutes), and basting with the marinade each time. Set aside for about 10 minutes before slicing. Slice against the grain in 1/4-inch-thick slices.

Serves 10–12 (depending on the size of the roast).

# Gabby's Roasted Leg of Lamb Au Poivre

1 leg of lamb (about 5 lbs.), boned
4–6 T soft green peppercorns, drained well
4–6 sprigs of fresh rosemary
4–6 sprigs of fresh mint
4–6 cloves garlic, pressed or minced
1 C dry red wine
1/2 C soy sauce

2 bay leaves
2 cloves garlic, cut into slivers
3–4 T Gabby's Own Mustard (*see chapter 7, Sauces and Dressings, for this recipe*)
Heavy kitchen twine for tying rolled lamb

Remove any fell from the outside of the roast; it is probably best if you have your meat cutter bone the lamb. Lay out the lamb in a large shallow glass baking dish, cut-side down.

In a small bowl, combine the peppercorns, herbs, wine, soy sauce and bay leaves. Pour this mixture over the meat, lifting it so that the marinade gets underneath the meat; place some of the herbs under also. Cover with plastic wrap and place in the refrigerator to marinate at least 12 hours.

Remove the meat from the marinade, roll the roast and tie with the twine in several places. Make small slits into the meat with a paring knife and slide slivers of garlic into each cut. Place the roast on a rack in a shallow baking pan. Spread the mustard over the roast, along with the peppercorns removed from the marinade. Pour the marinade into the roasting pan. Bake in a preheated 325° oven for 18–20 minutes per pound, basting several times, for a nice medium doneness. Serve with the juices from the pan.

Serves 8.

# Gabby's Mustard-Herbed Lamb Glaze

1 medium leg of lamb, boned and
    trimmed of all fat and fell
2–3 sprigs of fresh rosemary
6 large cloves garlic, finely chopped
Salt and fresh ground pepper, to taste
1/2 C honey
1/2 C Gabby's Own Mustard or your
    favorite prepared mustard (for
    "Gabby's Own Mustard," see
    chapter 7, Sauces and Dressings)

1 T dried minced onion flakes
1 T dried parsley flakes
1 tsp. garlic, finely chopped (bottled)
1/2 tsp. Worcestershire sauce
1/4 tsp. ground ginger

Lay out the prepared lamb, cut-side up. Place the sprigs of rosemary lengthwise over the lamb. Arrange the chopped garlic over the lamb also. Liberally salt and pepper the cut side. Using a heavy twine, tie the lamb in the shape before boning. Run your BBQ spit, lengthwise, through the lamb, then tighten the spit prongs at both ends of the meat. Turn on the rotisserie and start cooking.

In a small saucepan or mixing bowl, combine the remaining ingredients and mix well. After the lamb is lightly browned, start brushing the glaze over the roast and continue, several times, until reaching the desired doneness (I prefer medium, about 145-150° internal temperature). Remove the meat from the spit, discard the sprigs of rosemary, then slice the meat against the grain into 1/4-inch thick slices.

Makes 6–8 servings.

# Herbed Lemon Lamb Kabobs

1 1/2 lbs. boneless lamb, trimmed well
    and cut into 1 to 1 1/2-inch cubes
1/2 C fresh lemon juice
1/4 C water
2 tsp. Worcestershire sauce
2–3 cloves garlic, pressed or minced
Zest from one lemon
1 T olive oil
1 tsp. oregano

1/2 tsp. thyme
1/2 tsp. rosemary
1/2 tsp. salt
1/2 tsp. fresh ground pepper or to taste
2 medium sweet onions, cut into
    wedges
2 medium green bell pepper, cut into
    chunks

Prepare the lamb as indicated, place in a medium-size glass bowl and set aside. In a medium-size mixing bowl, combine the remaining ingredients, except the onions and bell peppers, whisk well, and pour over the lamb. Cover the bowl and refrigerate to marinate at least 2 hours or up to 24 hours, turning often.

Just before grilling, remove the lamb from the marinade. Slide the lamb, onion wedges, bell pepper chunks alternately on long metal or wooden skewers. Place the filled skewers over hot coals, 4–5 inches from the heat source, brushing with the marinade and turning several times until lamb is done (5–6 minutes).

Makes 4 servings.

Serve with just about any side dish.

# Galway Bay Lamb and Vegetable Hot Pot

1 1/2 lbs. lean lamb cubes
2 large onions, halved and thinly
    sliced
1/2 lb. fresh green beans, sliced
2 large potatoes, peeled, halved and
    sliced
2 large carrots, peeled and sliced
2 large tomatoes, halved, chopped

2 large green bell peppers, seeded and
    chopped
1 1/2 tsp. salt
1 tsp. fresh ground pepper
1/2 C butter, cut into cubes
1/2 C hot water or beef stock
1 T Worcestershire sauce

Fill a 2 1/2-quart Dutch oven with two layers each of meat and vegetables in the order listed. Sprinkle with salt and pepper and dot with butter between the layers.

Combine the hot water/beef stock and Worcestershire sauce and pour over the meat and vegetables. Cover tightly and simmer over low heat about 1 1/2 hours or until all is tender.

Serves 4.

A wonderful old Irish harvest time dish.

# McBride's Leg of Lamb Marinade

1 whole leg of lamb, with all excess fat and fell removed
Several cloves garlic, cut into slivers
1/2 C Gabby's Own Mustard or your favorite (*for "Gabby's Own Mustard," see chapter 7, Sauces and Dressings*)
1/3 C soy sauce

1/3 C olive oil
1/4 C lemon juice
3 cloves garlic, pressed or finely minced
1 1/2 T fresh ginger, grated
1 tsp. dried rosemary
1 tsp. dried thyme

Prepare the lamb as indicated, then lay out and insert the garlic slivers deep into the center of the leg, using a small paring knife. Place the leg in a jumbo plastic kitchen bag. In a bowl, combine all remaining ingredients for the marinade. Pour the marinade into the bag, close and place in the refrigerator to marinate overnight, turning several times during the period.

Place the leg on a rack in a roasting pan and roast in a preheated 350° oven for 25–30 minutes per pound, basting with the marinade several times during the roasting period.

Serves 10–12.

An excellent recipe!

# Baked Oriental Game Hens

4 Cornish game hens, split in halves
1 C orange marmalade
4–6 green onions, chopped
2–3 cloves garlic, pressed or minced
3 T Huli Huli sauce
1 T Gabby's Own Mustard or your favorite (*for "Gabby's Own Mustard," see chapter 7, Sauces and Dressings*)

1 1/2 tsp. sesame oil
1 tsp. fresh ginger, grated
1 can mandarin orange sections, drained
Fresh parsley for garnish

Prepare the hens as indicated, wash well in cold water, then drain on paper toweling. Place the hens, cut side down, in a large sprayed shallow baking dish. In a medium-size mixing bowl, combine the next seven ingredients and mix well. Spoon this mixture over the hens, cover with plastic kitchen wrap and place in the refrigerator to marinate several hours before baking.

Remove from the refrigerator about an hour before baking. Bake in a preheated 375° oven, uncovered, for 1 hour, basting several times. Arrange the orange sections over all during the last 10 minutes of baking. Arrange the hens with the sauce on a large serving platter, garnish with the parsley and serve.

Serves 4–8.

A green vegetable, rice or noodles, and you've got a wonderful low fat dinner.

# Oriental Cashew Pork

1 lb. boneless pork loin, trimmed and cut into thin 1/4-inch strips
2 T straight sherry wine
2 T soy sauce
2 T cornstarch
1/3 C peanut oil
2–3 carrots, sliced on the diagonal
1 large green bell pepper, cut into chunks
1 can (4 oz.) whole water chestnuts, drained
2 cloves garlic, pressed or minced
1 bunch green onions, sliced on the diagonal
1/2 lb. snow pea pods, strings removed
1/2 C unsalted cashew nuts
1/2 C defatted chicken broth
1 T brown sugar
4–6 C hot steamed short or long grain rice

Prepare the pork as indicated, then place in a small bowl. Combine the sherry, soy sauce and cornstarch, mix well, and pour over the pork, stirring well. Let this mixture marinate about an hour before cooking.

In your oriental wok, heat 2 tablespoons of oil over high heat. Add the marinated pork and liquid and stir fry about 3 minutes. Remove from the wok and keep warm.

Wipe out the wok and heat the remaining oil. Add the carrots and stir fry 2 minutes, then add the bell pepper, water chestnuts and garlic. Continue to stir fry for 2 more minutes, then add the green onions, snow peas and cashews. Return the pork to the wok along with the broth and brown sugar (combined). Stir fry until sauce thickens. Serve over mounds of hot steamed rice.

Serves 4–6.

# Gabby's Shrimp Fried Rice and Veggies

2 T peanut oil
1 medium onion, halved and sliced
3–4 cloves garlic, pressed or minced
2–3 tsp. fresh ginger, grated or to taste
1/2 head napa cabbage, sliced and
    chopped
4 C steamed long or short grain rice
3/4 C green onion, sliced into 1-inch
    pieces

1 C fresh pea pods, crisped
1/2 C soy sauce or tamari
1/4 C chicken stock or broth
1/2 lb. tiny bay shrimp, cooked
2 T peanut or canola oil
4–6 large eggs, lightly beaten

In a wok, heat the oil over high heat, add the onion, garlic, and ginger, and stir fry a couple of minutes. Add the cabbage and continue to stir fry until cabbage is limp. Add the cooked rice, green onions, and pea pods, and heat through, then add the soy sauce or tamari and chicken stock or broth. Stir fry constantly, adding the shrimp.

In a separate wok or skillet, heat the remaining oil over medium heat. Prepare the eggs, then pour into the hot pan and cook as an omelet until soft set, turning once. Lay out on a cutting board and sliced into 1 1/2-inch squares. Add the egg squares to the wok and stir into the mixture. Serve immediately with soy sauce or tamari on the side.

Serves 4–6.

Yes, you'll love it!

# Nutty Oriental Chicken

2 T peanut oil
1/2 C walnuts, lightly chopped
1/2 lb. chicken breasts, boned, skinned and cut into bite-size chunks
1 small carrot, thinly sliced on the diagonal
1–2 cloves garlic, pressed or finely chopped
1/2 medium green bell pepper, cut into bite-size chunks
1/2 C green onions, sliced into 1-inch pieces

1/4 lb. fresh pea pods, crisped
1 tsp. fresh ginger, cut into small match sticks
2–3 T soy sauce
1 T mirin or sherry wine
2 tsp. brown sugar
1/4 C water
1 T cornstarch
1 large firm fresh banana, sliced into chunks
2–4 C steamed short or long grain rice

Heat the oil in your wok over high heat. Add the walnuts and stir fry until browned. Add the chicken pieces and continue to stir fry 4–5 minutes. Add the carrot, garlic, bell pepper, green onions, pea pods and ginger. Stir fry this mixture about 4 minutes.

Combine and add the soy, mirin/sherry, brown sugar, water and cornstarch. Bring the mixture to a boil and cook 1–2 more minutes, then add the banana chunks and warm slightly. Serve over the steamed rice.

Serves 2.

# Quick and Easy Surf-and-Turf Stir Fry

1/2 lb. large shrimp, peeled and
    deveined
1/2 lb. flank or top round beef steak
1 1/2 T cornstarch
1/4 C mirin (sweet cooking rice wine)
2 T sesame oil
2 T soy sauce
1 large clove of garlic, pressed or
    minced
1 tsp. fresh ginger, grated

3 T peanut oil
2 C bok choy, sliced
1 C fresh bean sprouts
1 bunch green onions, sliced
    diagonally into 1-inch pieces
1/2 C fresh mushrooms, sliced
1/4 C chicken broth
2 T cornstarch
2 T oyster sauce

Prepare the shrimp and beef as indicated in a medium-size mixing bowl, sprinkle with the 1 1/2 tablespoons of cornstarch, mixing to coat well, and set aside. Combine the mirin, sesame oil, soy sauce, garlic and ginger. Mix well, then pour over the shrimp-beef mixture, mixing well. Cover and marinate in the refrigerator for 30 minutes to 1 hour.

Heat the oil in your wok over high heat. When oil is hot, add the marinated mixture and stir fry 1 minute. Add the vegetables and stir fry about 2 minutes. Combine the broth, the 2 tablespoons of cornstarch and the oyster sauce and pour over all in the wok. Stir fry until the sauce thickens and vegetables are tender crisp. Serve with steamed rice, and garnish with toasted sesame seeds.

Serves 4.

# Stir Fried Hot and Sour Chicken

2–3 boneless chicken breasts, skinned
    and sliced crosswise into
    1/2-inch strips
3 T seasoned rice vinegar
2 T soy sauce (your choice)
1 T Karo syrup
1 T cornstarch
3/4 tsp. red pepper flakes
1 tsp. sesame oil
2 T peanut oil

1 large onion, halved and sliced
1 T fresh ginger, grated
2–3 cloves garlic, pressed or minced
1 large red bell pepper, sliced into
    1/4-inch thick strips
1 large green bell pepper, sliced as
    above
3–4 small red Szechwan peppers
    (optional)
1/3 C chicken broth

Prepare the chicken breasts as indicated and set aside in a medium-size bowl. In a small bowl, combine the vinegar, soy, syrup, cornstarch and pepper flakes and whisk well. Whisk in the sesame oil. Pour this mixture over the chicken strips and toss well to coat.

In your wok, heat the peanut oil over high heat, then add the onion, ginger and garlic. Stir fry this mixture about 1 minute. Add the bell peppers and peppers and continue to stir fry another minute. Add the chicken, marinade and chicken broth. Cook this mixture until the chicken is done (3–4 minutes). Serve with hot steamed rice.

Serves 4.

# Lemon Chicken Stir Fry

1 1/2 lbs. chicken breasts, skinned,
    boned and cut into bite-size pieces
2 eggs, beaten
6 T cornstarch (divided)
2 T Japanese-style soy sauce
1 tsp. sesame oil
3/4 tsp. garlic powder

1 C chicken broth
1/2 C red currant jelly
1/2 C lemon juice
2 T catsup
1/3 C peanut oil
Napa cabbage, shredded for garnish

Prepare the chicken as indicated and place in a medium-size bowl. In a small bowl, combine the beaten eggs, 2 tablespoons cornstarch, soy sauce, sesame oil and garlic powder. Mix well and pour over the chicken, stirring to coat; set aside to marinate at least 10 minutes.

In a small saucepan, combine the broth, 2 tablespoons cornstarch, currant jelly, lemon juice and catsup. Bring the mixture to a boil, stirring, then reduce heat and simmer until the mixture thickens. Cover and keep warm.

In your wok, heat the peanut oil over high heat. Remove the chicken pieces from the marinade and sprinkle with the remaining cornstarch. Carefully add the chicken to the hot oil and stir fry until cooked through and crispy golden brown. Place the shredded cabbage on a medium-size serving plate and arrange the cooked chicken. Pour the warm sauce over all and serve immediately.

Serves 4 (when accompanied with side dishes).

# Oriental Sweet and Sour Shrimp

2 T peanut oil plus more for frying
1 medium green bell pepper, cut into
    cubes
1 small carrot, thinly sliced diagonally
1 small onion, cut into cubes
1 large clove garlic, pressed or minced
4 T sugar
4 T seasoned rice vinegar
2 T ketchup
1 T light soy sauce

1/2 C chicken broth
1 T cornstarch dissolved in 2 T of
    water
1/3 C unbleached all-purpose flour
1/4 C cornstarch
1/4 C water
1 extra large egg
1 tsp. salt
1 lb. medium-size shrimp, peeled and
    deveined

Heat 2 tablespoons peanut oil in a medium saucepan. Add pepper, carrot, onion, and garlic; saute until pepper and onion are tender. Combine the sugar, vinegar, ketchup, soy and broth, mix well, and add to the sauteed mixture. Bring mixture to a boil and stir in dissolved cornstarch. Reduce the heat to low and cook until thickened.

Mix flour, cornstarch, water, egg, and salt in a medium bowl. Add the prepared shrimp and coat well. Heat 1/4-inch of the peanut oil in your wok. Drop the shrimp one at a time into the hot oil and fry until lightly browned. Pour the sauce over all and serve.

Serves 4.

# Island Chicken, Kailua-Style

8 chicken breasts. skinned and boned
2 T olive oil and butter combination
1 tsp. Schilling's saltless garlic and
    herb seasoning
Salt and fresh ground pepper, to taste
1 C orange juice
2 T lemon juice
2 T soy sauce

2 T cornstarch
1/2 C light brown sugar
1 fresh pineapple, peeled, cored, cut
    into chunks
2 fresh papayas, halved, seeded, peeled
    and cut into chunks
2 fresh firm bananas, peeled and cut
    into chunks

Prepare the chicken breasts as indicated and set aside. In a large non-stick skillet, heat the oil and butter over medium-high heat; add the chicken and roll in the oil mixture. Sprinkle with the seasonings. Lightly brown the chicken over both sides, then place in a shallow baking dish and pour the pan drippings over all. Bake in a preheated 350° oven for 30–40 minutes.

During the baking period, combine the fruit juices, soy sauce, cornstarch and brown sugar in a saucepan. Heat until the mixture thickens, stirring. Stir the fruit into the sauce, pour over the chicken and return to the oven to bake an additional 10–15 minutes.

Serves 8.

A simple island recipe reduced in fat grams for lighter eating.

# Gabby's Szechwan Almond Chicken

1 large chicken breast, boned, skinned and cut into bite-size strips
3 T peanut oil
3/4 C blanched slivered almonds
1 C bok choy, sliced
1/2 C celery, sliced on the diagonal
6–8 oz. snow pea pods, chilled in ice water
1 bunch green onions, sliced on the diagonal
3 T mirin (sweet cooking rice wine)

2 T soy sauce
2 tsp. cornstarch
1 T light corn syrup
1/2 tsp. fresh ginger, grated
1–2 tsp. sambal oleck (oriental hot chili sauce)
4–6 firm ripe roma tomatoes, cut into wedges
Hot steamed long or short grain rice, chow mien noodles or soft fried noodles for each serving

Prepare the chicken as indicated. In your wok, heat the oil over high heat. Add the chicken and stir fry about 4 minutes or until chicken is done. Remove the chicken and in the remaining oil (you may need to add more), add the almonds, bok choy and celery. Stir fry about 2 minutes, then add the pea pods and green onions. This mixture should stir fry about 3 more minutes.

During the stir-fry time, combine and whisk the mirin, soy, cornstarch, syrup, and ginger. Add the sambal oleck to the stir-fried mixture. Pour the soy mixture into the hot wok and cook 1 more minute before stirring. Stir to mix the thickened sauce over all. Serve with your choice of rice or noodles.

Serve 2–4.

# Fried Catfish and Hush Puppies, Southern-Style

2–3 lbs. small fresh catfish fillets
2 C cold milk
Canola oil for deep frying
1 1/2–2 C yellow cornmeal
    (stone-ground preferred)
1 T fresh ground black pepper
1/2 tsp. cayenne or red pepper
1 tsp. salt

1 T (scant) baking powder
1 T granulated sugar
1/2 tsp. salt
1/2 tsp. black pepper
Pinch cayenne or red pepper
1 small sweet onion, minced
1 extra large egg, beaten well
1/2 C fresh buttermilk

**Hush puppy ingredients:**
1 C yellow cornmeal
1/2 C all purpose flour

Place the fillets in a large shallow baking dish and pour the milk over them. Let the fish marinate in the milk while you heat the oil to 375° in a large skillet or sauteuse pan. Place the cornmeal, both peppers, and salt in a plastic bag. Drain the fillets and place them one at at time in the cornmeal mixture, shaking the bag to coat each fish well. Carefully place fish in the hot oil (not too many at one time) and fry until golden brown on both sides. Remove and drain well on paper towels, keeping hot until all are done.

During the cooking time, prepare the hush puppies, combining all of the dry ingredients in a large bowl, mixing well. Add the onion and egg, stirring together with the buttermilk. In the same hot oil, drop the batter by the tablespoonful, cooking until golden brown. Drain on paper towels and serve hot with the catfish fillets.

Serves 6. Cold slaw is the only other addition—really great! (*Try the "24-Hour Slaw" recipe in chapter 3.*)

# So, Ya Don't Like Fish?

2–3 lbs. white fish of choice (bass, halibut, turbot, etc.), skinned, boned and cut into bite-size cubes (choose your favorite fresh or saltwater white fish)
6–8 strips of thick-sliced bacon, diced
1 medium sweet onion, chopped
1 medium green bell pepper, finely chopped
1 large clove of garlic, pressed/minced
2 C seasoned fresh or dried bread crumbs
Mrs. Dash lemon pepper seasoning
2–3 T olive oil

Prepare the fish as indicated, then rinse in cold water and drain on paper towels. In a large skillet, fry the bacon until crisp, then remove from the pan and drain on paper towels. Discard all but 3 tablespoons of the bacon fat and heat it over medium-high heat; add the onion, bell pepper and garlic. Saute until onion is tender, then remove from pan.

Roll the fish cubes in the crumbs and season further with the lemon pepper. Add remaining oil to the pan, heat, then add the fish, browning well on all sides. Add the reserved bacon and vegetable mixture and continue to cook a couple of minutes. Sprinkle with lemon juice, if desired, and serve immediately.

Serves 4.

# Shrimp Italianne

2 lbs. large (U-20-30) shrimp, boiled, shelled and deveined
3 T olive oil
3 cloves garlic, pressed or minced
4 green onions, chopped
3 ribs celery, chopped
1 medium green bell pepper, finely chopped
2 T fresh parsley, finely chopped
2 tsp. capers, rinsed and drained

1 T cornstarch
1 can (8 oz.) chunky tomato sauce
1/2 tsp. oregano
1/2 tsp. basil
1/2 tsp. Italian seasoning
1/2 tsp. fresh ground pepper or to taste
1 1/2 C mozzarella cheese, shredded
3/4 C seasoned bread crumbs (buttered, optional)

Prepare the shrimp as indicated and arrange in a large shallow baking dish, or, if desired, in individual au gratin dishes or ramekins. In a large skillet, heat the olive oil over medium-high heat, adding the garlic, onion, celery, bell pepper, parsley and capers. Saute the mixture until the celery is just about tender.

Reduce the heat and stir in the cornstarch. Add the tomato sauce and all the seasonings. Simmer about 10 minutes, then pour over the shrimp. Top all with cheese and crumbs. Bake in a preheated 350° oven about 20 minutes or until lightly browned and bubbly.

Serves 4–6.

This is so delicious when prepared with Florida's rock shrimp—but they are wonderful any way you fix 'em.

# Sesame-Baked Red Snapper

1 egg white, beaten
2 tsp. Worcestershire sauce
1/8 tsp. Tabasco sauce or to taste
1–2 cloves garlic, pressed or minced

1 lb. red snapper or rock fish fillets
2 T sesame seeds
1/4 C corn flake crumbs
Fresh ground pepper, to taste

Combine the egg white, Worcestershire, Tabasco and garlic in a small mixing bowl and stir to blend well. Place the fillets in a shallow baking dish and pour the liquid mixture over all. Cover and marinate in the refrigerator at least 30 minutes or overnight.

Combine the sesame seeds and corn flake crumbs and dredge the fillets in the mixture. Place the breaded fillets in a sprayed shallow baking dish. Bake in a preheated 350° oven for 15–20 minutes, or until lightly browned.

Makes 2–3 servings … *healthy* servings.

# Oriental Gingered Salmon

2–4 lbs. skinless salmon fillets (I prefer sockeye, king or silver salmon)
1 bunch green onions, finely chopped
3 T fresh ginger, grated
3 T light vegetable oil (canola)

1/4 C dark or light soy sauce
1 T brown sugar
1 tsp. mirin (sweet cooking rice wine)
1 tsp. sesame oil
1/4 tsp. fresh ground pepper

Lay out the salmon in a large shallow glass dish. In a small bowl or 2-cup measure, combine all remaining ingredients and mix well for the marinade. Pour the marinade over the salmon, cover with plastic wrap and place in the refrigerator for at least 1 hour or overnight.

The salmon can either be broiled or grilled. Place the fish about 4 inches from the heat source. Brush generously with the marinade several times during the cooking. Broil or grill about 10 minutes per inch of thickness.

Serves 2–4.

Trout fillets can also be used for this recipe, especially if they are good-sized.

# Gabby's Low-Fat Real Crab Cakes

1/2 C no-fat soda cracker crumbs (can also use the no-salt kind)

1 extra large egg, beaten (can also use egg substitute)

5 T low-calorie mayonnaise

2 T parsley flakes

1 T white or red Bermuda onion, very finely chopped

1 T celery, very finely chopped

1 1/2 tsp. Gabby's Own Mustard (*see chapter 7, Sauces and Dressings, for this recipe*)

1 tsp. Worcestershire sauce

1/2 tsp. Old Bay seasoning

1/4 tsp. fresh ground pepper

1/4 tsp. garlic granules

Pinch cayenne pepper

1 lb. crab meat (Dungeness or king—no substitutions here), picked of all cartilage

Sweet Hungarian Paprika for garnish

In a medium mixing bowl, combine all ingredients, except the crab meat, and mix well. Gently fold in the crab meat, breaking up any large lumps. Shape into eight cakes, sprinkle the paprika over both sides, place on a plate or cookie sheet, and cover with plastic wrap. Refrigerate at least 1 hour before baking.

Place the cakes on a sprayed shallow baking sheet on the second rack under your preheated broiler; broil until golden brown on both sides.

Makes 4 servings (2 crab cakes each).

Like I said, this recipe is low fat—in fact, there are only about 350 calories per serving.

# Oriental Steamed Halibut

1–1 1/2 lbs. fresh halibut fillets (about 1 1/2-inches thick), skinned
2 T fresh ginger, grated
2 T sesame seeds, toasted
1 T seasoned rice vinegar
1 T Japanese-style soy sauce

Several sprigs of fresh cilantro
2 T peanut oil
2 cloves garlic, pressed or minced
1 1/2 tsp. sesame oil (can be chili-sesame flavor)

Lay out the fillets, prepared as indicated; using a sharp filleting knife, make deep slices on the diagonal over the top of each fillet. Combine the ginger, sesame seeds, vinegar and soy, mix well, and spread over the top of each fillet, working into the cuts.

Place the fillets in a bamboo steamer or on a plate to sit over steaming water in a wok. Arrange the sprigs of cilantro over the fillets. Bring about 3 inches of water to a boil in the wok. Place the steamer or steamer rack over the water and cover. Let the fish steam 10–15 minutes, depending on the thickness of the fish.

During this cooking time, heat the peanut oil and garlic over low heat until the garlic lightly browns; stir in the sesame oil. Remove the fish to a serving plate, then drizzle the seasoned oil over all and serve immediately.

Serves 4.

# Gabby's Mustard-Dilled Salmon Fillets

6–8 fresh salmon fillets (4–5 oz. apiece), skinned
1 C dry white wine (can use non-alcoholic cooking wine)
1/2 C butter, melted
1 C sour cream
1/4 C chives, finely chopped

1–2 T Gabby's Own Mustard (*see chapter 7, Sauces and Dressings, for this recipe*)
1 T fresh parsley, finely chopped
1 tsp. dill weed
1/8 tsp. ground white pepper

Place the salmon fillets in a shallow glass baking dish and pour the wine over all. Marinate the fish in the wine for 15 minutes prior to broiling. Remove the fish and pat dry on paper towels. Brush both sides of each fillet with the melted butter, and place on a broiling rack. Broil, second rack down, under a preheated broiler, 5–7 minutes, depending on the thickness of the salmon.

As the fish broils, prepare the sauce by combining the remaining ingredients, stirring well to blend. Spread over the fillets about 2 minutes before removing from the oven.

Serves 6–8.

The sauce can also be served cold on the side.

# Braised Fish Fillets with Tomato and Fresh Basil

2 T olive oil
4 fish fillets, cut 1-inch thick (sea bass, orange roughy, halibut or swordfish)
Salt and fresh ground pepper, to taste
1/2 C (lightly packed) fresh basil, chopped

1/3 C onion, minced
1 clove garlic, pressed or minced
1/3 C dry white wine
1/3 C chicken broth
1 C ready-cut tomatoes with juice
2 T heavy whipping cream
Fresh basil sprigs for garnish

In a large heavy skillet, heat the oil over medium-high heat. Season the fish with salt and pepper. Place the fillets in the pan and brown lightly about a minute per side. Reduce the heat to low. Sprinkle the basil and onion over the fish. Cover skillet tightly and braise the fish about 8 minutes. Carefully transfer the fish to a serving platter and cover to keep warm.

Increase the heat to high, add the wine and let reduce to a tablespoon (about 3 minutes). Mix in broth and boil until mixture is reduced by half (about 2 minutes). Stir in the tomatoes and continue to cook until the sauce thickens. Stir in the cream and season with more salt and fresh ground pepper, if desired. Spoon the sauce over the fish and garnish each piece with a sprig of basil.

Makes 4 servings.

# Grilled Chilean Sea Bass

1 1/2 lbs. Chilean sea bass fillets (a very firm snow white fish of mild but distinctive buttery flavor)
6–8 cloves garlic
1/4 C lemon juice
2 T light (canola) oil

2 T straight sherry wine
2 T fresh basil leaves
1 tsp. sweet Hungarian paprika
1 tsp. fresh ground pepper
1 tsp. salt

Trim all the fillets to an equal thickness, slice into four equal-sized serving pieces, and place in a shallow glass baking dish. Combine all of the remaining ingredients in a blender or food processor. Pour this marinade mixture over the fish, cover with plastic wrap and refrigerate for 30 minutes.

Grill the fish on a sprayed grill until it is opaque in the center and slightly springy to the touch. Turn and continue to grill 4–5 more minutes.

Makes 4 servings.

Sea bass—also known as Patagonia toothfish—just might be one of the top five seafoods available in today's marketplace. Superb!

# Mexican Lime-Garlic Prawns

12–15 large (U-15) prawns, peeled and deveined
Juice from two fresh limes (divided)
2 cloves garlic, pressed or minced
1–2 fresh serrano chilies, seeded and finely minced
1/2 tsp. salt
2 C fresh mangos, peeled, seeded and diced

1 medium sweet onion, finely chopped
1 red bell pepper, finely diced
2 fresh jalapeno peppers, seeded and finely minced
1 small bunch fresh mint, finely chopped
4–6 wooden skewers
4–6 C hot steamed rice

Prepare the prawns as indicated and place in a medium-size bowl. In another bowl, combine half of the lime juice, garlic, chilies and salt. Whisk well and pour over the prawns. Cover and marinate in the refrigerator at least an hour or up to 2 hours.

Prepare the mangos as indicated and combine with all remaining ingredients, except the skewers and rice. Mix well, cover and hold in the refrigerator until it is time to grill the prawns.

Place the shrimp on the skewers and grill about 2 minutes per side, brushing with the marinade. Serve with the mango salsa and steamed long grain rice.

Serves 4–6.

Great for lighter summer fare.

**Chapter 6**

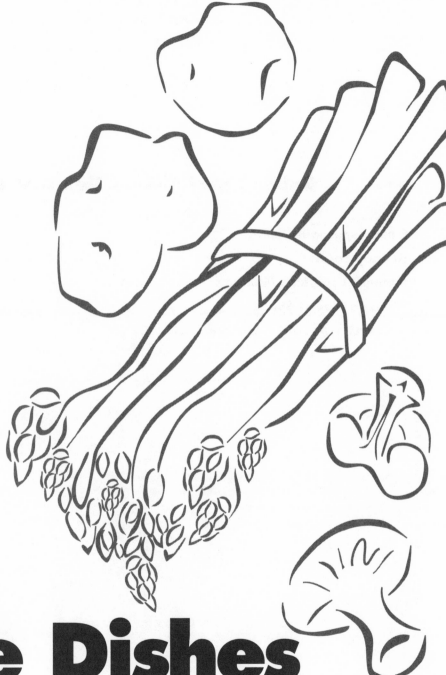

# Side Dishes

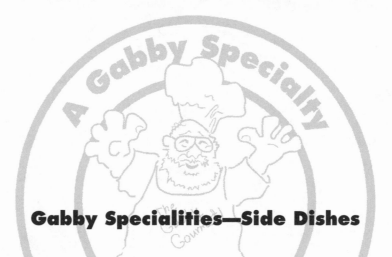

## Gabby Specialities—Side Dishes

# Baked Artichoke-Stuffed Tomatoes

2 large fresh firm tomatoes
4 T olive oil (or you can use the
    marinade from the artichokes)
1 medium sweet onion, chopped
1 C marinated artichoke hearts,
    drained and chopped
1/3 C fresh parsley, finely chopped
1/2 tsp. salt

1/2 tsp. fresh ground pepper
1/4 tsp. thyme
1/4 tsp. marjoram leaves
1/4 tsp. sweet basil
dash cayenne pepper
1 C fresh bread crumbs (can be
    seasoned)

Prepare the tomatoes as indicated, then scoop out the pulp. Place the shells upside down in a small baking pan with about 1/2-inch of hot water. Place the pan in a preheated 300° oven and bake for 10 minutes.

In a medium-size skillet, heat the olive oil or marinade over a medium-high heat. Add the onion and saute until golden in color. Add the chopped artichoke hearts and continue to saute 1 minute. Add all remaining ingredients and continue to saute until heated through.

Remove the tomato shells and drain on paper towels. Fill each tomato shell with the artichoke mixture, rounding, then place in the baking dish (drained of water). Return to the oven and bake until heated through, 10-15 minutes.

Makes 4 servings.

Make sure the tomatoes are at their peak.

# Fresh Asparagus Italian

1/4 C melted butter and olive oil
combination
1 lb. fresh asparagus spears, trimmed at
the tender spot
1/4 C red onion, minced
1/4 C celery, finely chopped
1/4 C fresh parmesan or asiago cheese,
grated or shredded

1 can (14 1/2 oz.) Italian-style stewed
tomatoes, drained
1 tsp. Italian seasoning
Salt and fresh ground pepper, to taste
1/4 C Gabby's Croutons, crushed (*for
this recipe, see chapter 3*)

Combine the butter and olive oil and pour over the bottom of a square 9 x 9-inch
shallow baking dish. Arrange the trimmed asparagus in the dish. Sprinkle the
remaining ingredients, in the order listed, over the asparagus. Bake in a preheated
375° for 40–50 minutes (depending on the thickness of asparagus) or until tender.

Serves 4.

This is really good and really shows off the wonderful asparagus flavor.

# Italian Wrapped Asparagus Spears

2 lbs. thin fresh asparagus spears, trimmed

6–8 slices of Italian prosciutto ham

1/4-1/2 C melted butter

1/2 C asiago or parmesan cheese, grated

Fresh ground pepper, to taste

Juice from 1/2 fresh lemon

Steam the asparagus or microwave for 4–5 minutes or until just barely tender. Wrap 4–6 spears of cooled asparagus in a slice of the prosciutto, then repeat until all spears are bundled.

Place the bundles in a sprayed shallow baking dish. Drizzle the melted butter over all, followed by the grated cheese and pepper. Bake in a preheated 350° oven for about 8 minutes. Sprinkle the juice over all and serve immediately.

Serves 4–6.

# Gabby's Steamed Asparagus with Caper Vinaigrette

1–1 1/2 lbs. fresh asparagus, tough
    ends removed
1/2 C olive oil
3–4 T garlic red wine vinegar
3 T red onion, very finely chopped
1 1/2 tsp. Gabby's Own Mustard(*see
    chapter 7, Sauces and Dressings, for
    this recipe)*

1 T capers, well-drained
2 T fresh parsley, finely chopped
Salt and fresh ground pepper, to taste
2 hard cooked eggs, sieved or very
    finely chopped

Prepare the asparagus as indicated and place in a shallow baking dish, adding the 1/4 cup of water. Seal with plastic wrap. Place in your microwave oven and cook for 7–7 1/2 minutes on high. Drain well and place the spears on an oblong serving plate and allow it to cool down to a warm serving temperature.

In a small bowl or 1-cup measure, whisk together all remaining ingredients, except the eggs, and pour over the warm asparagus. Garnish with eggs and serve.

Serves 4–6.

Ah, asparagus, the first sign of Spring!

# Spring's Fresh Asparagus and Mushroom Stir Fry

3 T peanut oil
3/4 lb. fresh tender asparagus
    (preferably small stalks), with
    tough ends removed and cut into
    1-inch pieces
1/2 lb. fresh mushrooms, sliced
4–6 green onions, sliced into 1-inch
    pieces
1/2 C pimento, cut into strips

2 cloves garlic, pressed or minced
1 tsp. thyme
1/2 tsp. salt (optional)
1/4 tsp. fresh ground pepper
3 T chicken stock or broth
1 tsp. fresh lemon zest, finely chopped
1/4 C fresh parmesan or asiago cheese,
    grated

In your wok, heat the oil over high heat. Add the prepared asparagus, mushrooms and green onions. Stir fry this mixture about 2 minutes, then add the garlic and continue to stir fry 3 more minutes.

Stir in the seasonings and the chicken stock (dry white wine can be substituted, if desired), then cover and simmer for 3 minutes or until all the vegetables are tender-crisp. Add the pimento strips and lemon zest. Turn the mixture onto a serving plate. Sprinkle the grated cheese over all and serve immediately.

Serves 4–6.

# Holiday Sprouts

1/4 C slivered almonds
4 C medium brussels sprouts
2 T herbed white wine vinegar
3 T (packed) brown sugar

1 T Gabby's Own Mustard (*see chapter 7, Sauces and Dressings, for this recipe*)
1 T butter

Place the almonds in a small dry skillet or fry pan and stir fry over medium-high heat until golden brown. Remove from the pan and set aside.

Remove the outer coarse leaves from the sprouts and wash them well in cold water. Place the sprouts on a wire rack over 1-inch of boiling water. Cover and steam the sprouts 15–20 minutes or until tender.

In a 10–12-inch skillet or fry pan, combine the remaining ingredients and bring to a simmer. Add the steamed sprouts and almonds. Stir to mix well. Remove to a serving bowl.

Serves 4–6.

Now, tell me you don't like brussels sprouts. These are really good!

# Gabby's Marinated Carrots

2 lbs. fresh carrots, peeled and sliced into 1/2-inch slices
Water for boiling
1/2 C light (canola) oil or a mixture of canola and olive oils
1/2 C garlic red wine or herbed wine vinegar
1 small bunch of fresh cilantro, chopped
4–6 cloves garlic, pressed or finely minced
1 1/2 tsp. ground cumin
1 1/2 tsp. sweet Hungarian paprika
Salt and fresh ground pepper, to taste

Prepare the carrots as indicated, place in a 2-quart saucepan and just cover with water. Bring the water to a rolling boil, cover, reduce the heat to low and simmer until the carrots are tender crisp. Drain well and place the warm carrots in a serving bowl.

In a small bowl, combine all remaining ingredients and whisk well. Pour the mixture over the carrots while they are still warm, stirring to cover all. Cover with plastic wrap and place in the refrigerator to marinate until serving. Can be served warm, room temperature or chilled.

Serves 4–6.

Great for a summer picnic or supper.

# Autumn Carrots

4 large carrots, peeled and ripple sliced
2 medium cooking apples, peeled and
    sliced
1/2 C dark raisins

2 T butter, cut into small bits
1 T brown sugar
1/2 tsp. ground cinnamon
1/2 C sliced almonds

Prepare the carrots as indicated, place in a saucepan and cover with water. Boil over medium-high heat until tender crisp, drain well and set aside.

At the same time, prepare the apples as indicated, then place in a medium-size saucepan, add 1/2 cup of water and cook until just tender. Add the raisins and continue to cook 3 more minutes, then drain well.

In a large mixing bowl, combine all remaining ingredients, except the almonds, stir well, then spoon the mixture into a 9 x 9-inch shallow baking dish. Arrange the almonds over the top. Bake in a preheated 350° oven for 10-15 minutes.

Serves 4.

# Honey-Nut Acorn Squash

2 medium acorn squash, sliced
   lengthwise
1/4 C honey
2 T butter

2 T walnuts or pecans, chopped
2 T raisins
2 tsp. Worcestershire sauce

Slice the squash lengthwise into halves and remove the seeds and fibers. Place each half, cut side down, in a baking dish with about 1-inch of hot water. Bake in a preheated 400° oven for 30–45 minutes or until soft.

Remove from the oven and discard the water. Return the squash, cut side up, to the pan. Combine the remaining ingredients and mix well. Spoon this mixture into the cavity of each half. Return to the oven and bake for 5–10 minutes.

Serves 4.

Great for holiday serving.

# Dressed Fresh Broccoli Spears

1 1/2 lbs. fresh broccoli spears
1/2 C water
1 carton (8 oz.) sour cream (can use
    imitation)
2 T butter (the real stuff)
2 T red onion, very finely chopped

1 T fresh lemon juice
1 tsp. Gabby's Own Mustard (*see
    chapter 7, Sauces and Dressings, for
    this recipe*)
1/4 C seasoned dry bread crumbs

Place the prepared broccoli in a large shallow glass baking dish and add the water.
Cover the dish with plastic wrap and cook in your microwave on high for 8–8 1/2
minutes or until desired doneness.

While cooking the broccoli, prepare the sauce by combining all remaining
ingredients, except the crumbs, in a small saucepan. Bring the mixture to a slight
simmer over low heat until heated through and the butter is melted. Place the
well-drained broccoli spears on a serving platter and pour the sauce over all.
Sprinkle the seasoned crumbs over all and serve immediately.

Serves 6.

# Gabby's Stuffed Broccoli Bake

1 1/2 lbs. fresh broccoli, trimmed and cut into 1 1/2-inch flowerets
1/2 C salted water
1 can cream of chicken soup
1 T flour
1/2 C sour cream (can use light)
1/4 C carrot, shredded
1 T onion, minced
Salt and fresh ground pepper, to taste
1 C Pepperidge Farm Herbed Stuffing Mix
2–3 T butter, melted

Prepare the broccoli as indicated, place in a shallow baking dish and add the water. Cover the dish with plastic wrap and cook on high in your microwave for 5 minutes (broccoli should still be crisp). Uncover and drain well.

In a medium mixing bowl, combine the soup, flour, sour cream, carrot, onion, salt and pepper. Add the cooked broccoli and stir well. Turn this mixture into the same shallow baking dish or a 2-quart casserole dish.

In a small bowl, combine the stuffing mix and melted butter. Arrange this mixture around the outside edge of the broccoli, making a 2-inch border. Bake, uncovered, in a preheated 350° for 30–35 minutes.

Serves 6 as a side dish.

# Gabby's Cheesy-Herbed Cauliflower

1 medium head of cauliflower (can also use brociflower)
1 C milk
1/2 C water
1 bay leaf
2 T butter or margarine
2 T flour
1/2 C cheddar cheese, shredded

1/2 tsp. lemon juice
1/2 tsp. thyme
1/2 tsp. Mrs. Dash Lemon Herb seasoning
2–3 T bacon crumbles or commercial bacon substitute
Fresh parsley, finely chopped for garnish

Trim all leaves from the cauliflower stalk and trim the stalk about 1/2 inch. Place the whole cauliflower head on a steaming rack in a 3- or 4-quart saucepan. Add the milk, water and bay leaf. Bring to a boil, cover, reduce heat and simmer about 20–25 minutes or until tender. Drain the cauliflower and keep warm, reserving the liquid in the pan.

In a small sauce pan, melt the butter over medium heat and add the flour to form a roux, stirring constantly about a minute. Remove from the heat and whisk in the cooking liquid, cheese, lemon juice, thyme and Mrs. Dash. Reduce the heat to low and continue to whisk the mixture over the heat until it is smooth and heated through.

Place the drained cauliflower in a large serving dish and ladle the sauce over the top. Sprinkle on the bacon bits and garnish with chopped parsley.

Serves 6 (depending on the size of the cauliflower).

# Fresh Cauliflower with Mushroom-Cheese Sauce

1 medium head of fresh cauliflower, trimmed
1/2 lb. fresh mushrooms, sliced
2 T butter
2 T flour
Dash ground white pepper
1 C milk
1 C medium-sharp cheddar cheese, shredded

1 tsp. Gabby's Own Mustard (*see chapter 7, Sauces and Dressings, for this recipe*)
1 tsp. dried marjoram
1 T fresh parsley, finely chopped
Sweet Hungarian paprika for garnish

Prepare the cauliflower as indicated and place in a medium-sized shallow dish. Pour in about 1/2 cup of salted water and cover with plastic wrap. Microwave on high for 8–10 minutes, depending on the size of the cauliflower (do not over cook). Drain well and keep covered until ready to serve.

While the cauliflower cooks, prepare the sauce. In a medium-size skillet, heat the butter over medium heat and saute the sliced mushrooms for about 3 minutes. Blend in the flour and pepper. Whisk in the milk and continue to whisk until the sauce thickens. Stir in the cheese, mustard and marjoram.

Place the drained cauliflower on a serving platter and spoon the sauce over all. Sprinkle the parsley and paprika over the top and sides and serve at once.

Serves 6–8 (depending on the size of the cauliflower).

# Peppers and Mushroom Saute

2 T butter and olive oil combination
1/2 medium red bell pepper, cut into julienne strips
1/2 medium yellow bell pepper, cut into julienne strips
1/2 medium onion, halved and sliced
1/2–1 lb. fresh mushrooms, sliced
1 clove garlic, pressed or minced

1/2 C Burgundy or other dry red wine
1 1/2 T brown sugar
1 1/2 T Gabby's Own Mustard (*see chapter 7, Sauces and Dressings, for this recipe*)
1 T Worcestershire sauce
Pinch salt
Pinch fresh ground pepper

In a medium-large fry pan, heat the butter-oil combination and when hot, add the bell peppers, onion, mushrooms and garlic to the pan. Saute the mixture until all the vegetables are tender crisp, stirring constantly about 5 minutes. Remove the vegetables and drain on paper towels.

Return the pan to the heat and add all remaining ingredients. Bring to a boil and let reduce by half, stirring occasionally. Return the sauteed vegetables to the pan and continue to cook in the sauce. Serve warm as a side dish.

Serves 2–4.

I like to serve shaved Parmigiana-Reggiano over this dish, adding a wonderful granular texture to the dish. Superb!

# Fresh Mushrooms Mock Souffle

8 thick slices of sourdough bread, trimmed and cut into 1 inch cubes

3–4 T butter and olive oil combination

1 lb. fresh mushrooms, sliced into 1/4-inch slices

1 medium onion, halved and coarsely chopped

1 medium red or green bell pepper, finely chopped

1/4 C celery, finely chopped (include some leaves)

1–2 cloves garlic, pressed or finely minced

1 C cream of mushroom soup

1 1/2 C milk

1/2 C mayonnaise

2 eggs, beaten

Salt and fresh ground pepper, to taste

1/2 C sharp cheddar cheese, shredded

Prepare the bread cubes as indicated. In a large skillet or fry pan, heat the butter-oil combination over medium-high heat. Add the vegetables and garlic and saute until the onion is transparent.

Mix together the remaining ingredients, except the cheese, and set aside. Place the bread cubes on the bottom and up the sides of a well-buttered 2-quart casserole. Mix together the sauteed mixture and the soup mixture. Slowly pour this mixture over the bread cubes. Cover and chill in the refrigerator over night.

Remove from the refrigerator 1 hour before baking. Bake, uncovered, in a preheated 350° oven for 40 minutes. Cover with the cheese and continue to bake for 10 more minutes.

Serves 4–6.

# Harvest Stuffed Zucchini

4–6 medium zucchini (8 inches long)
3 T olive oil
1/2 C onion, finely chopped
1/4 C green bell pepper, finely
   chopped
1–2 cloves garlic, pressed or minced
1–2 roma tomatoes, finely chopped
1/4 C pine nuts, toasted

2–3 T fresh parmesan cheese, grated
2 T dried parsley
1/2 tsp. Italian seasoning
Salt and fresh ground pepper, to taste
1/4 tsp. ground cinnamon or to taste
1/4 C seasoned bread crumbs
1/2 C fresh parmesan cheese

Wash the zucchini in cold water, then simmer in a couple of inches of salted water for 8 minutes. Let cool, then slice off the top 1/2 inch, lengthwise. Scoop out the centers of each, leaving a shell.

In a medium-size skillet, heat the oil over medium heat. Add the scooped out zucchini and all remaining ingredients except the 1/2 cup of parmesan. Saute this mixture for several minutes or until onion is tender. Stuff the mixture into the zucchini shells and sprinkle with the remaining parmesan cheese.

Place the filled zucchini on a sprayed baking sheet. Bake in a preheated 350° oven for 20 minutes or until all is heated through.

Serves 4–6.

# Gabby's Zucchini-Walnut Saute

4 T olive oil and butter combination
6 medium zucchini, coarsely shredded
2 medium shallots, chopped
2 cloves garlic, pressed or finely
    minced
3 T straight sherry wine

2 large tomatoes. peeled, seeded and
    coarsely chopped
4 T fresh parsley, finely chopped
3 T fresh basil, chopped
3/4 C walnuts, coarsely chopped
Salt and fresh ground pepper, to taste

Prepare the zucchini as indicated and place the shredded zucchini in a terry cloth towel; twist the towel to squeeze out excess water in the zucchini.

In a large skillet, heat the oil-butter combination over medium high heat. Add the zucchini, shallots and garlic to the hot pan, stirring and turning constantly. Add the sherry wine and saute until the liquid is reduced by two-thirds. Add the remaining ingredients, again stirring and turning until all is heated through and ready to serve.

Serves 6 as a side dish to just about any entree.

# Cheesy, Herbed Zucchini-Onion Bake

6 slices of thick sliced bacon, diced, fried crisp and well drained

2 T olive oil, butter, or a combination of both

6 medium zucchini, sliced into 1/4 inch rounds

1 large sweet onion, halved and sliced

2–3 cloves garlic, pressed or minced

1–2 large pimentos (canned or bottled), coarsely chopped

1 bay leaf

3 T fresh basil leaves, chopped

1/2 tsp. Italian seasoning

Salt and fresh ground pepper, to taste

2 eggs (or egg substitutes), whisked until fluffy and light

3/4 C Vermont Sharp White Cracker Barrel Cheese, shredded

3/4 C sour cream

1/4 tsp. Italian seasoning

1/2 C seasoned bread crumbs

1/2 C fresh parmesan cheese, shredded

Sweet Hungarian paprika, for color garnish

Prepare the bacon as indicated, drain well and set aside. In a large non-stick skillet or fry pan, heat the oil-butter over medium-high heat. Add the zucchini, onion and garlic. Saute this mixture until tender-crisp, then add the pimento and seasonings.

After 3 minutes, drain off the extruded liquid and arrange vegetables in a shallow baking dish. Sprinkle the bacon over all. In a medium-size bowl, combine the whisked eggs, cheese, sour cream and seasoning. Pour this mixture over the zucchini mixture, then combine the crumbs and parmesan cheese and sprinkle over the top, garnishing with paprika. Bake in a preheated 350° oven for 30 minutes.

Serves 6.

Great side dish!

# Italian Vegetable Toss

1/2 head fresh cauliflower, cut into
    flowerets
2 T olive oil
1 T butter or margarine
1 medium onion, chopped
2 cloves garlic, pressed or minced, or
    1/4 tsp. garlic powder
2 medium zucchini, cut into 1/4-inch
    rounds
2 medium yellow squash, cut into
    1/4-inch rounds

1 medium red or green bell pepper,
    coarsely chopped
1 medium tomato, chopped
1/2 tsp. oregano
1/2 tsp. sweet basil
Salt and fresh ground pepper, to taste
1–2 T herbed red or white wine
    vinegar
1/4 C fresh parmesan cheese, shredded

Steam the cauliflower about 5 minutes or until it is just tender-crisp. Meanwhile, in a large skillet, heat the oil and butter over medium-high heat. Add the onion and garlic and saute about 2 minutes, then add the zucchini, squash, pepper and steamed cauliflower. Saute this mixture 2–3 minutes, then add the tomato and seasonings. Splash in the wine vinegar, wait 1 minute, and sprinkle the cheese over all. Serve immediately.

Makes 6 servings.

# Summer Vegetable Montage

2 T olive oil
1 large sweet onion, coarsely chopped
2 cloves garlic, pressed or minced
2 C baby carrots
1 C zucchini, halved lengthwise and sliced
1 medium green bell pepper, diced
1 lb. fresh mushrooms, whole or halved
2 large tomatoes, cut into wedges
2 cans artichoke hearts, well-drained
2 C fresh sweet or lemon basil, coarsely chopped

2 T lemon juice
Salt and fresh ground pepper, to taste
1 C mayonnaise (prefer Best Foods)
1 C plain low fat yogurt
3 C fresh parsley, finely chopped
1 clove garlic, pressed or very finely chopped
1 T (scant) dried thyme leaves
1 T fresh basil, finely chopped
1 tsp. onion powder
Salt and fresh cracked pepper, to taste

Prepare all vegetables as indicated. Heat the oil in a large fry pan (preferably non-stick) over medium-high heat. Add the onion, garlic and baby carrots. Saute this mixture 4 minutes, then add zucchini and bell pepper. Saute another 4 minutes, then add the mushrooms, cover and cook an additional 3 minutes.

Remove the cover and add tomato wedges, artichoke hearts, basil, lemon juice, salt and pepper. While the vegetables cook, combine all remaining ingredients in a small bowl and mix well (this can be done up to a day before and chilled). When the vegetables are warmed through, place them in a large serving bowl, ladle the sauce over all, garnish as desired and serve immediately.

Serves 6–8.

# Gabby's Fresh Corn Off the Cob

10–12 ears of fresh corn, shucked
1/4 C fresh chives or green onion tops,
    finely chopped
1 T sugar

1 1/2 tsp. salt
1/4 tsp. ground white pepper
1–2 C heavy whipping cream

Prepare the corn as indicated, then cut the kernels from each cob. Combine the corn with the chives, sugar, salt and pepper. Mix well, then place in a sprayed shallow 9 x 13-inch baking dish. Pour the cream over all to just cover the corn. Bake, uncovered, in a preheated 350° oven for 1 1/2 hours.

Serves 6–8.

Really delicious!

# Swiss Corn Bake

2 pkgs. frozen whole corn
6 oz. evaporated milk (can be light)
1 egg, beaten
2 T onion, finely chopped
1/2 tsp. salt
1/4 tsp. fresh ground pepper

4 oz. Swiss cheese, shredded
1/2 C fresh (soft) seasoned bread
  crumbs
1–2 T butter, melted
Sweet Hungarian paprika for garnish

Following the package directions, boil the corn in salted water for 3 minutes, then drain well and place in a medium-size mixing bowl. Add the milk, egg, onion, salt, pepper and cheese; mix well and turn into a shallow baking dish. Toss the seasoned crumbs with the melted butter and sprinkle over the corn mixture. Garnish with the paprika. Bake, uncovered, in a preheated 350° oven for 30 minutes.

Serves 4–6.

I will use fresh corn off the cob when corn is in season. Good side dish!

# Roasted Herbed Potatoes

2 1/2–3 lbs. medium-size red new
  potatoes, cut in half
1/4 C olive oil
4–6 cloves garlic, finely minced
1 T dried parsley flakes, finely chopped

1 T dried marjoram leaves, crushed
1 T dried rosemary leaves
1 tsp. fresh ground pepper
1/4 C brandy (optional)

Prepare the potatoes as indicated, parboil in salted water for about 5 minutes and drain well. Place the spuds in a single layer in a dark shallow baking pan.

Combine the olive oil and all seasonings, then slowly drizzle this mixture over the potatoes, stirring to coat well. Bake in a preheated 375° oven, uncovered, for 30 minutes, turning several times. Add the brandy after baking 15 minutes. The potatoes should be slightly golden brown on the cut edges.

Serves 8.

If desired, roast beef or lamb drippings can be added during the baking period.

# Roasted Potatoes, Parsnips and Sweet Onions

6 medium russet potatoes, peeled and
cut lengthwise into 6 wedges
6 medium parsnips, peeled and cut in
half crosswise
6 medium sweet onions, peeled,
halved and cut into wedges
12 shallots, peeled and cut into wedges
3 cloves garlic, pressed or finely
minced

6 T unsalted butter, melted (can use
regular butter, too)
3 medium sprigs of fresh rosemary
3 medium sprigs of fresh thyme
1 tsp. salt, or to taste
3/4 tsp. ground pepper, or to taste

Prepare the potatoes, parsnips, onions and shallots as indicated. In a large
roasting pan, toss together all of the vegetables and garlic. Pour the melted butter
over all and stir will to coat. Scatter the fresh herbs over the top and season with
the salt and pepper.

Roast, uncovered, in a preheated 375° oven, turning the vegetables every
20 minutes, until all are crusty brown on the outside and tender inside (about
1 hour).

Makes 12 servings.

A great mixture of hearty vegetables and herbs.

# Gabby's Herbed Potatoes Au Gratin

2 lbs. baking size russet potatoes, peeled and thinly sliced
Salt and fresh ground pepper, to taste
1 C Swiss cheese, shredded
1–2 cloves garlic, pressed or finely minced
1 1/2 T dried rosemary needles, crushed just a bit

3–4 tsp. butter, cut into small bits
1 C heavy whipping cream or half & half (can also use Mocha Mix non-dairy creamer)
1 can cream of mushroom soup

Prepare the potatoes as indicated and wash the slices in cold water. Dry on paper towels. Lightly spray or butter a medium-size shallow baking dish and arrange the potato slices in layers, sprinkling the cheese, garlic, seasonings and butter between each layer.

Combine the cream and the soup, mixing well, and pour over the potatoes. Bake, uncovered, in a preheated 325° oven for 1 hour or until the potatoes are tender.

Serves 6.

This recipe can be prepared in advance, covered and held in the refrigerator for a couple of hours until baking time (be sure to cover tightly with plastic wrap).

# Baked Roquefort Potatoes

6 medium russet potatoes, scrubbed
1/2 C Roquefort or blue cheese,
   crumbled
1/4 C heavy cream
1/4 C green onion, very finely chopped

Salt and fresh ground pepper, to taste
1/3 C seasoned bread crumbs
3 T melted butter
1/4 tsp. sweet Hungarian paprika
1 clove garlic, very finely minced

Prepare the spuds as indicated and bake in a preheated 375° oven until soft to the squeeze. Cut off the top 1/3 of the potato, lengthwise, and scoop out the potato pulp into a large mixing bowl. Save the shells, covering with a terry cloth.

Whip the potato pulp with an electric mixer and then mix in the cheese. Slowly mix in the cream until the mixture is fluffy; add the salt and pepper to taste. Spoon the mixture back into the potato shells, rounding.

In a small bowl, combine the crumbs, butter, paprika and garlic. Sprinkle over each potato. Return the stuffed potatoes to the oven on a baking sheet and bake again at 350° until lightly browned (about 25 minutes).

Serves 6.

# Pepper-Jack Stuffed Potatoes

4 large (8-oz.) potatoes, scrubbed
2 T unsalted butter
2–3 large cloves garlic, pressed or
   minced
1 C Monterey Jack and jalapeno
   pepper cheese, shredded

3/4 C sour cream
2 T fresh cilantro, chopped
2 T green onions or fresh chives,
   chopped
Salt and fresh ground pepper, to taste
Chopped fresh tomato (optional)

Prepare the potatoes as indicated and bake in a preheated 400° oven for 1 hour or until tender. Cool slightly, cut in half lengthwise, and scoop out the potato pulp into a bowl. Set aside to cool.

In a small skillet, melt the butter over low heat, add the garlic and cook 1–2 minutes. Mash the cooled potatoes, then stir in the garlic-butter, cheese, sour cream, cilantro, 1 tablespoon of the chives, salt and pepper. Mix well.

Spoon the mixture back into the potato shells and place on a baking sheet. Return to the oven and bake until heated through (about 10 minutes). Remove and place on a serving platter and sprinkle with the remaining green onions/chives and chopped tomato (you can also add more cheese, too).

Serves 8.

*This is another great recipe celebrating June, Dairy Month, with my friends and sponsors from the Utah Dairy Council.*

# Gabby's Spuds O'Brien

6 large russet or red new potatoes,
  peeled and cut into 1-inch cubes
Salted water to cover potatoes
4 T butter
3–4 T flour
2 C milk
1/2 C green bell peppers, finely
  chopped
1/4 C green onions, finely chopped

1 small bottle diced pimento
1 tsp. salt
1/2 tsp. fresh ground pepper, or to taste
1/4 tsp. fresh nutmeg, grated
Tabasco sauce, to taste (optional)
1 C sharp cheddar cheese, shredded
3/4 C Ritz cracker crumbs, lightly
  buttered

Prepare the potatoes as indicated, rinse, place in a medium saucepan and cover with the salted water. Simmer the potatoes until tender, drain well and set aside in the pan.

In a 1-quart saucepan, melt the butter over medium heat, stir in the flour and cook for 2 minutes, stirring constantly. Whisk in the milk and bring to a simmer, continuing to whisk until thickened.

Stir in the bell peppers, onions, pimento, salt, pepper, nutmeg and Tabasco, and then stir in the cheese. Lightly spray a small 7 x 11-inch baking dish with Pam and pour in the potatoes. Pour the sauce over all and sprinkle the buttered cracker crumbs on top. Bake in a preheated 425° oven for 12–15 minutes or until bubbly.

Serves 6.

Everyone will like these.

# Gabby's Crabby Spuds

4 large russet potatoes, baked
1/4 C butter, room temperature
1/3 C half & half cream or milk
3/4 C sour cream
1/4 C green onions or chives, finely
    chopped

1 can (6 1/2 oz.) lump crab meat or
    equal amount of fresh or frozen
    crab, drained well
1 1/2 tsp. McCormick-Schilling Garlic
    Pepper
1 tsp. sweet Hungarian paprika

Bake the spuds as you normally would. Cool slightly, then slice each in half and scoop out the pulp into a large mixing bowl. Add the butter and mash or beat with an electric mixer.

When the potatoes are smooth, stir in the remaining ingredients and check for proper seasoning; add salt, if you like, but check first. Mound or pipe this mixture into individual ramekins. Place the filled ramekins on a baking sheet and bake in a preheated 400° oven for 15 minutes.

Fills 6–8 ramekins.

These can be made in advance and frozen for later serving. Place the filled ramekins on a baking sheet and place in your freezer. When frozen solid, place in a zip lock bag and use as you need. Bring to room temperature before heating through.

A great side dish for any occasion.

# Real Brunswick Stew, Georgia-Style

1/2 C butter (can also use margarine instead)

3 C cooked chicken (white and dark), chopped into bite-size pieces

3 C potatoes, peeled and diced

2 C smoked pork loin, chopped into bite pieces

1 large onion, chopped

2 cans (14 1/2 oz.) chicken broth

2 cans (14 1/2 oz.) Cajun-style stewed tomatoes

1 can (17 oz.) cream-style corn

1 pkg. (16 oz.) baby lima beans, drained

1 can (8 1/2 oz.) English peas, drained

1/2–3/4 C barbecue sauce (your favorite)

2 T Wright's liquid smoke

1–2 T Worcestershire sauce

2 whole bay leaves

Salt and black pepper, to taste

In a large Dutch oven, melt the butter over medium heat. Add the chicken, potatoes, pork, onion and broth. Bring this mixture to a boil, reduce the heat and simmer, uncovered, about 30 minutes.

Stir in all remaining ingredients and bring to a boil, reduce the heat and simmer, uncovered, for about 2 hours, stirring occasionally.

Makes 3 quarts.

Serve as a side dish to a southern-style barbecue.

# Gabby's Pignoli, Orzo and Rice Pilaf

3 T butter or butter olive oil
    combination
1/2 C orzo pasta (also called rosa
    marina)
1/2 C raw pignoli (pine nuts)
1 C long grain white rice (do not use
    instant)

2 1/2 C defatted chicken broth
1/4 C fresh Italian parsley (flat leaf),
    chopped
Salt and fresh ground pepper, to taste

In a heavy 2-quart saucepan, heat the butter over medium-high heat. Stir in the orzo and pignoli, stirring until both are golden brown. Stir in the rice, stirring until all is coated.

Heat the broth to the boiling point, then stir into the rice mixture. Add the parsley, salt and pepper. Cover, reduce the heat to low, and simmer 15–20 minutes or until all liquid has been absorbed and ingredients are tender. Place in serving bowl and serve immediately.

Serves 6.

# Gabby's Thanksgiving Yam Souffle

3–3 1/2 C baked and skinned yams
   (regular or red)
1/4 C butter or margarine
1/2 C sugar
2 large eggs
1/2 C milk

1 tsp. vanilla
Salt and fresh ground pepper, to taste
1/2 C (packed) brown sugar
1/3 C flour
1/4 C butter or margarine, melted
1 C pecan gems

Prepare the yams as indicated and, while still warm, place them in a large mixing bowl with the butter and mix with an electric mixer. Mix until smooth, adding the sugar, eggs, milk, vanilla, salt and pepper.

Pour the mixture into a 9 x 13-inch shallow baking dish. In a small mixing bowl, combine the brown sugar, flour, 1/4 cup butter/margarine and pecan gems, then sprinkle over the potato mixture. Bake, uncovered, in a preheated 350° oven for 30–35 minutes.

Makes 6–8 servings.

# Gabby's Corn Bread and Spicy Sausage Stuffing

10–12 C corn bread (2-day-old),
  crumbled (make 2 regular corn
  bread loaves)
1 lb. spicy bulk pork sausage, crumbled
  before cooking
1/4 lb. butter (or butter olive oil
  combination)
4 medium onions, finely chopped
1 1/2 C celery (with leaves), finely
  chopped
2–3 cloves garlic, pressed or finely
  minced

1/2 C fresh parsley (no stems)
2 T poultry seasoning
1 T fresh lemon zest, finely chopped
1 1/4 tsp. thyme
1/2 tsp. sage
2 tsp. salt, or too taste (optional)
1 tsp. fresh ground pepper, or to taste
1/2 C turkey broth (from boiling
  giblets)

Prepare the corn bread and coarsely crumble or cut into small cubes and set aside, covered, for 2 days. Crumble the sausage and brown in a large skillet, draining well. Combine the sausage with the stale corn bread, mixing thoroughly.

In the same skillet, melt the butter over medium-high heat. Add the onion, celery and garlic and saute about 10 minutes. Add the sauteed mixture to the bread-sausage mixture. Mix in the parsley, zest and seasonings. When well mixed, slowly stir in the broth to moisten evenly.

Half of the dressing will stuff an average-size turkey without packing. Place the remaining dressing in an ovenproof baking dish and cover with foil. Bake in a preheated 350° oven for 25–30 minutes. Do not over bake.

Happy holiday eating!

# Gabby's Southern-Style Corn Bread-Sausage Stuffing

1 9 x 9-inch square of corn bread,
   cooled
1 pkg. (6 oz.) herbed bread stuffing
   (Pepperidge Farm is a good one)
1 pkg. Jimmy Dean Light sausage
   (80% turkey meat)
2/3 C butter
2 large onions, chopped
4–5 ribs celery, chopped
1/2 medium green or red bell pepper,
   finely chopped

4 green onions, chopped
2 cloves garlic, pressed or minced
1/4 C dried parsley flakes
2–3 tsp. salt, or to taste
1 T poultry seasoning
1–2 tsp. sage
1 tsp. thyme
1 tsp. fresh ground pepper
Turkey broth (from boiling the giblets)

Prepare the corn bread the day before making the dressing. In a large mixing bowl, break up the corn bread and add the seasoned stuffing bread. In a medium-size skillet, crumble the sausage and saute until lightly browned; drain well on paper towels.

In a large skillet, melt the butter over medium-high heat. When toasty brown, add the onions, celery, bell pepper, green onions and garlic and saute until the onions are tender. Add this mixture to the corn bread mixture, along with the drained sausage, stirring well to blend. Add the herbs and seasonings, stirring well. Moisten the mixture to desired consistency. Dress the turkey with the mixture or mound in a shallow 9 x 13-inch baking dish. Cover tightly with foil and bake in a preheated 325° oven for 1 hour.

Serves 10 with leftovers.

# Chapter 7

# Sauces
# and Dressings

## Gabby Specialities—Sauces and Dressings

# Gabby's Own Mustard

| | |
|---|---|
| 1/2 C all purpose flour | 1/4 C granulated sugar |
| 1/2 C dry mustard (Coleman's is one of the best) | 3/4 C cider vinegar |
| | 1/8 tsp. salt |

This is really very simple to make. Just blend all of the ingredients together until the mixture is smooth. Pour the mixture into a crock or old mayo jar (with lid). Place in the refrigerator for 7 (count 'em, 7) days.

Every couple of days, shake the jar for a few seconds. After the seven days, stir and serve as you would any prepared mustard—maybe just not as much. In fact, *definitely* not as much!

Makes a 2-month supply, unless you really like to use lots of mustard.

This also makes a great gift. Pour the mustard into a decorative jar and top with a ribbon and a copy of the recipe. They will love you for it!

# Cranberry Sauce with Burgundy Wine

1 C Burgundy wine
1/2 C water
1/2 C granulated sugar
1 pkg. (12 oz.) fresh cranberries

1 T orange zest
Dash salt
1/2 C pecans, chopped

In a medium-size saucepan, combine the wine, water and sugar. Bring to a boil over high heat, stirring until sugar dissolves. Add the cranberries and continue to cook until the berries start to pop open, about 10–15 minutes.

Reduce the heat and add the remaining ingredients. Pour the mixture into a medium serving bowl. Place in the refrigerator and chill.

Makes 3 cups.

*Nutritional information for 2-tablespoon serving size: 46 calories, 0.6 grams protein, 1.8 grams fat, 8 grams carbohydrate, 0 grams cholesterol.*

# Lime-Cilantro Butter

1/2 lb. butter, softened
1 clove garlic, minced or pressed
1 tsp. chili powder

1/4 C roasted red bell pepper, minced
1 T fresh cilantro, minced
1 T fresh lime juice

Mix all of the ingredients well, making sure you mix in all of the lime juice.

Makes 1 cup.

Use as a condiment or a baste on vegetables, especially corn on the cob. For example, preheat your barbecue grill and spread the mixed butter liberally on the ears of corn, then wrap each in foil. Place on the grill and cook for 5 minutes, turning frequently.

# Black Bean Salsa

1 1/2 C cooked black (turtle) beans, drained
1/2 C red onion, finely chopped
1/2 C roma tomatoes, finely diced
1/4 C red bell pepper, finely diced
1/4 C green bell pepper, finely diced
1/4 C yellow bell pepper, finely diced
2–3 tsp. serrano or jalapeno chile, minced

2 tsp. fresh cilantro, chopped
1–2 cloves garlic, finely minced
1/2 tsp. ground cinnamon
1/2 tsp. ground cumin
2 T lime juice
1 1/2 T raspberry vinegar (can use red wine vinegar)
3 T olive oil

Prepare all of the ingredients as indicated and combine in a medium-size serving bowl. Cover and refrigerate at least 2 hours.

Makes 3 cups.

This is another great salsa that serves well with just about any seafood, especially marinated prawns, poultry, and meats. Or just break out the tortilla chips and use for dipping.

# Gabby's Green Chile Summer Salsa

4 large fresh firm tomatoes, skinned and chopped

2 medium fresh jalapeno peppers, seeded, deveined, and very finely chopped

1 can (4 oz.) chopped green chilies

1 large clove garlic, finely minced or pressed

1 medium white onion, finely chopped

1 T olive oil

4 T fresh cilantro, chopped

1/2 tsp. salt (optional)

1/4 tsp. oregano

1/8 tsp. ground cumin

Stick each tomato with a fork and dip into boiling water for just a few seconds or until the skin pops, then remove, skin and chop.

Place all of the ingredients, prepared as indicated, in a medium saucepan and simmer about 10 minutes. Cool to room temperature, then chill well before serving.

Makes about 2 1/2 cups and keeps well in the refrigerator.

# Gabby's Fresh Watermelon and Peach Salsa

2 C fresh sweet watermelon, seeded and finely diced

1 1/2 C fresh sweet peaches, skinned, pitted and finely chopped

1 C fresh tomato, finely chopped

1 small red Bermuda onion, finely chopped

1–2 red jalapeno peppers, very finely minced

1 clove of garlic, finely minced

3 T fresh cilantro, finely chopped

1 1/2 tsp. fresh mint, finely chopped

1 T dried oregano leaves

1/2 tsp. dried ground cumin

3 T seasoned rice vinegar

1 T extra virgin olive oil

1 tsp. salt or to taste

Prepare all of the fresh ingredients as indicated. It is best if these ingredients are all hand minced or chopped instead of processing in a food processor.

In a large mixing bowl, combine all of the ingredients. and mix well. Taste for proper seasoning and adjust as desired. Cover with plastic wrap and place in the refrigerator to chill until serving.

Makes just over a quart.

If you prefer less sweetness, use regular rice vinegar in place of seasoned. This is a wonderful condiment for roasted lamb or grilled white fish. Really wonderful and just as great on a tortilla chip. Try!

# Yogurt Cilantro Sauce

1 C plain non-fat yogurt
1/2 C fresh cilantro, finely minced
1/4 C (rounded) green onions,
    chopped
2 tsp. orange juice
1 tsp. fresh jalapeno pepper, finely
    minced

1 tsp. fresh orange zest
1/2 tsp. sugar
1/2 tsp. salt
1/2 tsp. fresh ground black pepper

In a small mixing bowl, combine all of the ingredients and mix well to blend. Cover and refrigerate. Before serving, taste for proper seasoning and adjust to your taste. Serve as a dipping sauce with quesadillas.

Makes about a cup of sauce (enough for 4 quesadillas).

# Tsatziki (Greek Yogurt-Cucumber Sauce)

2 cucumbers, peeled, seeded and
    shredded
2 C plain yogurt
1–2 cloves garlic, pressed or minced

1 T olive oil
1–2 tsp. lemon juice
1/2 tsp. salt
Pinch ground white pepper

Prepare the cucumbers as indicated and wrap it in a small towel, squeezing to remove the juice. Place the cucumber in a medium-size mixing bowl and add all of the remaining ingredients, stirring well to blend.

Makes about a quart.

This is the basic sauce that is served with the Greek gyros, but it can also be used as a salad dressing or as a dip with crusty French bread.

# Chilled Cucumber-Dill Sauce

1 C sour cream
2 T mayonnaise (the real stuff)
1 large cucumber, peeled, seeded, finely chopped, and squeezed of its juice
1 T sweet onion, very finely minced or grated

2 tsp. lemon juice
1 tsp. dry dill weed
1 tsp. Gabby's Own Mustard (*this recipe is found at the front of this chapter*)
3–6 drops hot pepper sauce
Sweet Hungarian paprika

In a small mixing bowl, combine all of the ingredients and mix very well. Place the mixture in a small serving bowl and spritz the paprika over the top. Cover with plastic wrap and refrigerate to chill several hours before serving.

Makes just over 2 cups (depending on size of cucumber).

This serves so well with most any seafood, but especially well with poached or baked salmon.

# Southwestern Tartar Sauce for Grilled Seafood

1/4 C light or fat-free mayonnaise
1/4 C light or fat-free sour cream
2 T fresh cilantro, minced
1 T red onion, minced
1 T small capers, drained well
1 T lime juice

2 tsp. fresh jalapeno pepper, minced
1/8 tsp. chili powder
2/3 lb. large sea scallops
2/3 lb. medium shrimp (U-20), peeled
    and deveined

In a small mixing bowl, combine all of the ingredients, except the scallops and shrimp, to make the tartar sauce; mix well. Cover and refrigerate until needed.

Thread 4 scallops and 5 shrimp, alternately, onto 4 12-inch bamboo skewers. Carefully coat the grill rack with cooking spray. Place filled skewers 4–5 inches from grey-hot coals or heat source. Grill, turning once, just until the shrimp are opaque and scallops are milky-colored, firm and opaque, about 3–4 minutes per side. Serve immediately with the tartar sauce.

Makes 4 servings.

# Gabby's Remoulade Seafood Sauce

3/4 C extra virgin olive oil
1 medium-small sweet onion, minced
2/3 C celery (with leaves), finely
   minced
1/4 C lemon juice
1/4 C Gabby's Own Mustard (*see this*
   *recipe at the front of this chapter*)
2 T fresh prepared horseradish

2 T green onions, very finely minced
2 T fresh parsley, finely minced
2 tsp. sweet Hungarian paprika
2 cloves garlic, pressed or finely
   minced
Pinch cayenne or red pepper
1 tsp. salt or to taste
1/2 tsp. fresh ground pepper or to taste

In a small mixing bowl, combine all of the ingredients and mix well to blend.
Cover with plastic wrap and refrigerate to chill well before serving.

Makes 2+ cups and can be stored in the refrigerator several days before using.

Serves well with just about any seafood, especially shrimp.

# Green Mayonnaise for Salmon or Trout

2–3 leaves of fresh spinach, no stems
2 T chives or green onion tops
2 T capers, drained
1 small clove of garlic, pressed or
    minced

1 T lemon juice
1 tsp. dried tarragon leaves
4–6 drops hot pepper sauce
1 1/2 C regular or light mayonnaise
    (don't substitute salad dressing)

Place all of the ingredients, except the mayonnaise, in your food processor or blender container. Process/blend for just a couple of seconds or until smooth.

Place the mayonnaise in a serving dish or bowl. Stir the blended mixture into the mayonnaise until well blended. Cover and refrigerate until ready to serve as a condiment to salmon or trout, fried, grilled, broiled, baked or poached.

Makes 1 3/4 cups.

If you're tired of the same old tartar sauce, try this.

# Gabby's Caper Sauce for Grilled Salmon

2 T butter
1/4 C onion (prefer sweet onion),
    finely minced
2 T flour
1/2 tsp. salt

1/4 tsp. ground white pepper
1 1/2 C milk
2 T lemon juice
2 T capers, drained
1 T fresh parsley, finely chopped

In a small skillet or saucepan, melt the butter over medium heat, then add the onion and saute until tender. Stir in the flour, salt and pepper, mixing well.

Whisk in the milk and continue to cook until mixture thickens. Stir in the remaining ingredients. Serve in sauce boat.

Makes 1 1/2 cups.

# Crab and Shrimp Cocktail Sauce

2 1/4 C catsup (your favorite brand)
l/4 C cider vinegar
l/4 C horseradish
l/4 C onion, finely minced
1 tsp. Gabby's Own Mustard (*see the front of this chapter for the recipe*)

2 C chili sauce (your favorite brand)
l/2 T fresh lemon juice
6 drops of hot pepper sauce
l/4 C celery, finely minced (use some leaves, too)
1 T Worcestershire sauce

Place all of the ingredients in a blender or food processor and blend/process until well blended. Refrigerate for at least a couple of hours before serving. This can be frozen for later use. Serve with crab or shrimp.

Makes lots!

# Sauce Bearnaise

1/4 C tarragon vinegar
2 T shallots, finely chopped
1 T dry tarragon
1 tsp. fresh tarragon leaves

1 tsp. fresh parsley, finely chopped
2 C Hollandaise sauce (*see the following recipe*)
Fresh ground pepper, to taste

In a small sauce pan, combine all of the ingredients, except the Hollandaise. Simmer over medium heat until most of the liquid is evaporated, then add the Hollandaise.

Makes 2 1/2 cups.

# Hollandaise Sauce

4 egg yolks
1/2 lb. unsalted butter, melted
1/2 oz. water
1 tsp. fresh parsley, finely chopped
1/2 oz. lemon juice (if you are using
    this to make the Bearnaise Sauce,
    use 1/2 oz. white tarragon vinegar
    in place of lemon juice)

Cayenne pepper or Tabasco sauce
    to taste
Worcestershire sauce to taste
Salt to taste

In a double boiler, combine the eggs and water over medium heat, whisking until the mixture thickens. Slowly drizzle in the melted butter until mixture thickens. Slowly whisk in the lemon juice and remaining seasonings. Keep warm until ready to serve (do not try to reheat).

Makes about 1 cup.

### For orange hollandaise:

Place 2 cups of orange juice in a saucepan and bring to a boil. Reduce the heat and simmer until reduced to about a 1/4 cup. Heat 1 cup butter until bubbly. Place 6 egg yolks and a teaspoon of salt in a blender and blend for a few seconds. While blending, add the orange syrup, then slowly add the melted hot butter. Blend until mixture is thick.

Makes about 1 1/4 cups.

# Chile Hollandaise Sauce

5 extra large egg yolks
2 T water
1 pinch salt
2 dashes Tabasco

Juice from 1/2 fresh lemon
1/2 tsp. Worcestershire sauce
12 oz. clarified butter
1 can (4 oz.) diced green chilies

Place all of the ingredients, except the butter and chilies, in your blender. Heat the clarified butter.

Turn the blender on medium speed. Slowly add the heated butter and blend until thick. Add the chilies and adjust the seasonings if necessary.

Makes about 1 1/2 cups.

Serve over eggs benedict.

# Creamed Mushroom Sauce

1/4 lb. butter
1 large onion, chopped
2–3 cloves garlic, pressed or finely
    minced
2 lbs. fresh button mushrooms, whole
    or sliced, depending on size
3–4 T fresh tarragon, chopped

1/4 C dry white wine
1 1/2 C sour cream
1 T flour
2 T fresh parmesan cheese, shredded
1/2 tsp. ground white pepper or
    to taste

In a large fry pan, heat the butter over medium-high heat. Add the onion and garlic. Saute this mixture about 5 minutes, stirring often. Add the mushrooms and tarragon and continue to saute an additional 5 minutes. Add wine and let liquid reduce to just a glaze. Reduce the heat to low.

Combine the remaining ingredients, mixing well. Stir this mixture into the mushroom mixture and heat through, but do not boil.

Makes about 1 3/4 cups.

This serves great with just about any red meat or fowl, and even vegetables. It's just a great complimentary sauce.

# Sesame Marinade and Dressing

3 T straight sherry wine
3 T light-style Japanese soy sauce
3 T seasoned rice vinegar
2 T Hoisin sauce (available in
    Oriental food stores)

1/2 tsp. fresh grated ginger
1/4 C water
2 green onions, finely sliced
1 T sugar
1 T Oriental dark roasted sesame oil

In a small mixing bowl, combine the wine, soy, vinegar, Hoisin and ginger and mix well. Add all remaining ingredients to the mixture and blend well.

Makes about 1 cup.

May be used as a marinade for steaks, or as a dressing for any type of tossed salad.

# A Super Italian Salad Dressing

1/4 C granulated sugar
1/2 C extra virgin olive oil
1/2 C light salad (canola) oil
1/2 C garlic red wine vinegar or
    herbed red wine vinegar
1 1/2 tsp. salt
1/4 tsp. fresh ground pepper

1 tsp. Gabby's Own Mustard (*see this*
    *recipe in the front of this chapter*)
1 tsp. sweet Hungarian paprika
1 tsp. dried oregano leaves
1 C catsup
1 clove garlic, pressed or minced
1 small onion, very finely minced

In a covered container (an old jar, crock, or Tupperware container), combine all of the ingredients (in any order). Cover tightly and shake well or until the mixture is well blended.

Let this mixture stand, at room temperature, for several hours, then strain into another container. Store in the refrigerator and it will keep well for several weeks.

Makes about 3 cups.

# Gabby's Mock Roquefort Dressing

1 pkg. (8 oz.) cream cheese, room
    temperature
2 C mayonnaise (don't use salad
    dressing)
2 C fresh buttermilk
1 tsp. Mrs. Dash Lemon Herb
    Seasoning Mix

1 tsp. garlic salt or æ tsp. garlic powder
1 tsp. onion salt
1 tsp. seasoned or fresh ground pepper
1 tsp. salt

Cut the room temperature cream cheese into small pieces and place in a medium mixing bowl. Add the mayonnaise and buttermilk and stir to blend. Add all remaining ingredients and stir once more.

Makes approximately 1 3/4 quarts.

*Note: This dressing should be lumpy.* Do not beat with an electric mixer or blend in a blender or food processor any more than just a second or two. This dressing can be served on just about anything—you name it!

# Gabby's Real Italian Dressing

1/2 C herbed wine or balsamic vinegar
1 T lemon juice
2 tsp. granulated sugar or Nutra-Sweet
    Spoonful
2 tsp. salt (optional amount, but
    should have some)
2 cloves garlic, pressed or minced
1–2 tsp. Gabby's Own Mustard (*see this*
    *recipe in the front of this chapter*)

1 tsp. fresh coarse ground pepper
1/2 tsp. oregano
1/2 tsp. anise seed, crushed
1/4 tsp. celery seed
1/4 tsp. marjoram
1/4 tsp. sweet basil
1 1/2 C olive or light olive oil (or you
    can use a mixture of half olive and
    half canola oil)

In a food processor or blender, all all ingredients, except the oil. Process or blend well, dissolving the salt and sugar.

While processing, slowly add the oil until it is well incorporated and homogenized. Place in a covered container and serve at room temperature.

Makes 2 cups.

Store in the refrigerator and it will keep well for several weeks.

# Homemade Low-Fat Ranch-Style Dressing

3/4 C plain low or no-fat yogurt
1/4 C low calorie mayonnaise
1 C buttermilk
1 T onion, finely minced
1 T fresh parsley, finely minced
1/4 tsp. dried basil

1/4 tsp. dried thyme
1/4 tsp. ground garlic
1/4 tsp. ground sage
1/4 tsp. salt-free seasoning (your favorite brand)

In a 2- or 3-cup mixing bowl, combine all of the ingredients in the order listed (first the yogurt, then mayonnaise, then buttermilk, and so on). Whisk well, then cover with plastic wrap and refrigerate until serving.

Makes 2+ cups.

The simplest of tossed green salads will taste great with the addition of this dressing. Now, don't pass up the opportunity to serve this dressing over baked potatoes or use as a dip for fresh vegetables. Best part, only 9 calories per tablespoon and so little fat.

# Gabby's Do-Everything Barbeque Sauce

1 C water
1/2 C catsup
1/4 C herbed red wine vinegar
2 T light vegetable (canola) oil
Juice from 1/2 fresh lemon
2 T brown sugar or Sugar Twin
2 T shallots or onion, very finely
    minced
2–3 cloves garlic, pressed or minced

1 tsp. Bovril (beef seasoning base)
1–1 1/2 tsp. chili powder
1 tsp. celery salt
1 tsp. instant minced onion
1 tsp. fresh ground black pepper
1/2 tsp. Wright's Liquid Smoke
    (optional)
1/4 tsp. cayenne (red) pepper (can use
    more or less)

Combine all of the ingredients in a 1-quart saucepan. Bring the mixture to a rapid boil, reduce the heat and simmer about 5 minutes.

Brush this sauce over just about anything you want to grill, from chicken, beef, pork (ribs, chops, roasts), and lamb to seafood (whole or steaks) and large prawns. This works best if brushed on during the cooking, but remember to always grill several inches (8–10) above the grey-hot coals or source of heat when using a brushing-type sauce.

Makes about 2 1/2 cups and will keep for some time, covered and refrigerated.

# Gabby's Red Sauce for Anything Italian

2–3 T olive oil
2 oz. pancetta (Italian bacon), finely chopped
2 medium white onions, finely chopped
2 cloves garlic, pressed or finely minced
1 medium rib of celery, finely chopped
1 lb. extra lean ground beef
1 can (28 oz.) ready cut tomatoes
1 can (14 oz.) ready cut tomatoes, drained

1 C dry red wine
1 medium carrot, finely shredded
1/4 C fresh basil leaves, finely chopped
3 T fresh Italian flat leaf parsley, finely chopped
3 T Italian-style tomato paste
1 T oregano (can also use Italian seasoning)
1/2 tsp. fresh grated nutmeg
Salt and fresh ground pepper, to taste

In a medium-size (8-cup) saucepan, heat the oil over medium heat, then add the pancetta, onions, garlic and celery. Saute this mixture, stirring often, until the onion is limp and transparent, about 5 minutes. Add the ground beef, crumbling as you add, and brown. Drain this mixture of all extruded grease and return the saucepan to medium heat.

Puree the 2 cans of tomatoes (small can drained) and add to the pan along with all remaining ingredients. Simmer lightly, uncovered, stirring often, over low heat about 1/2 hour (more if needed for proper consistency). Check for proper seasoning, then cool to room temperature before freezing or chilling for future use.

Makes about 2 quarts of sauce.

This sauce is perfect when you need a real Italian red sauce: try it on pasta, lasagna, meats, poultry, and seafood.

# Gabby's Quick and Easy Marinara

1/4 C extra virgin olive oil (I recommend the Sagra brand)

4 cloves garlic, pressed or very finely minced

3 T onion, very finely minced

4 cans (28 oz.) ready-cut Italian-style tomatoes, drained

1/2 C dry red wine

1/4 C carrot, finely shredded

1/2 C Italian-style parsley, finely chopped

1/2 C fresh basil leaves, coarsely chopped

2 tsp. dried oregano leaves

Salt and fresh ground pepper, to taste

In a large heavy sauce pot, heat the oil over medium-low heat. Add the garlic and onion and lightly saute about 2 minutes, then stir in the tomatoes, wine and carrot. Increase the heat to medium and let the mixture just bubble about 15 minutes.

Stir in all the remaining ingredients and test for proper seasoning. Simmer the mixture, uncovered, for about 20 minutes, stirring occasionally. This can be served immediately, chilled or frozen for later use.

Makes about 2 quarts.

# Gabby's Marinara Sauce for Jumbo Stuffed Shells

3 T olive oil
3 medium onions, finely chopped
2 cloves garlic, pressed/minced
1/4 C green onions, chopped
1 can (28 oz.) ready-cut tomatoes with juice
1 1/2 cans (15 oz.) chunky tomato sauce
1 can (6 oz.) Italian-style tomato paste

1/2 medium carrot, finely shredded
1/4 C fresh Italian parsley, finely chopped
3 T fresh sweet basil, finely chopped
1 T fresh oregano, finely chopped
1 bay leaf
Salt and fresh ground pepper, to taste
1/2 C dry red wine
1–2 C chicken or beef broth

In a large fry pan, heat the oil over medium-high heat. Add the onion and garlic and saute until the onion is just about tender. Add all remaining ingredients, except the broth, and bring to a simmer.

Add about a cup of the broth, reduce the heat to low and simmer, uncovered, for 1 to 1 1/2 hours, stirring and adding more broth as needed.

Makes about 1 1/2 quarts.

Use this sauce as indicated in my "Gabby's Jumbo Stuffed Shells" recipe (*found in chapter 4, Pastas and Pizzas*), but it can be also used in any recipe calling for a marinara sauce.

# Roasting Sauces

### Honey Sauce

2 C honey (your choice)
1/2 C butter
1/4 C orange juice
1 T Gabby's Own Mustard (*see this recipe in the front of this chapter*)
1/4 C cognac

Combine and heat all of the ingredients. Use the sauce as a baste for birds or ham, basting often during the roasting period.

### Cranberry Glazing Sauce

1 can (16 oz.) whole cranberry sauce
4 T butter
1/4 C frozen orange juice concentrate
2 T brown sugar
2 tsp. fresh orange zest
1/4 tsp. poultry seasoning

Combine and heat all of the ingredients. Use the sauce as a baste for birds, basting often during the roasting period.

# Honey-Mustard Glaze for Chicken or Pork

1 C Dijon mustard
1/4 C honey (your favorite)
1/4 C Schilling Salad Supreme

1/4 C water (more for a thinner glaze)
1/2 tsp. salt
1 tsp. garlic powder

Combine all of the ingredients and mix well.

Brush the mixture over whole, quarters or individual pieces of chicken just as the meat is finished cooking and you are ready to remove it from the grill. Make sure the glaze doesn't burn after brushing it on.

# Gabby's Creamed Horseradish Sauce

2 T horseradish (not horseradish
    sauce)
2 T mayonnaise
2 T sour cream
1 T tarragon wine vinegar
1/2 tsp. Gabby's Own Mustard
    (*see recipe found in the front of
    this chapter*)

1/8 tsp. salt (optional)
Dash cayenne or red pepper
1/2 C heavy cream, whipped
Sweet Hungarian paprika, for garnish

In a small mixing bowl, combine all of the ingredients, except the heavy cream and paprika. Mix until smooth.

Whip the cream, omitting any use of sugar or vanilla. Fold the whipped cream into the first mixture slowly—do not beat. Place the sauce into a serving boat, then refrigerate until ready to serve. Just prior to serving, add a dash of paprika and a sprinkle of parsley flakes over the top for garnish.

Makes 1 1/2 cups.

Great for a prime ribber or a regular roast of beef. Can also be served as a vegetable dip for hors d'oeuvres.

# Creamed Horseradish Sauce for Baked Ham

4 T horseradish
1 T sugar
2 tsp. prepared mustard (*preferably Gabby's Own Mustard—see the front of this chapter for the recipe*)
1 tsp. vinegar (your choice)

1/2 tsp. salt
1/2 tsp. ground white pepper
1/2 tsp. sweet Hungarian paprika
1/2 pint heavy whipping cream (unsweetened), whipped

In a small mixing bowl, combine all of the ingredients, except the whipped cream. Mix well, then fold in the whipped cream. Chill until ready to serve.

Makes enough to serve with 1 whole ham.

# Wonderful Sauces for the Holiday Hams

*Try one of these sauces on the next holiday ham.*

### Raisin-Rum Sauce

1 C raisins

1/2 C rum

3/4 C brown sugar

1/4 tsp. ground cinnamon

1 T butter

1/4 tsp. Worcestershire sauce

1/2 C water

5 whole cloves

1 tsp. cornstarch

1/4 tsp. salt

1 T herbed white wine vinegar

In a small sauce pan, combine the raisins, water, rum and cloves. Bring the mixture to a simmer for 10 minutes. Combine the sugar, cornstarch, cinnamon and salt and stir into the raisin mixture until thickened. Add the remaining ingredients, then place into a sauce boat and serve with sliced baked ham. Will keep, covered, in the refrigerator for several weeks.

### Raisin-Mustard Sauce

1/2 C (packed) brown sugar

2 T cornstarch

2 tsp. Gabby's Own Mustard (*see the front of this chapter for this recipe*)

1 C cranberry juice (can use light)

1/2 C orange juice

2 T lemon juice

1/2 C raisins

1/4 C bourbon or brandy (optional)

In a small saucepan, combine the first 3 ingredients, mix well, then whisk in all remaining ingredients and heat over medium heat. Cook the mixture cook, stirring constantly, until thickened. Serve warm.

# Chapter 8

# Desserts

# Gabby Specialities—Desserts

# Sundae Pie

1 C chocolate flavor syrup
1 1/2 C vanilla cookie crumbs
1 1/2 C flaked coconut
1/2 C pecans, chopped
1 tsp. vanilla
2 quarts ice cream (your choice of
    flavor), softened slightly

1/2 C chocolate flavor syrup
1/2 C maraschino cherries, drained
    and chopped
Whipped cream (optional)

In a large mixing bowl, combine 1/2 cup of the chocolate syrup, cookie crumbs, coconut and pecans. Press this mixture over the bottom and side of a 9-inch pie plate. Scoop 1 quart of the ice cream over the crust mixture and smooth out. Top with the remaining syrup. Place in the freezer, freezing until firm.

Top with remaining syrup, freeze until firm, then spread the remaining ice cream over the top. Drizzle the last 1/2 cup of syrup over all and return to the freezer until firm. Let stand at room temperature for 10 minutes before serving. Top each wedge with whipped cream and chopped cherries.

Makes 6 servings.

# Cinnamon Noodle Pudding

8 oz. uncooked medium-width egg
   noodles
1 C small curd cottage cheese
1 C plain yogurt
4 extra large eggs, lightly beaten

1 C golden raisins
1/4 C granulated sugar
1 tsp. ground cinnamon
1/4 tsp. salt

Boil the noodles, following the package directions, but don't add any salt. Meanwhile, in a large bowl, combine the remaining ingredients. Drain the noodles well and add to the previous mixture, mixing well.

Spoon the mixture into a sprayed 12 x 7-inch shallow baking dish. Bake, uncovered, in a preheated 350° oven until firm, about 35 minutes. Let stand for 10 minutes before serving.

Makes 6–8 servings.

# Fresh Strawberry-Rhubarb Marble

3 C fresh rhubarb, cut into 1-inch pieces
1/2 C (rounded) granulated sugar
1/4 C fresh orange juice
1/2 tsp. salt

3/4 C heavy whipping cream
3 C fresh strawberries, sliced and sugared
6 fresh whole strawberries

Prepare the rhubarb as indicated, then place in a medium-size saucepan, adding the sugar, orange juice and salt. Bring this mixture to a rapid boil, reduce the heat, cover and simmer about 7 minutes, or until the rhubarb is tender.

Remove from the heat and let the mixture cool. Pour the mixture into your food processor and process until pureed. Pour into a large bowl and chill completely. Whip the cream, adding sugar and vanilla, until stiff. Fold in the sliced berries. Fold this mixture into the chilled rhubarb mixture to appear marbled. Serve in stemmed parfait glasses topped with a whole berry.

Makes 6 servings.

# Low-Calorie Pumpkin Pie

1 can (16 oz.) solid-pack pumpkin
1 can (13 oz.) evaporated skim milk
1 large egg
2 egg whites
1/2 C biscuit mix (Bisquick)

2 T sugar
1/2 C NutraSweet sugar substitute
2 tsp. pumpkin pie spice
2 tsp. vanilla or 1/4 teaspoon dry
    vanilla

Lightly spray a 9-inch pie pan. Place all of the ingredients in your blender, food processor or mixing bowl. Blend or process for 1 minute or beat 2 minutes with a mixer. Pour the pumpkin mixture into the pie pan and bake in a preheated 350° oven for 50 minutes or until the center is puffed up.

We're talking 8 servings and only 114 calories in each slice.

# Summer Night's Fresh Fruit Platter

1 medium watermelon, halved and hollowed out, cutting the red portion into cubes
1 medium honeydew melon, cut into cubes
1 pint large fresh cherries
1 pint large fresh strawberries
1 pint large Thompson green or red flame grapes
2–3 apples, cut into wedges
1 fresh pineapple, cut into wedges

4–6 bananas, cut in pieces
1/2 C shredded coconut
2 C sour cream
2 T sugar
1/2 tsp. fresh grated nutmeg
1/4 tsp. ground cinnamon
1/4 tsp. ground cardamom
1/8 tsp. ground allspice
1/8 tsp. salt
1 tsp. vanilla
1/4 tsp. rum extract

Prepare all of the fruit as indicated, then arrange all in the hollowed out portion of the watermelon. Place on a serving platter along with the remaining fruit and sprinkle the coconut over all.

Place the sour cream in a small serving bowl. Combine and mix the sugar and spices, then stir this mixture into the sour cream; add the vanilla and rum extracts. Chill the fruit and the dip and serve as desired with party or toothpicks.

Makes lots!

This is so refreshing on a hot summer night!

# Gabby's Sherried Berries

2 pints fresh raspberries (can use combination of other berries also), washed and picked clean
4 egg yolks
1/2 C sugar
1/4 C dry sherry wine

1 T brandy
1/8 tsp. fresh nutmeg, grated
1/2 C sweetened heavy cream, whipped stiff
Fresh lemon zest, for garnish

Prepare the berries as indicated and refrigerate. In a medium-size mixing bowl, beat the egg yolks until thick and lemon colored, then beat in the sugar until ribbon consistency. Beat in the sherry, brandy and nutmeg.

Place the bowl over barely simmering water and stir constantly until the mixture thickens. Pour this custard-like mixture into a clean bowl and chill. Just before serving, beat the cream until stiff, then fold in the custard mixture. Divide the berries into tall stemmed parfait or wine glasses. Spoon the custard cream over all and garnish each with fresh lemon zest.

Serves 4–6.

If you have to ask about calories … don't!

# Bread Pudding with Lemon-Raisin Sauce

4 C whole wheat bread cubes (8–10
    slices of bread)
4 extra large eggs, slightly beaten
2 3/4 C milk
1/2 C (packed) light brown sugar
1 1/2 tsp. ground cinnamon
1/2 tsp. ground cardamom
2 T lemon juice
1/2 C granulated sugar

1/4 C (packed) light brown sugar
2 T cornstarch
3/4 C water
1/4 C lemon juice
1/4 C dark raisins
2 T nut meats (your favorite)
2 T butter or margarine
1 T fresh lemon zest, finely chopped

Place the bread cubes in a lightly sprayed 9-inch baking dish. In a medium-size bowl, combine the eggs, milk, 1/2 cup brown sugar, cinnamon, cardamom and 2 tablespoons lemon juice, mix well and pour over the bread cubes. Bake in a preheated 350° oven for 45 minutes or until a knife inserted in the center comes out clean.

During the baking period, prepare the sauce. In a small saucepan, combine the granulated sugar, 1/4 cup brown sugar, cornstarch and water, then gradually stir in the cold water and 1/4 cup lemon juice. Heat this mixture, stirring over medium heat until the mixture boils. Reduce the heat and continue to cook until the sauce appears clear and thickens. Stir in the raisins, nut meats, butter and zest. Serve warm over the still-warm or room-temperature pudding.

Makes 6 servings.

# Gabby's Golden Delicious Cobbler

5 C golden delicious apples, peeled,
    cored and sliced
Juice from 1 fresh lemon
1/2 C pecan gems
1/2 C (rounded) granulated sugar
2 T all-purpose flour
1/2 tsp. ground cinnamon
1/2 tsp. fresh nutmeg, grated

1/4 tsp. salt
1/4 C (1/2 stick) cold butter
1 C all-purpose flour
1/4 C granulated sugar
1 tsp. (rounded slightly) baking
    powder
3 T cold butter
3/4 C sour cream

Prepare the apples as indicated and place in a large mixing bowl, squeezing the lemon juice over all and stirring well. Stir in the pecans, sugar, flour, cinnamon, nutmeg and salt. Arrange the apple mixture in a sprayed 1 1/2-quart souffle dish. Dot the top with the 1/2 stick of cold butter, cover and bake in a preheated 400° oven for 15 minutes.

During the baking period, combine the flour, sugar and baking powder in a medium-size mixing bowl. Using a fork or pastry blender, cut the 3 tablespoons of butter into the mixture. Stir in the sour cream until well blended. Remove the apples from the oven and drop the pastry mixture by tablespoons over the apple mixture. Return the cobbler to the oven, uncovered and continue to bake about 30 more minutes.

Serves 4–6.

# Fresh Peaches and Berries Cobbler

4 C fresh peaches, peeled, seeded and
    cut into wedges
2 C fresh berries, (raspberries,
    blueberries or blackberries)
2/3 C all-purpose flour
1 3/4 C granulated sugar
1/4 tsp. cinnamon
5 extra large eggs
1 tsp. vanilla

2 C milk
1/2 C heavy whipping cream
1 C all-purpose flour
1/2 C granulated sugar
1/2 tsp. ground cardamom
6 T butter
1 tsp. vanilla
Half & half cream or sweetened
    whipped cream

In a lightly sprayed 9 x 13-inch shallow baking dish, arrange the prepared peaches and berries of choice. In your food processor or blender container, combine the 2/3 cup flour, sugar, cinnamon, eggs, vanilla, milk and 1/2 cup whipping cream and process until all is blended. Pour this mixture over the fruit, then bake, uncovered, in a preheated 400° oven for 30 minutes.

During the baking period, prepare the topping. In a medium-size mixing bowl, combine the 1 cup flour, sugar and cardamom. Using a pastry blender, cut the butter into the mixture. When the mixture resembles a streusel in consistency, stir in the vanilla.

Remove the baked mixture from the oven and sprinkle the topping over all and return to the oven for an additional 15 minutes or until the topping is lightly browned. Place on a cooling rack and let cool to just warm before serving. Serve with chilled half & half cream or whipped cream.

Serves 8–10.

# Gabby's Apple Pie Crisp

4 large cooking-type apples (Granny, Rome, Golden Delicious), peeled, cored and sliced

Juice from 1/2 fresh lemon

1/3 C granulated sugar or Sugar Twin substitute

1 tsp. ground cinnamon

1 C regular oat meal

3/4 C all-purpose flour

1/2 C light brown sugar

1 tsp. ground allspice

1 tsp. apple pie spice

1/2 C butter, softened to room temperature

1 9-inch unbaked pie shell

Prepare the apples as indicated and place in a medium-size mixing bowl. Pour the lemon juice over all, then stir in the granulated sugar and cinnamon, stirring to mix well, then set aside.

In another medium bowl, combine the oat meal, flour, brown sugar and spices, mix well, then cut in the softened butter until the mixture is crumbly. Arrange the apple mixture in the pie crust. Spoon the crumbly mixture over the apples and tamp down a bit. Bake in a preheated 375° oven for 55–60 minutes. Crust should be golden and crusty over the top.

Serves 6–8.

Serve a wedge of this with a slice of sharp cheddar cheese.

# Sour Cream Apple Crisp

6 C cooking apples, peeled, cored and
    sliced (preferably Granny Smith or
    Golden Delicious)
1 C sour cream
2 C granulated sugar (divided)
3 T cornstarch
1 tsp. cinnamon

1/2 tsp. ground allspice
2 eggs, beaten
3 C quick oats
1/2 C brown sugar
1 C pecans, chopped
1 C butter, melted

Prepare the apples as indicated and place in a large mixing bowl. Add the sour cream, 1 cup sugar, cornstarch, spices and eggs and mix well with the apples. Arrange this mixture in a sprayed 9 x 9-inch shallow baking dish.

In a separate mixing bowl, combine the oats, brown sugar and pecans, plus the remaining 1 cup of sugar and mix well. Pour the butter over all and mix well again. Spread this mixture evenly over the apple mixture. Bake in a preheated 350° oven for 60 minutes. Should be crispy over the top. Let set for 15 minutes (or longer) before serving.

Serves 6–8.

Old-fashioned, summer dessert.

# Nutty Sugar Cookies for Christmas

1/4 lb. butter (the real stuff), softened
   to room temperature
1 C brown sugar (packed)
1 extra large egg, beaten

1 1/2 C flour
1 C pecan gems
1 tsp. vanilla (can use lemon extract, if
   you desire a different flavor)

In a medium-size mixing bowl, combine the softened butter and sugar and cream until fluffy (low speed on mixer). Beat in the egg and gradually mix in the flour. Stir in the remaining ingredients.

Drop by teaspoonfuls onto a lightly sprayed baking sheet. Bake in a preheated 350° oven for 9–10 minutes.

Makes 2–3 dozen chewy cookies.

An easy cookie for the holidays.

# Chocolate Nut Mocha Butter Cookie Logs

1 C unsalted butter, softened to room
    temperature
1/2 C granulated sugar
1/2 tsp. salt
1 large egg yolk
2 1/4 all-purpose flour

2 tsp. instant coffee granules
1 tsp. water
6 T whipping cream
1 1/2 C semisweet chocolate chips
1 C toasted filberts or pecans, finely
    chopped

In a large mixing bowl, cream butter, sugar, salt and egg yolk with an electric mixer. Gradually beat in the flour. Dissolve the instant coffee in the water, then work into the dough.

Divide the dough into quarters, then wrap separately in plastic wrap. Refrigerate 1 hour or up to 2 days. Remove the dough from the refrigerator and divide each quarter in half. Knead dough lightly to make pliable. On a lightly floured board, shape each portion into a strand about 12 inches long. Cut each strand into 8 pieces. Arrange 1 inch apart on a parchment paper-lined or ungreased cookie sheet. Bake in a preheated 350° oven until lightly browned, 14–16 minutes.

Heat the whipping cream 45 seconds in a microwave, then stir in the chocolate chips. Mix until mixture is smooth (if necessary, microwave another 25–30 seconds to totally melt the chips). Dip one end of each cookie in the melted chocolate, then in the chopped nuts. Let stand until the chocolate is firm.

Makes 64 logs.

# Frosted Carrot Cookies

1 C (packed) light brown sugar
1/2 C butter-flavored Crisco shortening
1/4 C granulated sugar
1 egg
1/2 tsp. vanilla
2 1/4 C all-purpose flour
1 T apple pie spice (can use 2 tsp.
    cinnamon, 1/2 tsp. ground ginger
    and 1/2 tsp. nutmeg)
1 1/2 tsp. baking powder

1/2 tsp. salt
1 1/2 C finely shredded carrots
1 C walnut gems
1 C golden raisins (can use dark)
1 pkg. (3 oz.) cream cheese (softened)
2 T butter (softened)
1/2 tsp. vanilla
3 C powdered sugar
Walnut gems for topping each cookie
    (optional)

In a large mixing bowl, combine the brown sugar, Crisco and granulated sugar and cream well with an electric mixer. Beat in the egg and vanilla.

Combine the flour, spices, baking powder and salt and add gradually to the creamed mixture, mixing on low speed just until well blended. Stir in the carrots, walnuts and raisins.

Drop by rounded tablespoons on a lightly greased or sprayed baking sheet, 2 inches apart. Bake in a preheated 375° oven for 10–12 minutes or until edges are lightly browned. Let cool 2 minutes, then remove to a cooling rack to cool completely.

In a medium-size mixing bowl, combine remaining ingredients, except the walnut gems, mixing until smooth on low speed (add the powdered sugar slowly). Spread on the tops of the completely cooled cookies. Sprinkle a few of the walnut gems over each frosted cookie, then cover and refrigerate.

Makes about 3 dozen cookies.

# Mocha Chips 'n Bits

1 C butter-flavored Crisco
3/4 C granulated sugar
1/2 C (packed) light brown sugar
2 T milk
1 T instant coffee crystals
1 tsp. vanilla
2 eggs
2 1/3 C all-purpose flour

1 1/2 T unsweetened cocoa powder
1 tsp. baking soda
1/2 tsp. salt
1 C pecans, coarsely chopped
1 C vanilla milk chips
3/4 C dark raisins
3/4 C flaked coconut

In a large mixing bowl, combine the shortening, sugars, milk, coffee and vanilla. Beat with an electric mixer at medium speed until all is well blended. Beat in the eggs, one at a time.

Combine the dry ingredients and add to the creamed mixture at low speed, mixing just until well blended. Stir in the remaining ingredients. Drop rounded tablespoonfuls of dough 2 inches apart onto ungreased baking sheets. Bake at 375° for 10–12 minutes. Cool 2 minutes on baking sheets before removing to cooling rack.

Makes about 3 1/2 dozen cookies.

# Chocolate Swirl Delights

1 1/2 C brown sugar
1/2 C granulated sugar
1/2 C butter (the real stuff)
2 eggs
2/3 C sour cream
1 tsp. mint flavoring
2 C all-purpose flour
1/2 tsp. baking powder

1/4 tsp. salt
1/2 C semisweet chocolate chips
1/4 lb. butter
4 T cocoa
6 T milk
Dash salt
1 tsp. vanilla
2 C powdered sugar

In a large mixing bowl, cream together the brown and granulated sugars and 1/2 cup butter, then mix in the eggs, sour cream and mint flavoring.

Whisk together the flour, baking powder and salt and stir into the creamed mixture. Melt the chocolate chips and swirl into the dough. Drop by the tablespoonful onto a lightly sprayed baking sheet. Bake in a preheated 350° for 12–15 minutes. Remove and cool completely.

Meanwhile, make the fudge frosting. In a saucepan, combine the 1/4 pound butter, cocoa, milk, salt and vanilla and bring to a boil. Remove from the heat and stir in the powdered sugar. Drizzle the fudge frosting onto the cooled cookies.

Makes about 3 dozen cookies.

*A wonderful addition to your St. Patrick's Day celebration. Thanks to my friend Karen Udy (formerly with the Utah Dairy Commission) for this easy recipe.*

# Topsy-Turvey Delights

| | |
|---|---|
| 2 C Wheat Chex brand cereal, crushed to 1 1/4 cups | 1/2 tsp. ground cinnamon |
| 1 C flaked coconut | 1/2 C (1 stick) butter |
| 1/2 C golden raisins | 1/2 C (packed) brown sugar |
| 1/2 C flour | 1/4 C honey |
| 1/2 tsp. baking powder | 1/2 C semisweet chocolate chips |
| | 1/2 tsp. vegetable shortening |

Lightly spray 36 miniature muffin cups. In a large mixing bowl, combine the cereal, coconut, raisins, flour, baking powder and cinnamon and mix well.

In a small saucepan, combine the butter, brown sugar and honey. Cook this mixture over medium heat, stirring until the butter melts and the sugar is dissolved. Pour the butter mixture over the cereal mixture, stirring until well combined. Place a tablespoon of the mixture into each prepared muffin cup. Press firmly over bottom and sides. Bake in a preheated 350° oven for 12–14 minutes or until golden brown. Let cool in the pan 10 minutes. Loosen edges and remove. Cool completely.

Melt the chocolate chips and shortening in a saucepan over low heat, stirring until smooth. Remove from the heat. Dip the bottoms of the cups into the chocolate, allowing the excess chocolate to drip off. Cool chocolate side up. If desired, decorate with almonds, pecans, powdered sugar, dried fruit, cake decorating candies or white chocolate drizzle.

Makes 32–36 delights.

# Frosty Fresh Strawberry Squares

1 C all-purpose flour
1/4 C light brown sugar
1/2 C butter
1/4 tsp. fresh nutmeg, grated
1/2 C walnut gems
2 egg whites

2 T lemon juice
3/4 C granulated sugar
2 C fresh strawberries, hulled and
   sliced
1 C whipped cream (whipped with
   vanilla and sugar)

In a medium-size mixing bowl, combine the flour, brown sugar, butter, nutmeg and walnut gems, stirring to blend well. Spread mixture in a shallow 9 x 13-inch baking pan. Bake in a preheated 350° oven for 20 minutes, stirring occasionally. Remove from the oven and set aside to cool.

Remove about 1/3 cup of the mixture, then spread the remaining over the bottom of the same pan. In another mixing bowl, combine the egg whites, lemon juice, granulated sugar and strawberries. Beat the mixture with an electric mixer at low speed until stiff peaks form (it takes about 10–12 minutes).

Whip the cream and fold it into the strawberry mixture. Spread this mixture into the baking pan and top with the reserved 1/3 cup of nut mixture. Place in the freezer overnight or for at least 6 hours before serving. Cut into squares and garnish each with a fresh berry.

Makes 12–15 squares.

Something different for that first lug of spring berries.

# Cranberry Crumb Bars

1 1/2 C firmly packed light brown
  sugar
1 1/2 C all-purpose flour
1 1/2 C uncooked quick oats
1 C butter-flavored Crisco shortening
1 tsp. baking powder
1 tsp. cinnamon

1/2 tsp. ground cloves
1/2 tsp. salt
1 can (1 lb.) whole berry cranberry
  sauce
1 C walnut gems
1 tsp. orange peeling zest

In a large mixing bowl, combine all of the ingredients except the cranberry sauce, walnuts and zest and mix at low speed with an electric mixer until well blended and crumbly. Press half (about 2 1/2 cups) of the mixture into a sprayed and floured 9 x 13-inch baking dish. Bake in a preheated 350° oven for 10 minutes.

In a small bowl, combine the cranberry sauce, walnuts and zest, mix well, then spread evenly over the baked crust. Sprinkle the remaining crumb mixture over the cranberry filling and press down gently. Return to the oven and bake 20–25 minutes or until the crust is golden brown. Do not over bake. Run a spatula around the edge of the pan to loosen. Let cool completely, then cut into bars. Refrigerate until ready to serve.

Makes 9–12 bars.

A very festive look and taste.

# Apple Crumb Bars

1 1/2 C quick oats (not instant or old-fashioned)
1 C all-purpose flour
1 tsp. ground cardamom
1/4 tsp. salt
3/4 C butter-flavored Crisco
3/4 C (packed) light brown sugar
1 T (plus 1 tsp.) milk

3 1/2 C Granny Smith apples, peeled, cored and sliced (3–4 medium apples)
2 T fresh lemon juice
2 tsp. cornstarch
3/4 tsp. ground cinnamon
1/2 tsp. ground allspice
1/4 tsp. salt

In a medium mixing bowl, combine the oats, flour, cardamom and salt. In another bowl, cream together the shortening and brown sugar; when light and fluffy, add the milk, blending well. Gradually blend in the dry mixture, forming a crumb mixture. Press half of the mixture into a greased or sprayed 9-inch square baking pan. Bake in a preheated 350° oven for 10 minutes.

Prepare the apples as indicated, place in a medium-size bowl and sprinkle the lemon juice, cornstarch, cinnamon, allspice and salt over all. Spoon the apple mixture over the partially baked base. Sprinkle the remaining crumb mixture over the apples and press topping gently into apples. Return to the oven and continue to bake 40–45 minutes or until top is browned and apples are tender. Let cool completely, then cut into 1 1/2-inch square bars. Store air tight in the refrigerator.

Makes 25 bars.

# Caramel Layer Chocolate Squares

50 light caramels
1/3 C evaporated milk
1 German chocolate cake mix
1 pkg. (6 oz.) chocolate chips

1/3 C evaporated milk
1 C nuts, chopped
3/4 C margarine or butter, melted

In the top of a double boiler, melt the caramels with 1/3 cup evaporated milk, then set aside. Mix the cake mix, 1/3 cup of evaporated milk, nuts and melted margarine/butter with a wooden spoon. The mixture will be stiff.

Generously grease and flour a 9 x 13-inch baking dish. Press 1/2 of the dough over the bottom of the dish, reserving the other half for the topping. Bake the bottom layer in a preheated 350° oven for 6 minutes.

Remove from the oven, sprinkle with the chocolate chips, then spread the caramel mixture over the chocolate chips. Top with the remaining dough (sprinkle and pat to cover). Return to the oven and continue to bake for 15–18 minutes. Cool slightly and refrigerate until ready to cut into squares and eat.

Makes 9–12 squares.

*One of the many recipes that annually delight visitors to the Festival of Trees.*

# Orange Creme Brownies

3/4 C all-purpose flour
1/4 tsp. baking powder
1/4 tsp. salt
1 pkg. (6 oz.) semisweet chocolate
    morsels
1/2 C butter, cut into small pieces
1/3 C granulated sugar

3 T orange juice
1 tsp. fresh orange zest (peeling)
1 tsp. vanilla
2 eggs
1 1/3 C (about 6 oz.) walnut gems
Orange Creme (*recipe follows*)
Chocolate Icing (*recipe follows*)

Line the bottom and sides of a 9-inch square baking pan with foil, allowing foil to overhang slightly. Butter the foil, then set aside. On a square of waxed paper, combine the flour, baking powder and salt. In a small saucepan, combine the chocolate morsels, butter, sugar and orange juice. Cook, stirring over low heat until chocolate and butter are melted, then remove from the heat. Stir in the orange zest and vanilla.

Using a wire whisk, beat in the eggs, one at a time. Add the reserved flour mixture, beating until smooth. Stir in the nuts. Spread the mixture in the prepared pan. Bake in a preheated 325° oven 23–25 minutes or until wooden pick inserted in the center comes out clean. Cool completely on a wire rack. Spread with Orange Creme. Refrigerate until firm, about 15 minutes, or place in the freezer about 5 minutes. Spread the warm Chocolate Icing over the Orange Creme. Using a knife, score the Chocolate Icing layer in 36 (1 1/2-inch) squares. Refrigerate until Chocolate Icing is firm, about 25 minutes, or place in the freezer about 5 minutes. Remove from the pan by lifting the foil edges, then cut into squares. Refrigerate up to 4 days or wrap and freeze up to 1 month.

Makes 3 dozen brownies.

*Another special holiday confection from Karen Udy and the Utah Dairy Commission.*

## Orange Creme (for Orange Creme Brownies)

1/2 C butter, softened
2 C confectioners sugar
1 tsp. fresh orange zest (peeling)
1 tsp. milk
1 tsp. vanilla

In a small mixing bowl, beat the butter and sugar until light and fluffy. Beat in the zest, milk and vanilla.


## Chocolate Icing (for Orange Creme Brownies)

1 pkg. (6 oz.) semisweet chocolate morsels
1 T butter
1 T vegetable shortening

In a small saucepan, combine all ingredients, stirring over very low heat until all ingredients are melted and blended.

# Boter Koek

1/2 lb. butter, melted
2 C granulated sugar
2 C flour
Pinch salt

2 eggs, beaten
2 T almond extract
1 1/2 C sliced almonds

In a mixing bowl, combine and mix all of the ingredients, except the almonds and a small amount of the beaten egg to brush over the top. Spoon the mixture into a shallow 9 x 13-inch baking dish and press to the sides. Brush the top with the small amount of beaten egg, then sprinkle the sliced almonds over the entire top. Bake in a preheated 350° oven for 25–30 minutes. Let cool, then cut into squares and serve.

Makes 15 squares.

A true Dutch dessert and so easy.

# Pumpkin Roll

3 large eggs
1 C granulated sugar
2/3 C solid pack pumpkin
1 tsp. lemon juice
3/4 C all-purpose flour
1 tsp. baking powder
2 tsp. ground cinnamon
1 tsp. ground ginger
1 tsp. fresh nutmeg, grated
1/2 tsp. salt
1/4 C confectioner's sugar
1 C pecan gems

**Filling:**
1 C confectioner's sugar
1 large pkg. (8 oz.) cream cheese
    (softened)
1 small pkg. (3 oz.) cream cheese
    (softened)
1/4 C butter (softened)
1/2 tsp. vanilla

Line a regular-size jelly roll pan with foil, greased or sprayed, and floured. Beat the eggs for 5 minutes in a large bowl on high speed. Gradually stir in the sugar and beat well. Add pumpkin and lemon juice. Sift or whisk the flour, baking powder, and spices. Add to the pumpkin batter, blending well.

Spread the batter in the prepared pan and sprinkle with the nuts. Bake in a preheated 375° oven for 15 minutes. Turn out of pan immediately onto a towel sprinkled with 1/4 cup confectioner's sugar, then remove the foil. Starting at narrow end, roll towel and cake together in jelly roll form. Cool and unroll. Combine the filling ingredients, beating until smooth. Spread the filling on top of cake, then re-roll. Cover and chill, seam-side down. Sprinkle with more confectioner's sugar, then slice and serve.

Makes 8–10 slices.

# Cream Cheese Pound Cake

1 1/2 C butter, softened
1 pkg. (8 oz.) cream cheese, softened
3 C sugar
3 C flour
4 eggs
1/2 C milk
1 tsp. vanilla
1 tsp. almond extract

**Optional sauce for topping:**
1 can (8 oz.) crushed pineapple
1 pkg. (3 1/2 oz.) instant coconut
    pudding
3/4 C milk
1/2 C sour cream

In a large mixing bowl, combine the butter and cream cheese, then cream until fluffy. Gradually beat in the sugar. Add the flour, alternating with the eggs and milk. Stir in the vanilla and almond extracts. Pour the batter into a sprayed or buttered and floured bundt or tube pan. Bake in a preheated 325° oven for 1 1/2 hours. Let cool in the pan for 20 minutes before removing from the pan.

You can serve this pound cake topped with fresh fruit and whipped cream, or make the optional sauce by processing all of the sauce ingredients in a blender or food processor for 30 seconds. Spread over the cooled cake and refrigerate for several hours before serving.

Serves 10–20, depending on how you slice it!

# Blender Pots de Creme

1 pkg. (6 oz.) semisweet chocolate
   chips
1 extra large egg

1 tsp. sugar
1 tsp. vanilla
3/4 C scalded milk

Place all the ingredients except the milk in a blender container. Cover and blend on high, then slowly add the near-boiling milk. Continue to blend at high speed for 2 minutes. Pour the mixture into 4 pot de creme pots or stemmed wine glasses. Chill until the mixture is set. Serve with sprigs of mint and whole berries of choice.

Serves 4.

A very easy recipe for the perfect spur-of-the-moment dessert. *And one of the many great recipes from The Overlake School Cookbook, published back in 1984.*

# Pumpkin Spice Cake

3/4 C (3 sticks) cold butter
2 C flour
1 C sugar
1 tsp. baking soda
2 tsp. pumpkin pie spice
Zest from 1 fresh orange
1 C canned pumpkin

1 egg, beaten (can do without or use
    egg substitute, if desired)
1 1/2 C buttermilk or sour milk
1 C dark raisins
1/2 C walnut, chopped
1/2 C chocolate chips, chopped

In a large mixing bowl, combine the butter, flour, sugar and baking soda; using both hands, rub the butter into the dry ingredients, forming a crumbled mixture. Add the pumpkin pie spice and the zest and mix well. Add the pumpkin, egg and milk and stir in the raisins and walnuts.

Spread this mixture in a sprayed 12 x 10-inch jelly roll pan and sprinkle the chopped chocolate chips over the top. Bake in a preheated 375° oven for 25 minutes or until the cake springs bake when lightly pressed.

Makes enough for 15 kids.

# Blueberry Cake—the Best

1 1/2 C fresh blueberries, rinsed in
   cold water and picked of culls
1/4 lb. butter
1 C granulated sugar
2 extra large eggs (separated)
1 1/2 C flour

1 tsp. baking powder
1/2 tsp. salt
1/4 tsp. ground cardamom
1/3 C milk
1 tsp. lemon juice
2 tsp. granulated sugar

Prepare the blueberries as indicated and drain well. In a large mixing bowl, cream the butter and sugar with an electric mixer. Mix in the egg yolks, beating well. Combine the flour, baking powder, salt and cardamom and whisk to blend well. Beat the egg whites until stiff, but not dry. Stir the dry mixture into the creamed mixture, alternately with the milk. Fold in the egg whites, lemon juice and blueberries (lightly flour the berries before adding).

Pour the cake mixture into a sprayed and lightly floured 9 x 9-inch cake pan. Sprinkle the 2 teaspoons of sugar over top of the batter. Bake in a preheated 350° oven for 30 minutes. Let set in the pan on a rack 10 minutes before cutting into squares (best if left about an hour before serving).

Makes 9 servings.

# Judy's Rhubarb Cake with Brandy Sauce

4 C fresh rhubarb, cut into 1/2-inch
    pieces
3/4 C (plus 2 T) fresh buttermilk
1 1/2 C (packed) brown sugar
1/2 C butter, softened to room
    temperature
1 large egg
2 C all-purpose flour
1 tsp. baking soda
1/2 C granulated sugar

2 T butter, softened to room
    temperature
2 tsp. ground cinnamon
1/2 tsp. ground cloves
1/2 C brown sugar
1 T cornstarch
3/4 C water
2 tsp. butter
2 T brandy or bourbon

In a small mixing bowl, combine the buttermilk and rhubarb. In another small bowl, cream together the brown sugar and butter. Mix in the egg well. In a large mixing bowl, combine the flour and soda. Add the brown sugar mixture (the batter will be thick). Stir in the buttermilk and rhubarb. Mix until creamy.

Pour batter into a sprayed 9 x 13-inch shallow baking pan. Mix granulated sugar, 2 tablespoons of butter, cinnamon and cloves to form a crumbly mixture and sprinkle over the batter. Bake in a preheated 350° oven for 40 minutes or until cake tests done.

In a small saucepan, mix together the 1/2 cup brown sugar, cornstarch and water and cook over medium heat until thick and bubbly, about 5 minutes. Stir in the 2 teaspoons butter and brandy. Spoon this mixture over the slices of warm cake.

Serves 12.

Wow! If you have even a small liking for rhubarb, you'll just love this excellent dessert cake.

# Lemon Pecan Fruit Cake

1 lb. butter-the real stuff, softened
2 C granulated sugar
6 extra large eggs
4 C all-purpose flour (divided)
1 tsp. baking powder
2 oz. lemon extract

1 lb. pecans, chopped
1 lb. golden raisins
1/2 lb. mixed red and green candied
    cherries
2 1/2 lbs. candied pineapple

In a large mixing bowl, combine the softened butter and sugar. Cream this mixture, then beat in the eggs, one at a time. Whisk together 3 cups of the flour and the baking powder, then stir into the basic mixture, along with the extract.

Dredge all of the fruit and nuts in the remaining cup of flour. Fold the fruit mixture into the batter. Pour the batter into 2 sprayed loaf pans or 1 round angel food cake pan. Bake in a preheated 275° oven for 1 hour, then remove and cover with foil. Set the pans in a larger pan of hot water and return to the oven for an additional 1 hour and 45 minutes.

Makes 2 cakes.

This freezes very well for up to a year or more.

# Gabby's Macadamia Nut Fruit Cake

1 1/2 C butter, softened to room
    temperature
1 C granulated sugar
1 C light brown sugar
6 extra large egg yolks (save whites)
1 C milk
3 T brandy or rum (your choice)
2 T vanilla
3 1/2 C flour

1/2 tsp. salt
2 C golden seedless raisins
1 C dried fruit, chopped
1 C seedless dates, chopped
1 C fruit cake mix
1 1/2 C macadamia nuts, coarsely
    chopped
6 extra large egg whites
1/2 tsp. cream of tartar

In a large mixing bowl, combine the butter and sugars, then cream until fluffy and light. Beat in the egg yolks, one at a time. Combine the milk, brandy/rum and vanilla. Combine the flour and salt and whisk. Add both mixtures, alternately, to the creamed mixture. Stir in the fruits and nuts.

In another medium-size (and very clean) mixing bowl, beat the egg whites stiff, adding the cream of tartar. Fold the stiff whites into the basic batter mixture. Pour the mixture into 2 sprayed and floured regular size loaf pans. Bake in a preheated 275° oven for 2 1/2 hours. Let cool, then unmold and wrap with several layers of cheesecloth soaked in brandy, rum, port wine, Madeira or fruit juice. Wrap again with extra heavy foil, then store in a cool dry place (refrigerator is fine) for 2–3 weeks, resoaking several times during the storage period.

Makes 2 cakes.

These are well liked by all.

# Apple Upside-down Cake

**Topping:**
1/4 C butter, melted
1/2 C (packed) brown sugar
1/4 C pecan gems
2 C cooking-type apples, pared, cored
    and sliced
1 tsp. ground cinnamon
1 T fresh lemon juice

**Cake mixture:**
1/2 C butter, room temperature
3/4 C (packed) brown sugar

2 eggs
1 T fresh lemon zest, chopped
1 tsp. vanilla
2 C all-purpose flour
1 tsp. baking powder
1 tsp. cardamom
1/2 tsp. baking soda
1/2 tsp. ground cinnamon
1/2 tsp. fresh grated nutmeg
1/4 tsp. salt
3/4 C buttermilk

Pour the melted butter over the bottom of a 9-inch square baking pan. Sprinkle the brown sugar over the butter, the sprinkle the nuts over the sugar. Arrange the apple slices evenly in rows and sprinkle the cinnamon over the apples. Sprinkle the lemon juice over all, gently press mixture into the pan and set aside.

In a large mixing bowl, cream the soft butter and sugar until light and fluffy. Beat in the eggs, zest and vanilla. Combine all the dry cake ingredients, then add to the creamed mixture, alternately with the buttermilk. Starting and ending with the dry ingredients, mix well after each addition. Pour the batter evenly over the topping. Bake in a preheated 350° oven for 35–40 minutes or until a kitchen pick inserted in the center comes out clean. Cool 10 minutes in the pan, then gently loosen the edges with a knife. Invert the cake on a serving plate.

Serves 9–12.

Serve warm, cold, or room temperature, and with or without cream, milk or ice cream.

# Alaska's Bonanza Creek Supreme

2 C graham cracker crumbs (you can also use half graham and half Zwieback crumbs)
1/4 C granulated sugar
1/2 tsp. ground allspice
1/2 C butter, melted
2 1/2 C confectioner's sugar
2 extra large eggs, beaten
1/2 C butter, room temperature soft
1 tsp. vanilla

1 tsp. fresh ground nutmeg
4 fresh firm bananas, sliced
1 can (20 oz.) crushed pineapple, drained well
2 C heavy whipping cream
1/4 C (rounded) granulated sugar
1 tsp. vanilla
1/4 C walnut or pecan gems
Maraschino cherries, halved

In a medium-size mixing bowl, combine the crumbs, sugar, allspice and butter and mix well. Spread and press this mixture over the bottom and sides of a 9 x 12-inch shallow baking dish, forming a crust. Cover and chill.

In a medium-size mixing bowl, combine the confectioner's sugar, eggs, softened butter and vanilla. Beat this custard mixture until light and fluffy. Using a flat spatula, spread this mixture over the chilled crust. Arrange the sliced bananas over the custard mixture, then arrange the drained crushed pineapple over all. In a separate bowl, whip the cream, adding the sugar and vanilla while whipping. Spread the whipping cream over the top of the dessert. Sprinkle the nut gems over all, then arrange the halved cherries over all. Place in the refrigerator to chill through.

Serves 12–14.

This is one of the quick and easy desserts you'll want to use year round.

# Apple "Whatchamacallit"

2 C granulated sugar
1/2 C butter or margarine
2 extra large eggs
2 C flour
4 C cooking-type apples, peeled, cored
    and diced
1 tsp. fresh nutmeg
1 tsp. ground cinnamon
1 C pecan gems
1/2 tsp. baking soda
Pinch salt

**Lemon sauce:**
1/2 C granulated sugar
1 T cornstarch
1 T butter or margarine
1 C boiling water
Juice from 1/2 fresh lemon

In a large mixing bowl, cream the sugar and butter/margarine. Stir in the eggs. Combine the dry ingredients (salt, flour, nutmeg, cinnamon and soda) and whisk, then stir them into the butter mixture. Fold in the apples and nuts. The dough will be stiff, so you will have to really push to place it evenly in a 9 x 13-inch sprayed baking dish. Bake in a preheated 350° oven for 45–60 minutes. Remove from oven and allow to cool.

To make the lemon sauce, mix together the sugar and cornstarch. Add to the boiling water along with the butter/margarine and simmer for 5 minutes, whisking smooth. Add the lemon juice and continue to simmer 1 more minute. Let the sauce cool down to a warm temperature, then pour over the warm cake and serve immediately.

Serves 8–10.

It's just that easy and good!

# Hazelnut Apricot Torte

**Sugar pastry base:**
8 oz. "Softasilk" cake flour
5 oz. butter
Pinch salt
2 eggs, beaten
2 oz. sugar

**Sponge cake:**
4 oz. "Softasilk" cake flour
4 oz. sugar

4 eggs
Pinch salt
Capful of vanilla extract
4 oz. apricot glaze or jam

**Hazelnut mousse:**
1 qt. heavy whipping cream,
    sweetened and whipped
4 oz. hazelnut paste (available in
    professional baking stores)

Prepare the sugar pastry base by mixing the sugar and butter. Beat in the eggs and flour, then cover and let rest about an hour in the refrigerator. Roll out to 1/4-inch thick, then cut into a 10-inch circle. Bake in a preheated 400° oven for 10–14 minutes, then set aside. In a clean mixing bowl, prepare the sponge cake. Whip the sugar and eggs until thick and pale in color. Fold in the flour with vanilla and salt. Spread on a greased paper sheet pan. Bake 12 minutes at 400°. Allow to cool, then layer with apricot glaze or jam. Cut into 3 pieces, then cut around a 10-inch cake pan to form a circle. Place the circle of cake inside the cake pan and cut the remaining cake into 2-inch pieces and line around the inside edge of the pan.

Prepare the mousse by combining the whipped cream and the hazelnut paste. Fill the inside of the cake with the mousse. Cover with the cooled pastry base and place in the freezer for 24 hours. Remove from the freezer and invert onto a cake dish, then "paint" the remaining glaze over the outside of the torte. Decorate the top with your choice of fresh cut fruit and paint with more glaze. Chill until serving time.

# Cranberry Linzertorte

16 T unsalted butter
1/2 tsp. fresh minced lemon zest
3/4 C sugar
4 oz. hazelnuts or almonds, ground fine
1/4 C graham cracker crumbs
1 egg
1/4 tsp. vanilla
3/4 C all-purpose flour
1/2 tsp. ground cinnamon
Pinch ground cloves

1/2 tsp. baking powder
1/3 C sugar
2 T water
4 oz. fresh cranberries
1 C raspberry jam
1/2 C grated apple
1 tsp. fresh orange zest
1 tsp. fresh lemon zest
1/4 C strained apricot jam
2 T powdered sugar

Cream the butter and zest in a large mixing bowl. Process the sugar, nuts and graham crackers, then combine with the creamed butter, adding the egg and vanilla. Mix well. Whisk the flour, cinnamon, cloves and baking powder together, then add to the butter mixture and beat on low speed. Chill this dough at least 4 hours. Roll half the dough on a floured surface into an 11-inch circle. Fit this over a 9-inch fluted tart pan with removable bottom. Chill. Combine the sugar and water in a saucepan and dissolve over low heat. Add the cranberries, bring to a boil and cook 10 minutes, stirring occasionally. Add all remaining ingredients, except the apricot jam and powdered sugar, mix well, then spread over the crust. Roll out the remaining dough into a rectangle, cut into 3/4-inch strips with a ravioli cutter, then arrange in a lattice design over top of the tort. Bake in a preheated 350° oven for 30–35 minutes. Cool in the ring overnight. Melt the apricot jam and brush over the tart for a glaze. Dust the powdered sugar in a 1-inch border using a 7-inch plate as a stencil.

Makes 10 servings.

*Thank you Letty Flatt for this wonderful Deer Valley specialty.*

# Celebration Cheesecake

**Crust:**
2 1/2 C crushed creme-filled chocolate
    sandwich cookies (Tuxedo cookies
    work well)
2 T butter, softened

**Filling:**
3 pkgs. (8 oz.) cream cheese, softened
1 1/4 C granulated sugar
3 eggs
1/2 C mashed ripe banana

2/3 C heavy whipping cream
1 T lemon juice
2 tsp. vanilla

**Possible garnishes:**
1 1/2 C sweetened whipped cream
Chopped walnuts or peanuts
Red and green maraschino cherries
Hot fudge sauce, warmed
Mint sauce, warmed

Combine the crust ingredients and mix well. Press this mixture over the bottom and sides of an ungreased 9-inch springform pan. Refrigerate.

Now make the filling. In a large bowl, beat the cream cheese until smooth. Gradually add sugar, beating until smooth. Add eggs, 1 at a time, and the remaining filling ingredients, beating until the mixture is smooth. Pour the mixture into the chilled crust-lined pan. Bake in a preheated 350° oven for 55–65 minutes or until center is set. Cool to room temperature and remove the side of the pan. Refrigerate overnight.

To serve, garnish cheesecake with any of the garnishes.

Serves 8 with some left over.

# Great Grandma's Homemade Ice Cream

6 eggs, *very* well beaten
3 1/2 C granulated sugar
7 1/2 C milk
6 C cream
3 3/4 tsp. vanilla

3/4 tsp. salt
3 C fresh strawberries (2 cups mashed, 1 cup sliced)
Juice from 3 fresh lemons

In a large-size saucepan, combine the eggs, sugar and milk and cook over low heat, stirring constantly, until the mixture thickens and coats a metal spoon (160°). Remove from the heat and cool.

Add all remaining ingredients and chill well. When well chilled, place in your ice cream maker and follow the instructions.

Makes 1/2 gallon.

*Karen Udy, formerly with the Utah Dairy Commission, comes through again.* This is a superb homemade ice cream and will serve well any time of the year, but it's especially good in the summer.

# Tracy's Yummy Cream Pie

5 T cornstarch
1 C granulated sugar
1/4 tsp. salt
2 1/2 C cold whole milk
1/4 C heavy whipping cream
2 whole eggs or 3 egg yolks, beaten

3 T butter (the real stuff)
1 T vanilla
1 baked 9- or 10-inch pie shell
2 fresh firm bananas or 1 cup of
    shredded coconut
Whipped cream for topping

In a medium-size saucepan, combine the cornstarch, sugar and salt and whisk well. Add the milk and cream and cook over medium heat, stirring constantly until smooth and thick.

Remove from the heat and pour a small amount of the mixture into the beaten eggs and mix well. Stir the egg mixture into the milk mixture and return to the heat to cook for 1 minute. Remove from the heat and add the butter and vanilla, stirring well.

Slice the bananas over the bottom of the prepared and cooled pie crust. Pour the cream sauce over the bananas or mix the coconut into the sauce, then pour over the pie shell. Chill well before serving. Serve with dollops of whipped cream ... if you dare.

Makes 8 wedges.

*Tracy Christenson, KUTV's Sales Department, is our master pie baker and shares this absolutely sinfully delicious recipe that you have to try.*

# Index—By Chapter

## Salads, Soups and Chili

## Pastas and Pizzas

## Main Dishes

## Desserts

# Index—By Subject